A BRIEF GUIDE TO

THE SOUND OF MUSIC

PAUL SIMPSON

ROBINSON RUNNING PRESS

First published in Great Britain in 2015 by Robinson

A CIP catalogue record for this book
is available from the British Library.

ISBN 978-1-47211-874-5 (paperback)
ISBN: 978-1-47211-878-3 (ebook)

Typeset in Garamond by TW Typesetting, Plymouth, Devon
Printed and bound by CPI Group (UK) Ltd, Croydon, CR0 4YY

Robinson
is an imprint of
Constable & Robinson Ltd
100 Victoria Embankment
London EC4Y 0DY

An Hachette UK Company
www.hachette.co.uk

www.constablerobinson.com

First published in the United States in 2015 by Running Press Book Publishers,
A Member of the Perseus Books Group

Books published by Running Press are available at special discounts for bulk purchases
in the United States by corporations, institutions, and other organizations.
For more information, please contact the Special Markets
Department at the Perseus Books Group, 2300 Chestnut Street,
Suite 200, Philadelphia, PA 19103, or call (800) 810-4145, ext. 5000, or e-mail
special.markets@perseusbooks.com.

US ISBN: 978-0-7624-5614-7
US Library of Congress Control Number: 2014946281

9 8 7 6 5 4 3 2 1
Digit on the right indicates the number of this printing

Running Press Book Publishers
2300 Chestnut Street
Philadelphia, PA 19103-4371

Visit us on the web!
www.runningpress.com

Printed and bound in the UK

Paul Si⸻ ⸻ on a wide variety of topics, with his recent books including an acclaimed overview of conspiracy theories, a history of spying since the Second World War, anthologies of prison breaks and air disasters, and examinations of the careers of J. R. R. Tolkien, C. S. Lewis and Stephen King, as well as the world of L. Frank Baum's Oz. He has been a conductor, musical director and church organist for thirty-five years and currently runs two choirs near his home in a small village north of Brighton, England.

Recent titles in the series

According to my parents, music was my first love; I suspect it will be my last. It has always been a central part of my life, and it's appropriate that this celebration of The Sound of Music *should be dedicated to all the members of the choirs, music groups and dramatic societies with whom I have worked over the years. Thank you all for the music I've been lucky enough to share.*

CONTENTS

'Now the Lord had said unto Abram: Get thee out of thy country, and from thy kindred, and from thy father's house, unto a land that I will show thee.'

Genesis 12.1 (King James Version)

INTRODUCTION

Everyone has certain fixed memories of growing up which we maintain are true, even when presented with evidence to the contrary. I firmly recollect that there were some things which must have been laid down by law regarding what was shown on TV at Christmas in the UK without fail during the 1970s – we had to follow the plucky chaps as they dug their way to short-lived freedom in *The Great Escape* (although my mother developed an uncanny knack of ensuring that somehow my sister and I never saw the scene where they are all machine-gunned in a field); there was a James Bond film which everyone sat down to watch (with certain members of the family passing sarcastic comments about 007's ability to survive); and there was *The Sound of Music* – which most years I must admit I avoided. Three hours of nuns yodelling? I'd rather read the latest Alistair MacLean novel, or watch *The Amazing Spider-Man* or *Logan's Run* on another TV (little realizing their connections to the von Trapp saga).

However, in the years that followed I've come to appreciate the film considerably more, and now I can understand how its star Christopher Plummer – after many decades of referring to it as 'S and M' – finally succumbed to its charms. Whether it's the wonderful music of Rodgers and Hammerstein, or Julie Andrews' performance, which never plumbs the depth of saccharinity of which it is accused, or indeed the way in which the mood of the movie changes once the Nazis enter Austria – and those who criticize Andrews' acting really need to look more closely at the scene outside the von Trapps' home when they are confronting the Nazis – there's something there for most people (including pedants who point out, quite rightly, that travelling over the Alps from Salzburg would lead the von Trapps quite neatly into the Nazis' hands – Hitler's Berchtesgaden lies there!).

There are many people who adore the movie, and make the pilgrimage to Salzburg to visit the locations where it was filmed. After some years of negative feelings towards the musical – you suspect that its citizens would rather it be known for being the birthplace of Mozart than the home of Maria – the Austrian city has finally started to embrace its legacy and there are plenty of organized 'Sound of Music Tours' as well as opportunities to make your own way around with specially compiled guidebooks. If you want, you can stay at the actual von Trapp villa (although be warned; if you do so, you'll need a car to get back into Salzburg – it's quite a way out); many hotels, like the one that we stayed in during my research trip, run the movie constantly on one of the TV channels. As you wander around, you're bound to run into people re-creating scenes from the film – a group of teenage American girls decided to sing 'Do-Re-Mi' on the steps in the Mirabell Palace gardens despite the April rain as we passed by.

2015 marks the fiftieth anniversary of Robert Wise's nearly three-hour-long account of Maria von Trapp's story, but the movie wasn't the first – or indeed the last – version of that epic tale. *A Brief Guide to The Sound of Music* recounts the true story of the von Trapp family, which took place over a considerably longer period than the later versions would have you believe, and is markedly different to the story we know so well, and looks at the two West German movies that were made about the family's travels in the mid-1950s.

The award-winning original stage production from 1959 is then examined in detail, before we take a close look at the creation of Robert Wise's film of that show, released six years later, and its own legacy, as well as the subsequent careers of those who took part in it. The von Trapp story also became the focus of a forty-part Japanese anime in the early 1990s, which is described in detail since it is the least easily available version of the story. It reworked Maria's history, sometimes taking it even further from the truth, other times perhaps coming closest to the 'real' Maria of all the different adaptations. A round-up of other productions – notably the one in Salzburg itself, the Sing-a-long extravaganzas, and the various 'talent shows' – concludes the volume.

In her autobiography, Agathe von Trapp – the eldest daughter of the family – recounts how she resented *The Sound of Music* for the way in which it altered her family history (the first names and ages of all the children were altered, but the surname retained), but in time she came to realize that the creators of the stage and film versions had managed to stay true to the spirit of her family's story. Hopefully this volume will demonstrate how they did so, and explain why this enchanting story has captivated so many generations.

Paul Simpson
August 2014

AUTHOR'S NOTE: WHEN IS A BOOK NOT A BOOK?

That may sound like the start of a typical Rodgers and Hammerstein song, but the term 'book' is used in two different contexts in *A Brief Guide to The Sound of Music*.

In a musical, the 'book' (or the 'libretto') is the proper name for the narrative structure of the story – including the dialogue (and attendant stage directions) which isn't sung.

'Lyrics' is the correct term for the words of the songs.

So, Lindsay and Crouse wrote the book for *The Sound of Music* stage musical, to which Rodgers and Hammerstein added lyrics and music – but all their work was based on the original book penned by Maria von Trapp. Ernest Lehman then wrote the screenplay for the 1965 movie which incorporated all of the above!

Film and play titles in this book are italicized; song titles are in quote marks. 'The Sound of Music' therefore refers to the title song; *The Sound of Music* denotes the whole musical (whether it's the stage or screen version will be clear from context).

PART ONE: THE TRUE STORY OF THE VON TRAPP FAMILY SINGERS

I

THE VON TRAPPS BEFORE MARIA

The form is overstamped with multiple official markings, indicating the small piece of paper's voyage through the many levels of American bureaucracy. It is Certificate of Arrival number 3 242161, issued by the US Department of Justice, Immigration and Naturalization Service on 18 June 1943.

> I hereby certify that the immigration records show that the alien named below arrived at the port, on the date, and in the manner shown, and was lawfully admitted to the United States of America for permanent residence.
>   Name: Maria Augusta von Trapp
>   Port of entry: Niagara Falls, N.Y.
>   Date: Dec. 30, 1942
>   Manner of arrival: C. N. R. R.
>   I further certify that this certificate of arrival is issued under authority of, and in conformity with, the provisions of the

Nationality Act of 1940 (Pub. No.853, 76th Cong.), solely for the use of the alien herein named and only for naturalization purposes.

In witness whereof, this certificate of arrival is issued Jun 18, 1943.

It marked the end of the von Trapps' quest to become part of their adopted land, the United States of America. Unlike their fictional counterparts in the stage show and the movie, they hadn't had to clamber over mountains to escape from the Nazis, nor, as was suggested in the lurid anime based on their story, were some of them smuggled out of Austria inside a coffin. As the younger Maria explained in 2003, 'We did tell people that we were going to America to sing. And we did not climb over mountains with all our heavy suitcases and instruments. We left by train, pretending nothing.' Was it all theatrical hype then? No – the true story of the von Trapp family is as fascinating as the fiction later created around them.

The von Trapp saga didn't begin with a young novice entering a convent in Salzburg, unsure of who she was or her place in the world. Although Maria is a key part of the jigsaw, the story actually began nearly a century before the von Trapps became Americans, when English engineer and draughtsman Robert Whitehead arrived in Trieste on the Adriatic coast, which at that time in the mid-nineteenth century was part of Austria. The great-grandfather of seven of the von Trapp children, Whitehead was born in Bolton on 3 January 1823, and quickly showed a love of mechanics. He was apprenticed, aged sixteen, to his uncle's engineering factory and additionally trained at the Mechanics' Institute in Manchester. He married Frances Maria Johnson in 1846, and the newly-weds emigrated to Marseilles for Robert to work for Philip Taylor & Sons at their shipyard. He stayed there for a couple of years before moving to Milan (then part of the Austrian Empire), to work as a consultant engineer. After becoming embroiled in the surge of Italian nationalism in 1848, he moved his family with him from Milan to Trieste. There, he became technical director of a marine engineering firm, Stabilmento Strudthoff, and his work came to the attention of the owners of Fonderia Metalli, a metal foundry in Fiume (modern-day Rijeka, in Croatia), fifty miles or so away: notably, in 1856, Whitehead had designed and built the first cylindrical marine boiler in the Austrian Empire.

Renamed Stabilimeno Technico Fiumano, Whitehead's new employers became a major producer of marine steam boilers and engines, with one of their principal customers the Austrian navy, for whom Whitehead designed the engines for their new armour-plated screw frigate, the *Archduke Ferdinand Maximilian*. In 1864, Whitehead was introduced by Mayor Giovanni de Ciotta to Fregattenkapitan Giovanni de Luppis, a former officer in the navy who had come into possession of papers belonging to an officer of the Austrian Marine Artillery; these outlined the idea of using a small boat carrying a large charge of explosives, powered by a steam or air engine and remotely steered by cables to be used against enemy ships. That officer (whose name is no longer known) had not been able to do anything with the idea before he died, but had passed the papers to de Luppis who worked up a prototype, known as the *salvacoste*. The model was powered by a spring-driven clockwork mechanism and steered remotely by cables, but before the navy chiefs would take it further, they decided that it needed to have a better propulsion system.

Brought on board to help achieve this, Whitehead wasn't able to make de Luppis's idea work – at least in its current form, despite months of work refining both the motive power and the steering gear. However, he was convinced that at its core there was a good notion, and when he realized that the weapon needed to travel beneath the surface the whole time – so that it would hole the ship it was attacking below the waterline and thus sink it – he became inspired, and spent hours working with his twelve-year-old son John on a prototype. Meanwhile, his engines for the *Ferdinand Max* performed beyond expectations in the naval conflict between Austria and Italy that erupted in 1866 (even if Austria went on to lose the overall war with Prussia), and Whitehead capitalized on the attention this brought to promote his new weapon – the 'fish' torpedo. He hadn't yet perfected it, but the Austrian navy were interested enough to encourage Whitehead to continue work. Over the next couple of years, his daughter Alice fell in love with Count Georg Hoyos, a young Austrian naval officer, and Whitehead was created a baron for his services to Austrian engineering.

The solution to the outstanding problem with his variant of the torpedo came to Whitehead in his sleep towards the end of 1868, and the Austrian navy were quick to purchase the completed weapons, although their parlous finances following the war meant they couldn't buy exclusive worldwide rights. With the help of his new son-in-law, Count Georg, and son John, Whitehead was able to interest the British in the invention, and the scientists at the Royal Laboratory at Woolwich Arsenal were able to refine Whitehead's work, which was also continuing at Silurifico Whitehead, the new name for the factory after Whitehead and Hoyos bought it out in 1872.

The following years saw Whitehead's reputation and fortune grow, although after the loss of his wife in 1883 he entered semi-retirement, and his family took over the business (although he still managed to manipulate the British into buying the latest development of the torpedo in 1889). He was able to incorporate the new invention, the gyroscope, into the torpedo controls in 1895, which increased the weapon's accuracy. However, although his fortune began to dwindle – partly due to the mismanagement of his estate at Worth – Whitehead's children and grandchildren continued to prosper. Alice's daughter Marguerite married Count Herbert Bismarck in June 1892, although both his son John and eldest daughter Frances predeceased him, as did Count Georg. Robert himself died on 14 November 1905, with the inscription on his grave at Worth noting that 'His fame was in all nations round about'.

Not long after Robert's death, the Silurifico Whitehead came up for sale, and it was purchased jointly by Vickers and fellow weapons company Armstrong, Whitworth & Co., who turned its machines to the production of new submarines – including the Austrian navy's U-5 and U-6 craft. In 1908, the Imperial and Royal Austro-Hungarian Navy sent Kapitanleutnant Georg von Trapp to study the design and construction of both torpedoes and submarines – and the young officer caught the attention of Robert Whitehead's eighteen-year-old granddaughter, Agathe, who was living at the Villa Whitehead, overlooking the factory.

Georg Johannes Ritter von Trapp was born in Zara on 4 April 1880, the son of an Austrian naval officer who died when Georg was four. He and his two siblings were brought up in Eisenach and Graz, and Georg attended the naval academy in Fiume at the age of fourteen. After graduating, he and his classmates took a schooner, the SMS *Saida II*, around the world, visiting Australia, China and Egypt, where Georg was told by a fortune teller in the market that he would have two wives, ten children, and 'you will see two world wars, and you will live to be one hundred years old'. Only one of these predictions failed to come true. His career in the navy progressed smoothly: he was sent to China on the SMS *Zenta*, where he was caught up in the Boxer Rebellion, and became a trusted young officer.

Agathe Whitehead was invited to perform at the opening ceremony for the U-5 submarine in 1909, and at the party following the launch, she danced with the dashing young Georg von Trapp. They fell in love, and became engaged; however, because Agathe was still only nineteen, they waited until 14 January 1911 before marrying and moving to Pola, where Georg was stationed. A house, which would become known

as the Villa Trapp, was built near Monte Paradiso, outside
Pola, with stunning views of the Adriatic. Their eldest child,
Rupert Georg von Trapp, was born that November; their first
daughter, Agathe, arrived in March 1913. In order to inform
Georg of the safe delivery of their third child, Maria, in
September 1914, Agathe had to send a coded telegram ('SMS
Maria arrived') since personal messages were not permitted
in time of war – and, following the assassination of Archduke
Franz Ferdinand the previous June, Europe was now at war.

Georg had spent some time on U-boats before the outbreak
of the First World War in June that year, but when he was
offered the chance to command one for the conflict, he turned
it down, believing that accepting command of a torpedo boat
would mean he was in the thick of the action. This turned
out not to be the case, and in April 1915, he was not disappointed to be reassigned to the U-5 – the submarine that had
brought him and his wife together – even if he knew he would
miss his crew on the torpedo boat. Once back beneath the
waves, he was a calculating and clever skipper; within days of
his assignment, he carried out a daring underwater torpedo
attack on the French battleship, the *Léon Gambetta*, moving
outside his assigned territory to do so and risking the capture
or destruction of his own U-boat to bring down the enemy
ship. His actions in destroying the *Léon Gambetta* made
the Allies believe the Austrian navy was considerably better
equipped than they had believed, and made him famous at
home.

Agathe and the children moved to the Whitehead summer
home (the Erlhof) in Zell am See in the interior of Austria,
away from the coast, for the duration of the war, living with
Agathe's mother and her two sisters, Mary and Joan. Four
of the von Trapp children were born there: Maria, Werner in
December 1915 (named after Georg's brother, who was killed
in action the previous May), Hedwig (July 1917) and Johanna,
in September 1919 after the war was over. Towards the end
of the war, the older children began formal lessons, although

their first governess Fräulein Zeiner left them to enter a convent; they also had a live-in piano teacher.

Georg kept a journal of his war service, and wrote it up in 1935 as *Bis zum letzten Flagenschuss* – 'To the Last Salute'. (The title refers to the final time that the Austro-Hungarian flag was raised: 2 November 1918, nine days before the Armistice that brought the First World War to an end.) Translated by his granddaughter into English in 2007, the book provides a very vivid account of life beneath the waves, as well as the privations of those within the Austro-Hungarian Empire as the war progressed, and the depth of shame felt when the Empire surrendered.

The family moved out from the Erlhof once Georg rejoined them, taking over the Hotel Kitzsteinhorn from Agathe's brother Franky. Although by no means rich, they were still able to afford a cook, two maids, a governess for the two older children and a nanny for the three younger ones. They stayed there for about a year and a half, but once the Kitzsteinhorn became flooded when the nearby lake rose too high, they decided to find a new home, and moved to the Martinschlössl, which belonged to another of Agathe's brothers. Their furniture was collected from the Villa Trapp (although Georg couldn't oversee the operation himself, since the house was now in Italy, and he was not permitted to enter the country), and only a few weeks after they moved in, Martina, the last of Georg and Agathe's seven children, was born.

According to the accounts given by the children – notably by young Agathe in her autobiography – this was a happy time, and although they had needed to give their father time to rest when he returned during his wartime furloughs, he was happy to join in with their play. The children were tutored in the morning, and did homework in the early evening; they learned to sing and appreciate classical music. The only minor conflict came when their governess Fräulein Freckmann took the children to Mass on a Sunday when Georg wanted to go on a picnic. Freckmann was Catholic, instilling in the youngsters a fear of missing Mass, and they defied their father; he wasn't best pleased but calmed down eventually – some years later, he too converted from his Lutheran upbringing to the Catholic Church.

Over Christmas 1921, their mother Agathe fell ill with scarlet fever, probably catching it from baby Martina, although four of the other children were also sick. With the help of her sister-in-law Connie (Werner's widow) and her daughter (known as Connie Baby), who had come to stay to be safe from the conflict in Ireland, she nursed the children, before being taken to the Sanatorium Loew in Vienna because her case was so severe. She eventually returned home the following August, seriously weakened, and late in the evening of 2 September 1922, she died.

After Agathe's death, Georg looked for work outside the house, but he soon quit a job with the Danube Steamship Company, when he realized how prevalent corruption was within it. After Connie went to live with Agathe's mother in Vienna, soon after Agathe's passing, Georg hired a housekeeper, and a nanny for the younger children, while the older children started to attend local schools. Georg spent time in Hungary with his brothers-in-law, but regularly returned home to be with his children, and treated them to visits to the sights of Vienna, including the circus, the opera and the funfair at the Prater with its enormous Ferris wheel.

One major idea that Georg contemplated never came to fruition: he asked Rupert and young Agathe if they would like to go on a sailboat around the Pacific islands, which he had visited as a young man. Although he painted a tempting mental picture of the way of life, neither of his children liked the idea – Rupert later told his sister it was because there was no Catholic church there, and they had to go to church on a Sunday!

Georg's suggestion that the family move to Salzburg was, however, greeted with considerably more enthusiasm, and, with the help of money realized from the Whitehead estate in

Fiume, Georg was able to purchase a house in Aigen, a suburb to the south-east of central Salzburg. (The Villa Trapp later became Heinrich Himmler's headquarters when he was in Austria; however, it is now a hotel open to paying guests.) Situated near the railway line into Salzburg, and surrounded by huge gardens, the estate was far too large for a voice to be heard calling from the house. Georg therefore devised a system of distinctive calls on his bosun's whistle that denoted each of the children, or called all of them simultaneously. This also helped when the children were in their rooms, behind closed thick wooden doors – and while the septet might have pretended that they were sailors on their father's submarine, he never had any intention of treating them like young members of the military.

Georg arranged for a playhouse to be built in the woods, and a veritable menagerie of animals started to grow – a dog (put down after it attacked local deer), bees, chickens, and a baby goat were all acquired at various times. He accompanied his children on the guitar as he taught them songs he had learned over the years, and tutored Rupert and Maria in the accordion, Johanna and Maria the violin, and Agathe the guitar. The family would then play together in a group, even going away on a camp in the summer of 1926 to join with other families to make music.

Although his wife had told Georg before she died that he ought to remarry, according to his daughter Agathe in her autobiography, Georg did not feel that this was right. She notes that there were attempts to pair him off with an Austrian countess, a distant relative of her mother's, but these came to nothing. The first person in whom he really showed any interest was Maria Augusta Kutschera, a twenty-one-year-old teacher whom he hired to assist Maria ...

2

IN LOVE WITH GOD: MARIA BEFORE THE VON TRAPPS

Maria von Trapp wrote a number of books about her life, and while the most commonly known, *The Story of the Trapp Family Singers* (often reprinted simply as *The Sound of Music*), recounts a great deal about her time meeting Georg von Trapp and his seven children, far more detail about her own story can be found in her later books, particularly the 1972 volume simply entitled *Maria*.

Maria Augusta Kutschera was born on a train travelling between the Tirol and Vienna on the night of 25 January 1905. Her mother Augusta (known as Gusti) was returning to Vienna from a visit to her home village, but her waters broke earlier than anticipated, and young Maria arrived with the assistance of the train conductor (a father of nine who was used to helping in such circumstances). Her mother died of pneumonia when Maria was two, and her father left her in the care of an elderly cousin in Vienna who brought her up as best she could alongside her own now grown-up children. Maria had occasional contact with her father before his death when she was nine, and felt that she was always a disappointment to him – from her descriptions of her interactions with him, it is clear that he did not understand younger children, and that he would probably have enjoyed her company when she was older. (Her father had a son, Karl, from his first marriage – that wife had also died – but he had no interest in Maria when she was younger. Karl and Maria did eventually make contact when they were adults and met infrequently over the years before Karl's death in 1948.)

Over the next few years, Maria Kutschera was abused by her guardian – 'Uncle Franz', the son-in-law of the cousin who had looked after her – who would beat her for any perceived or imagined misdemeanour. Eventually she decided to enjoy her life, playing truant to go hiking in the countryside, and when she did go to school, cheeking the staff (to the extent that one teacher, when Maria was fourteen, called her out in front of the class and told her, 'I wish on you a daughter exactly like yourself'.) After finishing school, she decided that she wanted to go to the State Teachers' College of Progressive Education, but her 'uncle' was not willing to finance her further education – so Maria decided to raise the money herself during the holidays by working with her friend Annie at hotels in the holiday resort of Semmering. She faced down Franz when he came to bring her home, and thereafter had nothing more to do with him.

Maria and Annie passed the entrance exam to the college, and because Maria was an orphan and had done very well in the exam, she was given a scholarship, which covered board, lodging and tuition. She took a job working as a seamstress on alternate Saturdays, which paid for everything else. She indulged her love of music by attending Masses at the various local churches where musical settings by Mozart and Haydn would be performed by the choirs, or even on occasion by the Vienna Philharmonic Orchestra and the Vienna Boys' Choir.

Maria's own faith wasn't strong (or even very much in existence) at this point; she even became the de facto leader of the 'non-Catholic' girls at the college, trying to prove that you didn't need to be religious to live a good life. However, on Palm Sunday (the week before Easter) in the last of her four years at the college, she found herself listening to the Jesuit preacher, Father Kronseder, when she'd been expecting to be hearing Bach's St Matthew Passion. When she challenged him on his beliefs as he left the pulpit, Kronseder took her aside and told her to meet him there on the Tuesday – and despite the fact her friends were going skiing the next day, Maria was back at the Jesuit church, engaging with the priest – and finding herself converting.

For the remainder of her time at the college, Maria was a committed Christian, and when she went hiking in the mountains after graduating, she found herself called, she later explained, to give all she enjoyed to her Lord – which meant in practical terms that she would give up her outside interests and spend her time as a nun, serving God. Impetuously she took a train to Salzburg, arriving there at 6.30 a.m., and asked a passing monk which was the strictest convent in the area. He directed her to the Benedictine Abbey of Nonnberg, high above the town.

It's rather surprising that those who have told Maria's story in other media have not drawn on her account of her arrival at Nonnberg (although the Japanese anime does come close). Around 7.30 in the morning, she arrived at the gates, and asked to see the 'boss'. Over her left shoulder was a coil of rope from her mountain climbing; in her right hand was an ice pick. On her back was her heavy knapsack. She was deeply tanned from being outside so much, and probably smelled, since she had come straight to the abbey after travelling on the overnight train. She was taken to a big room bisected by a large grille; on the far side were paintings of previous abbesses.

Maria had to wait some time before a small, frail nun

entered and smiled kindly at her. When asked what she could do for Maria, the young student announced that she had come to stay. 'Has somebody sent you, my child?' the nun asked. 'If anybody had sent me, I wouldn't be here,' Maria replied. 'I haven't obeyed anybody yet.' The Reverend Mother must have seen something special about the figure in front of her; she immediately admitted Maria to the abbey.

While Maria may have believed that she was ready for the abbey, the abbey certainly wasn't ready for her. While Saint Benedict may not have specifically given a rule against sliding down the banisters, or taking the steps two at a time, the nuns felt it necessary to rectify the omission by creating rules just for Maria to ensure that – at least for a tiny part of the time – she was acting as a candidate should. She could understand why one shouldn't whistle worldly tunes, but what was wrong with repeating the Benedictine chant that way? Why should she not be allowed to speak save during one precious hour between 1 and 2 p.m.? And if the rules stated that if a postulant contradicted her superior, she had to kiss the floor in repentance, wouldn't it make sense to kiss the floor first and then say what she wanted to say – in fact, it saved time if she just kissed the floor straightaway!

Even nearly five decades later, Maria could still clearly remember the list she made of her first Lenten resolutions: 'I will not whistle. I will not slide down any banisters. I will not go up on the roof and jump over the chimney. Fourth, I will not tickle anybody and make them laugh out loud in a time of deep silence.' (On the written list, the Reverend Mother had added, 'Good for you, Maria.') There was a serious side as well: Maria used her qualification, and became a respected teacher at the local school, praised by the area superintendent and entrusted with the classes' annual May outings.

Then one day shortly afterwards, as she was grading her students' papers, Maria was called to the Reverend Mother's office. The abbess had received a visitor – a widower, named Captain Georg von Trapp.

3

A LESSON FOR MARIA

Maria Kutschera's arrival at Villa Trapp and the unusual courtship between her and Captain Georg von Trapp forms the core of both the play and the movie of *The Sound of Music* – certainly of the part prior to the Nazi invasion of Austria. However, the true story is markedly different, not least because it actually took place a decade earlier than indicated in the movie: the pair met in the mid-1920s, not the mid-1930s. Much was to befall the von Trapp family in the period that is covered in the movie with a jump cut from the wedding bells pealing out to the bells heralding the Anschluss.

In the autumn of 1926, Georg von Trapp was concerned about the health of some of his children. While most had recovered well from the attack of scarlet fever which had been responsible for the death of their mother, both Maria and Werner suffered after-effects, with heart murmurs that meant they shouldn't do too much. (Ironically, both of them lived to their tenth decade, passing aged 99 and 91 respectively.)

Eventually, it reached the point that Maria couldn't manage the forty-five-minute walk to and from school, and would need to be home-schooled. Georg asked the school whether there was an older student who might be able to come and live with them and help Maria with her work, so she wouldn't need to repeat the year. The school didn't have anyone suitable, but did suggest the teacher of the fifth grade who was a candidate at the Nonnberg convent.

Georg von Trapp duly went to see the Reverend Mother who could see that this might solve a problem she had with her Maria – not the disciplinary one, which regularly reared its head with the young novice, but a medical situation. Maria had been suffering from headaches, which the doctor felt could be attributed to the sudden change from a very outdoor life to the cloistered existence of the convent. He had suggested that Maria should go somewhere she could take normal exercise for a year or so, and the opportunity to assist Captain von Trapp seemed like an answer to prayer.

Maria, however, was not impressed with this. She was aware that her place on earth was to find out the Will of God and to do it, but she couldn't really believe that this meant she had to leave Nonnberg for an extended period (the original book states it was eight months, from October to June, but then gives a figure of nine months in conversation between her and the Captain; her later autobiography claims she was told she would be away for ten months). She was not prepared to return to the outside world in such a way: she didn't even have anything to wear because once her candidacy had been agreed by the Chapter, her clothing was given away to the needy. All that was available was the dress worn by the most recent arrival, which had yet to be redistributed: an old-fashioned blue serge gown with some latticework around the neck and sleeves, which, together with a leather hat, heavy black shoes and black stockings, made Maria look like someone from three decades earlier.

After receiving the Reverend Mother's blessing, Maria said

goodbye to the three other young candidates with whom she had shared a room, and vowed that she would be back – soon. Carrying her guitar, and a satchel with some underwear and books, she made her way down the 144 steps into the town of Salzburg, heading for the bus station, where she found the bus for Aigen and soon found herself rattling through the countryside. After about twenty minutes, she was told she had arrived at her destination, although when she got off the bus, she couldn't see any sign of the Villa Trapp – all there seemed to be was an inn, with an elderly man outside who pointed her in the right direction.

At the front door of the huge house, she was greeted by Hans, the butler, who for a moment Maria believed must be the Captain himself; her recollections differed as to whether he shook her hand or not. In later life, Maria would claim that she was introduced to the children by the housekeeper, Baroness Matilda Mandelsoh, because the Captain wasn't there at the time, but in her original 1949 book, and in Agathe's autobiography, it's clear that it was Georg who showed her his offspring. After prospective employer and employee made their introductions to each other, Georg got out his bosun's whistle, and piped 'a series of complicated trills', explaining that it took too long to call his children by name, and so he had devised a different whistle for each of them. Six of the children duly came down the wide staircase, two abreast, and lined up in front of their father and Maria. To the children, Maria looked as if she had stepped out of a comic book; she was equally surprised – she had never seen such perfect little ladies and gentlemen, all dressed in blue sailor suits. The impasse and silence were only broken when Maria's hat fell off and rolled to Johanna's feet, at which point the little girl got a fit of the giggles.

After Georg had presented each child in turn, he took Maria to meet her charge and namesake, and then explained that the children had had twenty-six different nurses, governesses and teachers over the four years since the death of their mother.

She found out the rest of the von Trapp story a few days later when the Captain went away on a hunting expedition, and Baroness Matilda told her of his naval history, and how various people had been brought in to try to provide the best life for his children. The Baroness also explained that Georg's relatives were trying to persuade him to remarry, and that an engagement to Princess Yvonne would be announced soon. (The disparity between this version and Agathe's, related in chapter one, can easily be explained by such matters not being discussed in front of the children, hence Agathe was unaware of how close they were to gaining a stepmother at that time.)

Although Baroness Matilda tried to be something of a mother to the children, she saw her role as maintaining the discipline their father required. The youngsters were not allowed to play games in the huge gardens of the villa, because their hair would get caught up or their clothing torn – the Captain wanted his girls to wear sailor suits and nice shoes during the week, and silken dresses and white socks on Sundays, which, of course, had to be kept clean. When Maria suggested that they could buy playsuits and sandals for the children, the Baroness told her that it would not be possible – and when Maria suggested getting a volleyball net and other games items, the Baroness professed never to have heard of them, although she did think that the children might enjoy a game of croquet on the lawn.

By November, although Maria was starting to bond with the two children in her direct care (Johanna's teaching was also assigned to her) and was starting to become friendly with Agathe (who helped her with some of the chores she was assigned), she still didn't have that much to do with the older ones. On a wet Saturday, they all trooped into the nursery, and saw Maria's guitar. She started to play various well-known folk tunes, but they didn't know any of them; Maria therefore took it on herself to teach them, even if the Baroness's disapproval was evident. The fact that Maria seemed only to do this at times when the Baroness wasn't around may have added to the older woman's annoyance at the way in which a tutor hired to look after two of the children was involving herself with the whole family.

Shortly before Christmas, when the Baroness was away visiting a sick sister, Maria and the children rehearsed the various simple songs they had been learning, with young Maria on violin and Agathe on guitar. Their practice of the medieval carol 'In Dulci Jubilo' was interrupted by the arrival of Georg von Trapp who insisted on sitting down on the floor with his children (completely contrary to the way the Baroness had insisted he wanted them to behave) and asking Maria to join them. He was entranced by the children's singing and playing, and even borrowed his daughter's violin to join in with his own descant for some of the pieces. This was followed by the Captain helping Maria to create an Advent wreath for the family, which was put up in the nursery – or the 'living room' as it was rechristened for the purpose – and the family joining in together for the Christmas preparations and festivities. Maria was even given sets of outdoor clothing and boots for the children's use.

The spring of 1927 saw the family continuing to spend much more time together: previously, the older and the younger children were kept separate, as was the custom of the time, and some previous governesses and tutors had even tried to foment trouble between them. Now, Georg von Trapp was home far more often than previously, and enjoying skiing with his children, as well as playing volleyball (something Maria loved, even if not all the children did). He did take a trip away, acting as a hired captain to take a yacht from Bremerhaven to Genoa, happy that the children were doing well.

Then towards the end of March, Princess Yvonne came on a visit, and she wasn't quite what Maria had been expecting. The young novice had built up a romantic notion in her head of the princess being a figure out of Grimm's Fairy Tales, perhaps with blue eyes and blonde hair, who emanated love towards the young motherless children and their lonely father. While it would be unfair to say that the princess was more like some of Grimm's other creations, she certainly wasn't that interested in the children – as she told Maria in forthright terms the afternoon she arrived. She had already shown her disapproval of Hedwig's love of her new ski pants over lunch, after which she presented herself at Maria's bedroom door.

Yvonne explained that she was aware that the Captain was in love with Maria – which came as a shock to the young nun – but that she was straightening him out: he only *thought* he was in love with Maria, because of the excellent way she was with the children. Maria said she would have to return to Nonnberg immediately, but the princess couldn't see why she needed to run away: she wanted Maria to stay through the summer, keep the children occupied on the day of the wedding with a nice party (the last thing she needed was a group of unruly youngsters at the nuptials, after all), and then Maria would be free to return to Nonnberg when the children were sent off to boarding school in the autumn.

Maria was horrified at the prospect of the seven children being sent away from home, and couldn't understand why Yvonne would be marrying the Captain if that was her intention. The princess was bemused – did Maria think she was marrying the children? Hearing that, Maria realized that there was no place for her in the set-up at Villa Trapp, and determined to leave immediately. However, the princess knew how to manipulate Maria, and engaged the help of an elderly priest who explained to Maria that it was the Will of God that she stay with the von Trapps until she was received into the abbey. Reluctantly, she agreed to remain there.

Once Princess Yvonne had left, Georg von Trapp was hurt by Maria's new stand-offishness: she didn't want to do anything which might increase his feelings towards her, so was brusque to the point of rudeness. In May, Baroness Matilda broke her leg while attending her brother's wedding, and wasn't able to return for the rest of the year; the Captain therefore asked Maria if she would take over the Baroness's duties. (Agathe suggests in her autobiography that the antipathy between the Baroness and Maria led to the former's departure.) Maria agreed, but asked the Captain if he would do her a favour in return, and get engaged to the princess as soon as possible. He wondered out loud if he really was doing her a favour by doing that, and Maria mumbled about her impending reception at the convent, and the end of the school year approaching.

The Captain left the next day, leaving Maria in charge of the household. She sent him regular reports regarding the house and estate, but his replies did not confirm his engagement. Eventually, given that it would soon be time for her to return to Nonnberg, Maria asked bluntly when he would get engaged. Georg's reply said that he wished he could see her eyes when she read the announcement of his engagement. Maria was incensed by this, and wrote back immediately that her eyes were none of his business, and that she was sorry she had been mistaken in her belief that the Captain was a man of his word. The letter was sent by registered post.

It arrived with Georg von Trapp on the day that he had decided he was going to get engaged. Unknown to Maria, Yvonne had been presenting various obstacles to the engagement over the past few months, but Georg had now had enough. Just as he was starting his impassioned proposal, he was interrupted by the butler with Maria's letter. When he read it, he realized that he was in love with Maria, and he couldn't go forward with the engagement. The pair returned to Yvonne's castle in silence, and the Captain headed for home. (Rumours immediately began to spread that the only reason Georg broke off the relationship was because he had made Maria pregnant.)

However, he didn't tell Maria that his relationship with Princess Yvonne was over, and spent much of his time in his study, only coming out very occasionally, and not joining in as he had been doing previously. Less than a fortnight before

Maria was due back at Nonnberg, she noticed that the children were going in to see their father for what was clearly a brief conversation. Agathe recalled that her father asked if he should marry Maria, and she said that she thought that if it was the Will of God, he should. Some of the younger ones were obviously asked if they thought Maria liked their father – when they challenged her, Maria replied that of course she liked him. She was taken aback when she learned that there had been rather a considerable misunderstanding: Georg thought that the 'yes, I do' which was relayed back to him by the children was an acceptance of his marriage proposal to her!

According to the Captain, the children had held a council among themselves, knowing that Maria was shortly to depart, and had decided that the only way that Maria could be kept with them was for him to marry her. He had told them he would love to, but, bearing in mind both the letter, and the way she had been behaving, he didn't think she liked him.

Maria wasn't sure how to respond to the Captain's proposal; she couldn't see how she could be in the convent and married at the same time, but said she would seek the advice of the Mistress of Novices. Whatever she said Maria would consider as coming from God. Maria set off for Nonnberg immediately.

When the old nun explained what had happened to one of the sisters, Frau Rafaela, she left her for an hour before returning to bring her to the Reverend Mother. The most senior member of the community told Maria that the whole convent had prayed about Maria, and it became clear to them that it was the Will of God that she marry the Captain and be a good mother to his children. Still feeling rejected to an extent by the God to whom she had promised herself, Maria returned to Villa Trapp, and told the Captain that they had told her she had to marry him. The next morning, Georg informed the children of her decision and that they had been right: the only way for Maria to stay with them was for her to marry him.

The Captain then went away for a long period, to ensure that there was no gossip about the pair of them being under the same roof during their engagement. When he returned, two weeks before the wedding, Maria would go to the convent until their wedding day – the Saturday before Advent, 26 November 1927. Maria believed firmly that she was marrying for the sake of the children, and that was why Georg had asked her. Even shortly before the wedding, she couldn't really understand why she couldn't simply be a housekeeper to help bring up the children: her knowledge of relationships (particularly the physical side) was severely limited, and when one of the children was ill, she even suggested to Georg that he go on the honeymoon without her.

She soon began to settle in to her new role as stepmother to the children, adopting the name 'Mother' as opposed to Mamá, which was how they had addressed their mother, although it took a little longer for her to truly fall in love with Georg. She knew that he and his first wife had been very happy together, and she wanted him to feel that with her, so she asked how she could make him happiest. 'By being exactly like Agathe,' was Georg's reply, which Maria took to mean that she should mimic how Agathe had behaved. She stopped going for bicycle rides with Georg, because Agathe wouldn't have done that; she took up knitting, because that's what Agathe did.

This lasted ten days before Georg asked what was bothering her, and why she was behaving so out of character. In tears, Maria explained that it was because she wanted to become like Agathe. Georg realized how his young bride had misinterpreted his request. He told her gently that he wanted her to be as kind as his first wife, not to imitate her – and from that moment, Maria knew she was in love.

4

A VIRTUE OF NECESSITY

Every summer, Salzburg holds a festival, to which many of the world's elite musicians travel, and the proximity of the von Trapp villa to the centre of town made the family very popular with their extended family and friends, many of whom asked if they could stay for the duration of the summer 1928 event. Maria was keen to experience the festival and thought the family would enjoy it. However, the children ended up spending their time as tour guides, visiting all of the town's famous monuments on multiple occasions, and there was no argument from them when Maria decided that they would not spend future summers at the festival.

There was another reason why she wouldn't want to have a lot of strangers around the following year. Although Maria didn't initially believe that her maternal role would be any more than as a stepmother to Agathe's seven children, she and Georg quickly ended up with two daughters of their own – Rosmarie, born 8 February 1929, and Eleonore ('Lorli'), who arrived on 14 May 1931. There is some confusion over Rosmarie's date of birth: in her Declaration of Intention for Naturalization in 1944 (given under oath), Maria stated that it was in 1928, not 1929, a fact she repeated in her Petition for Naturalization four years later. However, it's clear from Maria's 1972 autobiography that she was not pregnant at the time of her wedding and Agathe's book confirms the definite 1929 date for the birth.

The two girls' arrival helped to cement the family bonds – just as the two eldest children, Rupert and Agathe, began to spread their wings after graduating from school in the spring of 1931. After a summer spent with family in England, Rupert went to the University of Innsbruck, while Agathe studied English and became a tutor for a time, although this wasn't particularly successful.

The family enjoyed holidays away together, and in the summer of 1932, Georg decided to take his family sailing along the Adriatic coast. Italy had cancelled the black list that prevented him from entering the country, so he, Maria and all bar the two smallest children headed for Trieste, together with a couple of other young friends. Along the way, they visited the town of Zara, where Georg was born, and Maria was able to negotiate the rental of a house there for the coming winter.

When they returned in September, they discovered that the house came with the use of a small yacht, the *Alba Maris*, which could only sleep four people. A couple of days before Christmas, Georg and Maria were accompanied by Martina and Maria on an overnight trip to a small bay. At the time Zara was a small Italian enclave within Yugoslavia, so inevitably, the *Alba Maris* was being sailed through Yugoslav waters, and it came as no surprise that they were hailed and boarded by Yugoslav patrol officers wanting to see their passports. Everything was pleasant until the officers saw the von Trapps' Italian passports – their nationality had been changed from Austrian to Italian following the end of the Great War because they had been born in what was now Italian territory. Martina's sketches and Georg's camera aroused suspicions that they might be Italian spies, and they were brought to the Yugoslavs' headquarters.

Georg was taken away separately, but Maria was determined not to be separated from her husband. She persuaded a soldier to take her to where Georg was being held, and managed to convince the official to whom she was delivered that she was very frightened – although she was clearly more composed than she appeared since she made sure she wasn't locked in a room by inserting her foot between the door and the door frame when he tried to shut her in. Eventually the official relented and took her to see Georg, only to find him playing cards with the other inmate in the prison, a murderer. Georg was freed, although he was asked to return to the patrol station to sign a piece of paper. Believing this might be a trick, he asked if the patrol officers could bring the paper to the *Alba Maris*, which, to the family's surprise, was done, and they were freed.

The family stayed in Zara during the winter of 1932–1933, but the following summer they decided to rent out their house in Salzburg during the festival, and stay on the island of Veruda, near Pola. Again, Georg and the children with him – Hedwig, Werner and Agathe this time – ran into problems, and Maria and the others were left wondering for three days what had happened to them; the telegrams that Georg had despatched to explain their delay because of bad weather had not arrived.

His wife was not in the best of moods anyway: she was suffering from kidney stones, which required an operation in Vienna. She spent weeks recuperating, accompanied initially by three chicks Georg brought in, named Caspar, Melchior and Balthazar, and then by a turtle called Glöckerl ('little bell'), who ended up staying at the hospital after her release in September.

That was the last carefree summer that the von Trapp

family would have for many years. Within hours of Georg and Maria's return to Salzburg, the Captain received a long-distance telephone call from the Whitehead family home in Zell am See. 'The banking house Lammer and Co. is bankrupt,' came the message. And with it went the vast majority of Georg von Trapp's money, in part inherited from his late wife.

They weren't destitute, but savage economies needed to be made speedily. Six of the eight servants were sent away; the car was sold; and the majority of the house was shut up to keep the costs down. Rupert was still at Innsbruck, in premedical school, but quickly accepted that he would have to work his way through university, rather than rely on money from home; the other children were all happy to muck in and help, now that there weren't any servants.

Maria asked for prayer help from the nuns at Nonnberg, although Frau Rafaela had a more practical solution to their problems: why not ask the archbishop for permission to open a chapel on the estate, and rent out rooms to the priest who would be looking after that, and to students from the Catholic university? A downstairs room was converted into a chapel, and within a year the house was full of students and professors, including Professor Dillersberger, whose duty it was to say Mass daily before heading to the university. When he had to go away for Easter 1935, he asked a young friend if he could stay and take Mass in his place.

Father Franz Wasner was more than happy to do so; he was even happier when he heard the singing of the von Trapp family – they had maintained their tradition of regular choral practice for their own pleasure – but he had some ideas for improvement. He was the assistant director of the seminary at Salzburg, and spotted errors in the way in which the von Trapps sang the Gregorian chant for the Mass; over breakfast, he was able quickly and efficiently to show them the correct manner. Maria promptly asked him if he would be willing to work with them on the areas that they couldn't handle themselves.

Throughout the summer of 1935, Father Wasner increased the family's repertoire, adding motets and Mass settings by medieval composers to their church music as well as secular pieces he found in the library at Salzburg. Singing practice could go on for up to four or five hours a day, both inside and outside the house.

By August 1936, the von Trapps were tackling complicated motets by Johann Sebastian Bach and Orlando Gibbons. They were going through these one Saturday evening out in the park when they heard light applause coming from behind the pines; to their amazement, and embarrassment, it was the highly acclaimed singer Lotte Lehmann. The world-famous soprano was visiting to see if it might be possible to rent the Villa Trapp for the period of the Salzburg Festival the following year, and by chance had heard them singing. She couldn't believe that the family simply sang for themselves, and was adamant that they should share their gift with the world, giving concerts – she even suggested that they should follow in her footsteps and travel to America. The first step would be competing in the festival for the group singing contest being held the next day.

Georg was equally adamant. It would not be appropriate for the family of a baron and an Imperial Austrian Navy officer to appear on stage. However, he reckoned without the force of Lehmann's personality; she made the necessary phone calls and arranged for the late entry. Not believing for a moment that they had any chance, the family sang three songs – and won first prize. Georg, however, did not remain around for the prize-giving – he was too embarrassed.

However, much as Georg might have wished it, this was not the last time that his family sang in public – as a result of their festival success they were asked to sing on the local radio station. This they did the following Saturday, and among the audience was Kurt von Schuschnigg, the Chancellor of the Austrian Republic, who wrote, inviting them to sing at a formal reception for national and foreign dignitaries, alongside the Vienna Philharmonic Orchestra. Even though the family really felt they didn't want to do this, their soul-searching couldn't find a good reason to turn it down.

They were a hit at the event at the Belvedere Palace. The seven oldest children and Maria performed their repertoire, conducted by Father Wasner, with the director of the Vienna Boys' Choir adding his voice to those calling for them to begin performing regularly. Their family hobby was about to become their profession.

An ad hoc series of concerts was arranged for the 1936/1937 season, with two further performances in Vienna. At the first, American contralto Marian Anderson was performing in the large hall, but reviewers came down to listen to the von Trapps in the smaller auditorium during the intermission, leading to reviews in the papers hailing 'the lovely miracle of the Trapp Family'. In the summer, they hired the chamber music hall (the Wiener Saal) at the Mozarteum, the Academy of Music, and received an equally rapturous reception, led by Lotte Lehmann, who sat in the front row. Afterwards, the family was inundated with impresarios from multiple countries in Western Europe – and even one from America – demanding that they continue their singing. A tour of Western Europe was arranged for the autumn of 1937, with a contract for four-teen concerts in America proposed for the following year, running until March 1939.

Come September 1937, the family choir was preparing for their first major European tour. They still didn't have a proper title: they had been billed variously as 'The Trapp Family Sings', 'The Trapp Family Choir', 'Choir Concert by the Family von Trapp-Salzburg'. The Mozarteum director, Professor Bernhard Paumgartner, had advised them to sort out an official name, and suggested 'The Salzburg Chamber Choir Trapp' (which was shortened to 'The Chamber Choir Trapp' prior to their emigration to America). Paumgartner also suggested that they should add some instrumental pieces to provide some variety, and since three of the girls already played the recorder, pieces for this were prepared. Father Wasner was permitted to find a substitute for his duties so he could accompany them; Rupert and Werner (who was now away at college studying agriculture) were able to arrange some time off from their studies; and friends of the von Trapps agreed to look after the two younger children.

The Salzburg Chamber Choir Trapp was a success wherever it went in Europe. The family performed in front of Queen Mary at the Austrian Legation in London that December, and also appeared in Paris, Brussels and The Hague. They travelled down into Italy, singing in Milan and Turin, and then for the Holy Father himself, Pope Pius XI (appropriately performing Mozart's 'Ave Verum' to honour the most famous composer from their home town), at the Vatican, before spending ten days in Assisi. They returned home in mid-January 1938.

Two months later, the Third Reich invaded Austria.

5

A HASTY DEPARTURE

German Chancellor Adolf Hitler had long dreamed of uniting his country with Austria, and in March 1938 he achieved his wish. Austrian Chancellor Kurt von Schuschnigg had tried to negotiate a peace with Hitler the previous month at a meeting at Hitler's retreat, the Berchtesgaden, just the other side of the Alps from Salzburg, but the Führer was in no mood for negotiation. He told von Schuschnigg in no uncertain terms that he was going to solve the 'so-called Austrian problem' one way or another and made various demands that were unacceptable to the Austrian chancellor and its president, Wilhelm Miklas. However, when Hitler ordered his army to carry out manoeuvres on the border, Miklas caved in. Nazis were released from prison, and a pro-Nazi Minister of the Interior was appointed. Nazi flags began to proliferate around Austria.

It was clear to every Austrian that their country's end was nigh, and on the night of 11 March, the von Trapp family were listening to music on the radio in the library at the villa when an announcement was made by von Schuschnigg. He explained that the German army was at the borders, with tanks and troops ready to invade Austria. The country didn't have the capability to avert the invasion, and resistance would be futile – indeed, it would simply bring about a terrible bloodbath. (Georg von Trapp sent him a telegram wishing him God's blessing and protection soon after the radio broadcast.) Within minutes of von Schuschnigg's capitulation, the Nazis entered Austria, apparently summoned by a telegram from von Schuschnigg's replacement as chancellor. Hitler himself visited his birthplace at Braunau am Inn and entered Vienna on the afternoon of 14 March, the day after the Anschluss (union) of Austria and Germany was ratified by the Austrian government. Ninety-nine per cent of the German and Austrian people voted yes in a plebiscite held to approve the Anschluss on 10 April; the Nazi grip was tight from the moment they entered the country.

Changes could be felt immediately at every level. On 12 March, Hans, the von Trapps' faithful butler, privately told Georg that he had (illegally) been a member of the Nazi party for many years, and that he would be required to report anything and everything that he heard from the family to his new masters in Berlin. When Agathe and some of her siblings cycled into Salzburg that afternoon, they saw German troops parading over the bridges across the Salzach – bridges which were already festooned with the red Nazi flags bearing the swastika. Little things were altered, apparently simply to disconcert the population and remind them that everything was different: one-way streets were turned into two-way streets, and vice versa, and then renamed. Children were encouraged to inform on their parents, and an air of dread started to hang over the once-happy town.

A Gestapo officer came to the villa, asking the Captain to display the Nazi flag at the house; Georg said they didn't have one, but would be happy to hang some oriental rugs outside if their new governors felt that the house needed brightening up. The officer promptly sent a large flag back with some teenage Nazi supporters on motorbikes, but Georg never allowed it to be hung – although the housekeepers did put two small Nazi flags out of their own windows on the third floor. Georg announced to the family that he would put ground glass in his tea or finish his life on a dung heap before he sang the new German anthem (the Austrian anthem was banned with immediate effect after the Anschluss); when Lorli innocently repeated this at school, the frightened teacher warned Maria that they needed to be careful or she would have to report it. Maria warned Lorli that she mustn't say anything at school about what she heard at home, or everyone would be put in concentration camps, but when the little girl refused to join in with the 'Heil Hitler!' salute practice, she mentioned this threat to her teacher, who once again summoned Maria.

According to Maria, around this time, she was sent to see a specialist doctor in Munich because of kidney pains. He explained that she was once again pregnant, but that her body wasn't capable of sustaining the foetus. Maria had already had two miscarriages since Lorli's birth, and she and Georg were hoping for a miracle for the new baby they were going to call Barbara. The doctor wanted her to abort, but she refused.

While she and Georg were in Munich, they visited the House of German Art, an exhibition dedicated to the glory of Adolf Hitler, and found themselves in the restaurant seated at the table next to the Führer himself – and neither von Trapp was impressed by the man in whose hands Austria's destiny lay, seeing the crude and ill-mannered truth beneath his public persona. Georg had received a letter from the German Navy Department asking him to take over one of the new navy submarines. Initially the offer was tempting, but Georg was not willing to become a Nazi commander: it would be against God and against his country.

When they got back to Salzburg, Rupert was waiting for them: he had graduated from medical school just before the

Anschluss, and had been offered a prestigious place at a hospital in Vienna. Like his father, he realized that he would need to obey instructions to which he was inimically opposed; and, like his father, he was not prepared to do so.

There was a further decision to be made: a telephone call informed Georg that the Trapp family had been chosen as representatives from Ostmark – the Nazis' name for what had been Austria – to sing for Adolf Hitler's birthday on 20 April. If they accepted the offer, they would have Hitler's seal of approval, and would be safe from the repercussions of their actions. (They were also, at least temporarily, protected by the fact that all bar Rupert were still officially Italian citizens – the oldest von Trapp boy had taken back his Austrian nationality when he went to medical school.) However, inevitably, they would be forced to say the 'Heil Hitler!' that all of them were refusing to do, as well as appearing to support the restrictions the Nazis were imposing.

Georg called a family conference, on Hans's day off, so they could speak freely. As one, they refused to sing for the birthday celebrations. Georg warned them that refusing Hitler and his regime once was bad enough; to do it three times, as they would now be doing, was incredibly dangerous. They would have to leave their home and find somewhere new to live.

That, at least, is the rather romantic version of events that Maria laid out in her first autobiography. Unfortunately, events are unlikely to have happened quite that way. Far from being the last thing that the von Trapps refused to do for the new German state, the invitation to sing for Hitler's birthday in April would have been the first, coming a mere month after the Anschluss. Maria and Georg's visit to Munich can't have occurred before they knew of that invitation: they were seeing the doctor because of problems caused by her pregnancy – and she did carry the baby to term, giving birth to Johannes on 17 January 1939, so the earliest that they would have been going to the doctor is May, or possibly even June. That would also make sense of Rupert's graduation and subsequent job offer in

Vienna: by that time, the Nazis' naked anti-Semitism (which was considerably more open in the former Austria than it was in Germany itself) had led to the departure of many of the best doctors from the city. The anti-Semitism and proselytization of the Nazi creed increased almost exponentially within the schools across the summer term, which would have led to Maria's confrontations with the teacher. The combination of all these events, and the ever-growing closeness between Hitler's regime and that of the Italian fascist leader Mussolini, meant that the von Trapps' Italian identities would soon afford them little protection.

In early August 1938, Hans – whose loyalty to the von Trapps was constantly at war with his duty to his Party – warned Georg that he had heard that the Austrian borders were shortly going to be closed. No one would be able to leave the country. It was clearly now or never. Maria wanted one more sign of divine approval for the plan, and Georg opened the Bible, finding the passage from Genesis 12 in which the Lord tells Abram to leave his country and go to a land the Lord would show him (quoted as the epigraph to this book). The Chamber Choir von Trapp still had a number of engagements left to fulfil, many of which were due to take place in America. However, this time, instead of returning home after they completed their tour, the von Trapps would be hoping they had found their new home. Georg therefore asked each member of the family if they definitely wanted to leave Austria and go to America, and in turn they all replied that they did.

They wouldn't be travelling alone: it was clear that Father Wasner was tainted by his association with the von Trapps, and when the family approached the Archbishop, telling him in confidence of their plan to leave the country, they asked if he would be agreeable for Father Wasner to accompany them. The Archbishop gave his blessing.

Then followed two weeks of manic preparations. The initial plan was to go to France, but Father Wasner wasn't able to get a French visa – and then, after the Italians closed their borders to French citizens, the French followed suit, which would have prevented the majority of the von Trapps from travelling there. They therefore would have to go to Italy, and then make their way across Europe to England or another country where they could find a port for embarkation to America.

None of them wanted to leave their lovely house in Aigen to be used by the Nazis, so they arranged for the priests from the Boromaeum, a high school for boys who were contemplating the priesthood, to take it over: they had been forced out of their premises in the Salzburg suburb of Parsch by the Germans. Georg charged them the token sum of one schilling for the rental. (It made no odds: when the Nazis decided that they wanted to take over the house for Heinrich Himmler, they simply chose to ignore the rental agreement, and threw the priests out.)

As preparations continued, Lorli fell ill with appendicitis, and was operated on, in case she suffered another attack on the ship to America, when it could be potentially life-threatening. Just as they seemed ready to depart, Georg had a bad attack of lumbago, and was unable to move for a week. Once he was feeling better, he supervised the final cleaning of the house, and the handing over to the Boromaeum priests.

On their last day in Austria, the family had lunch at a local restaurant and in the evening went to church for a final blessing. They sang near the shrines at Maria Plain, a pilgrimage site in the north-east of the city, and then returned to the villa one last time. At 6 a.m., they said Mass, cleared the rooms they had been sleeping in, and set off on their journey to the train station.

To onlookers, it looked as if the von Trapp family were simply off on one of their regular mountain-climbing holidays in the South Tyrol: each of them had a rucksack on their back, and a large suitcase, inside which were their musical instruments (a spinet, four gambas and eight recorders), as well as one suitcase with baby clothes optimistically marked 'Barbara von Trapp'. They boarded the train south to northern Italy, and arrived in the little village of St Georgen, a couple of hundred miles away, after a few problems at the border when the officials wouldn't let them take their spinet through. They would have had even more problems if their delay had been a day longer – as Hans had warned, the borders were closed between Germany and Italy the next day.

There was another good reason for going to Italy: the Italian government had refused to send Georg's naval pension out of the country, so he had a large amount of back pay to collect when they arrived at St Georgen. This was what they needed to finance their trip across Europe to England; the American promoter of their tour, Charles Wagner, agreed to send them the money for the tickets for the boat. Once that arrived, they left St Georgen, and caught another train through Switzerland and France to the English Channel. After a rather choppy crossing they reached England, travelled by train to London, where they spent a few hours sightseeing, and then headed for Southampton. (Maria's accounts of this journey in her autobiographies are markedly different, and it seems, in her old age, that she confused their two trips to America, talking about the later trip on the SS *Bergensfjord* as if it happened here, rather than a year later; her original story and Agathe's account are broadly in agreement.)

The transatlantic boat was the *American Farmer*, and it would be their transport to a new life. It left Southampton on Friday 7 October 1938 at 6 p.m., with seventy-five passengers on board – ten of whom were extremely relieved that the most difficult part of their journey was apparently now behind them.

6

THE PERIPATETIC SINGERS

During the ten-day voyage from Southampton to New York, Maria took it on herself to start to learn English, asking her fellow travellers for the words for items, and quickly building up a basic vocabulary of words and phrases that they would need in their new life. Father Wasner arranged a couple of American songs for them to learn ('My Old Kentucky Home' and 'Old Black Joe'), and by the time of the final party to mark the end of the voyage, Maria had a very basic understanding of the language, and could, at the very least, try to make herself understood. The two oldest children already spoke English, having spent some of their holidays in the United Kingdom, and Georg had acquired a working knowledge.

One of Charles Wagner's assistants met the von Trapps at the quayside, and took them by taxis to the Hotel Wellington on Seventh Avenue and 55th Street, where they would be staying. There weren't any problems with immigration: the visas had all been sorted out well in advance. The family settled in to the hotel, immediately finding differences from their time in European establishments – for a start, leaving their shoes outside the door to be shined wouldn't achieve anything apart from possibly getting them stolen. Maria was amazed to learn that Georg's hat could be ironed at a shoemaker, while the boys discovered that their shoes were shined at the barber's!

Overall New York was something of a culture shock to the von Trapps, particularly Georg and Maria. At the time there were still elevated trains in central Manhattan, and Maria was scared when she had to walk beneath the lines; that was nothing to her fear of the subway or an escalator when she first encountered one in Macy's department store. However, they all quickly acclimatized, with the younger girls enjoying playing in the elevators at the hotel.

Maria had more reason to be concerned about another matter: her pregnancy with 'Barbara'. They hadn't told Charles Wagner about it, and a seamstress back in Austria had prepared various items of clothing for Maria that would conceal the truth.

The youngest girls, Rosmarie and Lorli, were too little to take on the demanding concert tour, so Wagner's office helped the von Trapps to find an inexpensive boarding school for them. The Ursuline Academy in the Bronx fitted the bill, and although Maria didn't want to leave them there (and regretted making a final trip to see them after they had just begun to settle in), there was little option.

Now rechristened 'The Trapp Family Choir', the von Trapps, together with Father Wasner, travelled around America in a big royal blue bus that had been specially out-fitted for them. As well as the thirty-two upholstered seats, there was a metal cot beneath the last two windows on the rear left in case anyone needed a lie down, and the choir's name was emblazoned on both sides and on the windscreen. Charles Wagner arranged a driver who would remain with them for both this tour and the next: Mr Tallerie was used to the idiosyncrasies of musical parties, but even he was occasionally flummoxed by Maria's requests for him to stop the bus when they were travelling at 60 miles per hour on the freeway because she had seen something she wanted to photograph!

The first concert was in Lafayette College, in Easton, Pennsylvania, and although, in hindsight, Maria accepted that the programme was too long, and too serious, the family gave it all they had, and the audience responded in kind. Their travels took them around the United States, and they found themselves briefly engaging with many different groups – although Georg, never comfortable in these circumstances, found a simple way of passing what appeared to be a polite comment: he gave each person a number as he was introduced to them, and the American ladies, hearing his polite German tones, were delighted. Maria was able to put her English lessons to good use, although telling a bishop to 'scram' when she simply wanted him to precede her through a doorway did provoke some hearty laughter, largely from the bishop himself.

Maria missed her two youngest children, and was petrified when Rupert rushed to tell Georg and Father Wasner some news he had heard late at night on the radio. Apparently, New York was in uproar, but no one could get any further information. It turned out that it was a false alarm: Rupert had simply tuned into Orson Welles' soon to be infamous live broadcast of H.G. Wells's *The War of the Worlds*, and, like some of those living in the New York area, had believed it to be true.

However, Maria was unable to continue concealing her pregnancy for much longer, and when Charles Wagner learned the news, he cancelled the concert tour immediately. They returned to the Hotel Wellington with no prospect of future income, but with three months still remaining on their visas. There they met up with an old friend, Mrs Pessl, the mother of a Viennese harpsichordist; she encouraged them to do a concert at the Town Hall, one of the prime locations in New York. Contralto Marian Anderson, who had appeared at the same time as the von Trapps in Vienna, had made her American debut there in 1935, and it had become known as the place for performers to make a mark on the New York scene. It would cost the von Trapps $700 to secure the hall, but it could multiply their earning potential. Through Mrs Pessl, they also secured the services of a publicist, Edith Behrens, who ensured that the public were well aware of the von Trapps' background long before the concert, held on 17 December.

The concert was a success. But even at this stage, the von Trapp story was becoming confused: *Time* magazine's report on 19 December talks about a 'patch-mustached Austrian nobleman' who came home from the Great War to 'his buxom wife, Frau Maria Augusta'. There they 'settled down to the serious business of raising their family' and 'developed the pleasant habit of making music together. On crisp Tirolese evenings they all gathered in the hall of their mountain castle to sing and play hoary Latin masses and lusty Tirolese folk songs.' After touring the whole map of Europe, the von Trapps decided to go to the US, and '[t]raveling all together in a specially chartered bus, Papa von Trapp, Mama von Trapp and the seven young singing von Trapps barnstormed the Middle West and South, surprised many a gas-station attendant with their dirndl dresses and Lederhosen'. Concluding that they are 'One of the world's most musical families', *Time* quotes 'ample, athletic Frau von Trapp: "We are having the time of our lives in God's own country."'

The day the *Time* report was published, the von Trapps went to the Central library at the invitation of Carleton Smith (director of the National Arts Foundation) and met Professor Otto Albrecht from the University of Pennsylvania, who was able to help them find a furnished house in Germantown, Philadelphia. They were able to move in before Christmas, and before the arrival of baby 'Barbara', who was born at home (something which came as a shock to Maria's new American friends, who were convinced that she had to have her child in hospital) on 17 January. 'Barbara' wasn't a girl: he was Johannes, and he completed the von Trapp family.

Charles Wagner was able to arrange a second concert tour for the following autumn, starting in September, and the family hoped that they would be able to eke out an existence giving occasional concerts before then. That of course depended on the American authorities allowing them to extend their visas, something they were assured by friends would simply be a formality. It wasn't: in February they were informed that they had to leave the United States by 4 March at the latest. Georg was able to secure twelve tickets for third-class passage on the *Normandie* heading to Southampton, but they weren't sure what they would do after that.

Looking back through the scrupulously maintained records he had kept, Georg saw that they had received an offer from a Danish impresario to give half a dozen concerts in Scandinavia. This might be their salvation, and Georg cabled him. On the morning of 2 March, forty-eight hours before they sailed on the *Normandie*, they received a reply: everything was ready for their first concert in Copenhagen on 12 March. The house in Germantown was packed up and the family headed to New York, where they embarked on the *Normandie*. It would be seven months before they returned.

The growth of the Third Reich was causing problems throughout Europe, as the von Trapps discovered when they arrived back. A pan-European war seemed increasingly likely, as Germany's territorial ambitions became ever clearer and refugees were treated with suspicion. Even with an established track record as a choir, the von Trapps found themselves only able to stay in countries for the period necessary to give their concerts. They travelled around Denmark, Sweden and Norway, and then were allowed to stay with friends, the president of KLM Airways and his wife, in Holland during June.

They separated during July: the older girls, along with Maria and Werner, dared to return to Austria for a short visit, staying with cousins of their mother, but Rupert, Georg and

Father Wasner didn't dare take the chance. Maria was horrified by the change in the country and its people in such a short
time, and was relieved to head back to St Georgen, where she
and Georg fulfilled a promise they had made while staying
there that they would bring baby 'Barbara' back to the shrine.
Everyone met back up safely in Amsterdam at the end of the
month, ready for another set of concerts in Sweden.

The Second World War began at the start of September,
and led to a premature cancellation of the rest of their tour,
since Hitler's blitzkrieg into Poland was making everyone in
Scandinavia very uneasy. Accordingly, their last concert was
held in Karlskruna, and Charles Wagner once again advanced
some money to enable them to purchase passage on the SS
Bergensfjord, the last ship to leave Oslo to take refugees to the
United States. Although Agathe recalled that the journey was
smoother because they were on the lowest deck, Maria was
less generous about the accommodation: the ship 'must have
been a first cousin of Noah's ark', she wrote in 1972.

There was a serious hiccup when the von Trapps arrived in
New York. Maria was so relieved to be back in a safe country
that she didn't think before she replied to the Immigration
Officer's standard question about how much time they
intended to spend in America. The answer should have been
'six months' as stated in their visas; instead, she said that she
was so glad to be there that she wanted to stay forever and
never leave. Her exact words differ slightly in her two volumes of autobiography, but that was the gist of it – and it
was enough to alarm the immigration officer, who promptly
pushed the family to the back of the queue (with the exception of Rupert, who had an immigration visa and so was
allowed in). They were then repeatedly questioned, and no
matter how many times they repeated that they were simply
there for their concert tour, Maria's comment had left the
impression that this was an emigration by stealth. They were
therefore taken by motorboat from the *Bergensfjord* to the
immigration headquarters on Ellis Island, where they were

separated from each other at night into men's and women's dormitories (Maria was able to get the lights switched off in the latter because of the new baby; the men weren't so lucky).

Rupert and Charles Wagner tried to find out what was happening, and, if nothing else, the family's incarceration on Ellis Island provided plenty of publicity. They were assured that it would simply be a formality, and they would be released soon, but on the fourth day, the judge in charge of appeals said that he didn't believe them. It looked as if the family were going to be returned to the *Bergensfjord* – but then the publicity paid off. Various friends of the von Trapps had seen the story, or been contacted by Rupert, Wagner or other friends, and they had put pressure on their senators and congressmen to vouch for the von Trapps' honesty. They were free.

7

BUILDING A REPUTATION

The Trapp Family Singers' second tour didn't get off to as strong a start as anyone had hoped, least of all Charles Wagner. The first concert saw them return to the Town Hall in New York, but the audience size was disappointing, a pattern that would be repeated as they travelled around. Wagner's 'pink envelopes' (he used pink stationery at the time) would be waiting for them as they arrived at the next hotel or concert hall, with a note inside expressing his sadness at how disappointingly they had done the previous time. Publicity was poor, and it was starting to look as if the tour might be cancelled because of lack of interest – but the originally booked twenty-four concerts did take place, ending at the Academy of Music in Philadelphia in December.

There, their friends Harry and Sophie Drinker, who were great fans of music even if not as proficient in the arts as their many acquaintances, offered the von Trapps the use of a house which had been used by Drinker's mother prior to her death.

There wouldn't be any rent: Harry Drinker simply wanted Father Wasner's assistance in translating Bach's chorales from German to English, a project he had undertaken some years earlier.

However, the von Trapps once again faced a serious problem: although expressing much regret, Charles Wagner told them that he did not want to renew his contract with them, since he felt they were better suited to Europe than America. The last thing that any of them wanted to do was return to the war-torn continent, so Maria asked Mrs Pessl to enquire how she could get in contact with F.C. Schang of Columbia Concerts, whom she had met and been impressed by at their first Town Hall concert the previous December. Mrs Pessl provided the telephone number, and Maria rang the promoter and asked if they could audition. A week later, they sang at the Steinway Hall for Schang and Mr Coppicus, one of the other managers of the Metropolitan Musical Bureau. To the family's disappointment, they too turned down the Trapp Family Choir.

Undeterred, Maria encouraged the family to rework the programme, and requested another audition – and once again they were turned down. This time, Maria wasn't going to take a blanket answer, and asked Coppicus's secretary why. She told her kindly that Mr Coppicus had said that they had no 'sex appeal'. Maria tried to find out what the phrase meant by looking in a book of musical terms, but couldn't see it there; she therefore went back to Schang's office, and asked to see him.

Schang didn't hold back. It wasn't the musicianship of the choir that was the problem, he explained. It was the music that they chose – such as a forty-five-minute-long Bach cantata, which simply wouldn't attract audiences, bar musical experts, to come to listen to them. An even bigger problem was the way that they looked: far too solemn, they came on and off stage as if they were at a funeral. He wanted them to change their clothes and wear some make-up.

Maria told him simply that they couldn't do that. She couldn't understand how in America, the so-called land of the free, they couldn't express their music in the way they wanted to. 'I thinked – America free country. Is not!' she said, and stormed out of the office.

Maybe it was the passion that she showed then – a passion which, as far as Schang was concerned, was simply lacking from the Trapp Family Choir performances – but as Maria waited for the elevator to return to her family, knowing she would have to break the news to them that their dream was over, the secretary asked her to return to Schang's office. There, Schang told her he was willing after all to give it a try for a year – as long as they could raise $5,000 for advance publicity. Thanks to loans from Harry Drinker and another rich woman who had offered her help after hearing the family sing at the Cosmopolitan Club in New York, Maria was able to produce two cheques for $2,500.

Schang was clear about what needed doing: the Trapp Family Choir had to become something marketable. And the first change was simple: the name was too 'church-y'. He therefore became manager of the 'Trapp Family Singers' – who now no longer had the threat of returning to Europe over their heads. As a result of the war, the United States government was no longer forcing anyone to leave, and their temporary visas could be renewed every six months.

Their first concerts were held before Christmas 1939 in the Town Hall, and included some of Freddy Schang's proposed changes: a new programme was devised, which included English and American Christmas carols, as well as other pieces, in the family's traditional musical style, which Father Wasner was able to locate. The main tour wouldn't begin until the following autumn, so the family had time to bed down in their new home, with a tutor found for the younger children. To raise the cash they needed to survive the summer months, they created the Trapp Family Handicraft Exhibit, with many members of the family showing they had other artistic talents beside the musical (all bar their mother and Rupert, who handled the exhibiting).

The new tour began in September in New York, and once again the little girls didn't accompany them, although this time they were able to stay at home with 'Tante Lene' – one of Maria's own teachers from her time in Vienna, who was also a refugee – and Martha, one of young Maria's school friends who had been acting as babysitter to Johannes during the Swedish tour, and ended up emigrating with them. (Johannes did come along, much to the delight of their driver, Rudi.)

In consultation with Freddy Schang, the programme had been lightened considerably: pieces like 'Sweet Honey-Sucking Bees' and 'Early One Morning' sat alongside the music played on the medieval instruments, and selections from the sacred works. And the Trapp Family Singers were going to try something very different as well: they were going to smile. This was something completely alien to them (Agathe recalls thinking it was an absurd idea at the time), but they were willing to give it a try – after all, since Schang had expressed his faith in them by booking over a hundred concerts, it seemed the least they could do.

The smiling certainly helped, and the audiences came to the concerts as the Trapp Family Singers criss-crossed America, but Schang was sure that there was something more that would help to endear the family to their audiences. Maria discovered it quite by accident at a concert in Denver, Colorado, shortly before Christmas 1940.

It was one of the rarer occasions when the Singers were indulging their more serious side. The emphasis of the programme was very much on the sacred music, and towards the end Maria felt a twinge of sympathy for those who had perhaps been expecting something nearer their now-normal repertoire. She therefore told Father Wasner at the end that she'd like to sing a Jodler – the proper name for a yodelling song. As they got started, Maria got a fly in her throat, which meant she didn't give a proper performance, so she told the audience what had occurred: 'What never happened before, has happened now,' she said. 'I swallowed a fly.' She was amazed by the laughter which greeted that explanation, and messed up the introduction to the encore she offered in apology – a mistake which also was greeted with waves of laughter. It didn't take her long to realize what had been missing: the family were used to singing for each other for their own pleasure, or for the pleasure of their guests. What they now did was extend that mantle to the audience, so they effectively became guests at a musical party thrown by the Trapp Family Singers.

The first tour under Schang's management was so successful there was no question about a follow-up the next year, and the family started to expand their repertoire further. The younger children started to travel along, receiving their tuition on the bus, with the house in Pennsylvania becoming a base. They also began to make recordings, initially for RCA Victor, and later for the Concert Hall Society and Decca Records. They gave up the tour bus, and started to use two large cars: a seven-seater 1935 Lincoln Continental and a large Cadillac, which had the advantage of giving them transportation during the months they weren't singing.

Used to the more temperate climate of Austria, the von Trapps suffered during the summers in Pennsylvania, and gratefully took up the offer of the use of a cabin in New Jersey (which nearly led to the death of Johannes, who waded out into a fast-flowing river and was only saved by Father Wasner happening to spot him at exactly the right moment). They were intrigued by another offer, this time of a tourist house in Stowe, Vermont, known as 'The Stowe-Away'. It seemed to fit exactly what they were after: Vermont's geography was far more what they were used to, and there were plenty of places for the family to go hiking without being constantly asked by passers-by if they needed a lift.

Realizing that this was the place they wanted to settle, they started to look for a place of their own in Vermont, and after spending a large amount of time discovering the discrepancies between real-estate advertisements and the actual state of the properties, Georg spotted Luce Hill, which seemed ideal. He knew that he'd be happy there – although at the time it wasn't for sale. However, the day after he saw it, the owner came to offer it to the family. The place was in what was known as 'fair repair' (in reality, one step away from collapsing), but it would provide them with the home they had been lacking since they left the Villa Trapp in September 1938.

It wasn't all good news for the family, however. Shortly before they were due to begin the next tour, Rupert and Werner received letters from the Draft Board, telling them to be ready to be called up; and as they progressed across country, mandatory gasoline rationing was introduced. The von Trapps' two cars were both gas guzzlers – achieving a mere ten miles per gallon – which meant that at each town they went to they needed to visit the local rationing board in order to gain more than the minimum, or they wouldn't be able to travel between performances. In March 1943, the two boys were taken to Hyde Park for their induction, and Maria was surprised to find that Freddy Schang had also been accepted into the army ranks.

The loss of Rupert and Werner cut to the core of the Trapp Family Singers. Their pieces were arranged for the specific make-up of the group: they couldn't simply remove the boys' bass and tenor lines from the harmony and sing the rest. Now they would be a women's choir, and would need to find music that was appropriate – or create completely new arrangements of the current material for the new line-up.

They were invited to give a concert in Bethlehem, Pennsylvania, ten days after the boys' departure, and the time was spent manically learning the new songs. To everyone's relief, the 'new' Trapp Family Singers received as good – if not a better – reception than they had before, and Maria sent a telegram to the boys saying: 'Battle of Bethlehem has been won'.

The spring and summer between concert seasons was spent

renovating their new home in Vermont, or indeed rebuilding large parts of it from scratch after the roof fell in – wartime regulations wouldn't allow them to build a new house, but they could alter the design of the parts they rebuilt. It was back-breaking work, but the family enjoyed the challenge, and the boys were delighted to see the progress when they came back on furlough.

Preparations for the new concert season included singing at the local Town Hall in a fundraiser for the schoolhouse roof, and Maria was rather surprised when the local townsfolk – the entire audience for the concert, since holidaymakers had left for the season – came up to shake them by the hand. The following weekend, many of the locals came to assist the von Trapps with their final work on the house: many had steered clear because of rumours that these 'Germans' were building something on the hill which wasn't as innocent as it looked.

Maria recalled that the season was prefaced with a feature in *Life* magazine: the reporters had come out to the new farm to find out what the von Trapps got up to when they weren't singing. It worked wonders for publicity, particularly the photo of young Johannes: many people knew them simply from that article. The magazine also gave coverage to their arrival in New York for their November concert; however, contrary to Maria's recollections, the feature in *Life* about 'The Trapp Family in Vermont' actually only appeared in the 8 November edition, some time after the tour had begun.

Whether aided by the article or not, the tour was another success: their concert in Minot, Dakota, was hailed as 'superb' by the Minot State College student newspaper for its 'precision of timing, entrance of voices . . . [and] clarity of diction'. The programme began with Mozart's 'Ave Verum', which displayed the singers' 'beautiful blend of voices, especially in the pianissimo passages' and concluded with 'America the Beautiful', sung in thanks by the von Trapps, as Maria explained, for the 'gratitude and love she and her family' had for the 'land of their adoption'. Since gasoline was simply not available, they travelled between concerts by train or bus where possible, although occasionally they had to improvise: when they discovered that one bus service which they expected to use was no longer operating, they asked one of the locals for help – and the only vehicle he could provide was a hearse!

During their Christmas 1943 break, the von Trapps learned that the local Army camp was going to be closing down, and they applied for permission to turn it into a singing camp, where they could hold 'Sing Weeks' like the ones Maria had participated in during her youth. Groups of between fifty and a hundred people could get together to make music and dance for a week to ten days. Their publicity manager in New York helped to spread the word: 100,000 green leaflets were sent out explaining: 'You are invited to enjoy a holiday of music-making with the Trapp Family Singers during the coming summer at the Trapp Family Music Camp in Stowe, Vermont.'

By May 1944, over a hundred people had already signed up, paying a ten dollar deposit each, and the lease was confirmed at the end of that month. Once again War Department regulations seemed designed to confound their efforts, and Maria found herself in hot water when it appeared that she had transgressed the law by using materials for the construction of the new facilities at the camp, which she shouldn't have done as they were officially required for the war effort, and was threatened with a $10,000 fine and a year in jail. However, the camp was made ready – albeit with a large number of teething problems along the way – and the first guests arrived on schedule in July. The next twelve months saw another concert tour, and a second round of Trapp Family Music Camps, during which the war came to a close; Rupert and Werner returned from their active service in Italy, and although Werner chose to return to the musical life, combining that with developing his knowledge of farming, Rupert elected to complete his medical training. He went back to school, at the University of Vermont, and not long after he became engaged.

* * *

Although the family had very much embraced their adopt-
ive country, they were still Austrian at heart, and when
they heard about the plight of the people back home in the
aftermath of the war, they were more than happy to help.
They received a letter (from the general in charge, according to Maria; from the chaplain in Agathe's version) which
asked if the Trapp Family Singers could do something for the
Austrians during their concert tours. They therefore set up a
charity – the Trapp Family Austrian Relief Inc. – which would
allow them to collect food, clothing and money, which would
be tax-deductible. Nearly forty years before Bob Geldof and
Midge Ure devised Live Aid, the von Trapps were doing their
piece in the battle against poverty.

Determined to raise as much as they could, every concert
contained what the children called 'Mother's Austrian Relief
Speech' in which she highlighted the situation, and said which
hotel (usually the wrong one!) they were staying in where
items could be left; the response surprised even them – mostly
positive, although, inevitably, there were some who wanted to
come to concerts to relax, not to be reminded of the problems
of the poor. It was the von Trapps' longest tour – over thirty
thousand miles and 107 concerts – and not only did they have
the stress of the performances, but they also had to collect,
package up and mail out the items they had collected to the
Catholic Army chaplains in Vienna and Salzburg who had
agreed to coordinate the effort at the Austrian end.

However, amid all of the hard work bringing some aid
to the people of Austria, there was heartbreak for the von
Trapps. During the 1946–1947 tour, when the Austrian Relief
effort was just starting, Georg began to fall ill, and although
he argued that he wanted to remain with his family, his condition deteriorated, and he was flown back from Denver to
New York to see a specialist. He was diagnosed with pneumonia, and when Maria flew up a couple of weeks later, she
was delighted to be told that he could be taken home to Stowe

as soon as she wanted. She and Georg spent the day making plans for the future, not realizing that the reason the doctor was allowing him home was because Georg was terminally ill.

The doctor broke the news to her that evening: Georg had a malignant tumour in his lung and he had three months left to live. The next day Maria took him home, and told Rupert everything. They brought in other local specialists, who disagreed with the New York doctor's diagnosis. Although Maria could see that Georg was weakening, she put her faith in the positive prognosis. Right up to the end, the local doctors assured her that he was simply suffering from asthma, and no one died from asthma; Georg's breathlessness was a nervous condition, rather than the precursor to death, which the New York doctor had described. But the original diagnosis was correct, and at 4.30 a.m. on 30 May 1947, Georg von Trapp died. Like many of his comrades from the U-boat service in the First World War, he had succumbed to lung cancer. He was buried in the grounds of the family home.

It was the end of an era, but not the end of the Trapp Family Singers.

8

THE TRAPP FAMILY SINGERS GO GLOBAL

The Trapp Family Singers continued performing for nearly nine more years after Georg von Trapp's death. During that time, the group underwent many changes, and their story became more widely known as a result of Maria's first book, which was published in 1949.

Georg's death marked the start of a bad period for the family – Maria used the analogy of the seven good years and the seven lean years from the biblical story of Joseph. Only a couple of weeks after the funeral, Rosmarie disappeared, unable to cope with the pressures of the past few months. 'When Father died I was eighteen, and after his death I had a nervous breakdown,' she recalled to an Israeli newspaper in 2006. 'I ran away from home in Vermont and when I came back, the doctors treated me with electroshock therapy. It was awful.' Maria didn't seem to realize how bad things were with her eldest daughter – this marked the start of a period of estrangement between them, perhaps not helped by Maria's rather insensitive comments in her book a couple of years later. Rosmarie didn't travel with the Trapp Family Singers, staying at home in Vermont.

Both Johannes and Hedwig suffered major illness, Lorli was hit by a pickup truck and a car reversing towards each other – only receiving a couple of broken ribs – and Maria suffered a final miscarriage. She was too unwell to travel to Fall River, Massachusetts for Rupert's wedding, although she did try to take part in the 1947–1948 tour – only to fall ill with a uremic condition, with convulsions and high blood pressure. She was so ill that on Christmas Eve 1947 she was given the last rites, but she recovered sufficiently to become an American citizen the following May. As part of that process, the family renounced their title and coat of arms, and began to live under the precepts of *Cor Unum et Anima Una* ('one heart and one soul'), as was exemplified by the first Christians in Jerusalem – and the Lodge was renamed Cor Unum.

Things started to look up then: after the war, the Villa Trapp in Aigen had been handed back to the von Trapps, but they didn't want to return there, particularly after they learned the story of Hitler ordering the deaths of a number of guards because he heard one of them singing a Russian folk song. The property was put on the market, and sold to a religious order in America. It became a seminary. With the money, the family were able to pay off their debts on their Vermont home, and considerably extend it. Werner fell in love with Martina's friend, Erika, and Martina herself fell for a Canadian lad. Johanna married and left the singing group the same year.

The concert tours continued, with lengthy trips across the entire United States (barring Alaska), as well as the Hawaiian Islands (which only became a state in 1959) and Canada. In early 1950, Freddy Schang told them they had been invited to give a three-month tour of South America, but the arrangements took until Good Friday to complete, and even then they weren't properly ready. The itinerary suggested some possible concerts, rather than the tight-knit schedule they were used to; arriving in Caracas, they discovered that far from being 'the country of mañana' (tomorrow), as they had been told, the posters all displayed the previous day's date for the concert. Their first concert in Buenos Aires was seen as a gateway for the others, and they had to learn an Argentinian piece quickly (since by law, all programmes had to include at least one such item), but they were a success. They also discovered how much of a melting pot South America had become in the immediate post-war years, meeting German prince Albrecht von Bayern among many other refugees from Europe.

Unlike most years, the summer of 1950 didn't see the von Trapps return to Cor Unum for a long period: in addition to the South American tour, they were scheduled to sing at the Salzburg Festival, their first official return to their home since their departure in 1938. Despite the escalating tensions over Korea, they made the journey, and were overwhelmed by the reception they received at the train station; Maria believed that someone famous, such as the conductor Toscanini, must be on the train with them. Despite their earlier reservations, the von Trapps stayed at their old house, which proved to be a bitter-sweet experience, as did the whole trip. Because of their work with the relief aid, they were fêted as heroes, but many hoped that they would be able to help more, or even take them back to America when they left. (Lorli did take someone home eventually – she met her husband-to-be during this trip.) However, this was a concert tour, and after three weeks in Salzburg (during which they did receive some negative reaction to their having fled the country), they moved on.

It wasn't one of their most successful trips. The European peoples were still struggling to cope with the realities of the post-war economy, and no matter their origins, the von Trapps were seen as Americans coming over. Promoters thought that they should go for the biggest venues available, but they failed to fill them. Concerts in England were cancelled; one in Wales stood out because the audience was composed of singers, who valued the performances. In the end, Maria called Freddy Schang and asked him to advance against their Christmas concerts. However, before they left Europe, they visited Rome, where, against all odds, they were permitted to sing in the tomb of Saint Peter, which had recently been discovered beneath the Vatican. Tragedy struck again the following year, when Martina died in childbirth, a year and a half after getting married. She was buried next to her father; because of the concert schedule, only Maria could go home to bury her stepdaughter.

The first tour to Hawaii took place in 1952, after a visit the previous summer to Cor Unum by Bishop Lane of the Maryknoll Fathers, who had carried out extensive missionary work around the world. As well as doing their usual concert tour, and interacting with many of the locals, the family visited the leper colony of Molokai where they not only sang for the sufferers from Hansen's Disease who lived there, but were treated to a concert by the patients themselves.

Further tours followed each year, with more additional non-family members assisting with the performances, as the von Trapp sisters had children and dropped out of the group. For the final extensive tour of Hawaii, the Fiji islands, Australia and New Zealand, which began in spring 1955, there were only six von Trapps: Agathe, Maria, Hedwig, Werner, Johannes and their mother – alongside four other singers. Agathe recalled that it was clear to everyone – except her mother – that this would be the last tour. Their reception wasn't as favourable as it could have been, at least initially, and because the southern hemisphere was in winter, there were various health issues. The family were often billeted in private homes rather than in hotels, which had its own problems, but slowly they got used to the conditions, and enjoyed meeting the Maoris to the extent that they started to include Maori songs and dances in their programme.

And that was it. When they got home after the seven-month-long tour and the singers were asked if they wanted to carry on – possibly to Japan – the answer was no. A final series of concerts was given over Christmas 1955, and then, on 26 January 1956, the last performance by the Trapp Family Singers took place in Concord, New Hampshire. Nine months later, the story of their escape from the Nazi regime would make the first of its many appearances on screen – but by then, the Trapp Family Singers had dispersed. (They did reunite briefly in 1959 to record, of all things, a selection of songs from *The Sound of Music*.)

Maria Augusta Kutschera von Trapp lived for a further thirty-one years; her third volume of autobiography, *Maria*, relates how she became involved with missionary work for some time before she returned to Vermont to run Cor Unum. This wasn't necessarily something that suited her talents, and eventually she passed the responsibility over to Johannes in 1969. She lectured extensively about her faith in God and her family's story.

She was awarded the Decoration of Honour in Gold for Services to the Republic of Austria in 1957, and five years later received the Siena Medal from the Theta Phi women's fraternity at the University of Michigan, which is given to those outside the fraternity who live up to the motto of Catherine of Siena: 'Nothing great is ever achieved without much enduring.' She was also given the Austrian Cross of Honour for Science and Art, 1st class, in 1967 for improving ties between Austria and America. Cor Unum burned down in a fire in 1980, and Maria lived long enough to see the new buildings completed before she died in 1987 after undergoing surgery for gangrene of the small intestine.

Rupert became a family doctor, and lived in Rhode Island until his retirement, when he returned to Vermont; he died in 1992, aged 80. Agathe and her friend Mary Lou Kane started a kindergarten together after the Trapp Family Singers disbanded, and worked and lived together for 37 years before retiring to Baltimore, Maryland. She was encouraged to write her memoirs by her family doctor, Janet Horn, partly because she was so 'rabidly negative' towards the musical and film of *The Sound of Music*. 'She believed you really need to accomplish something every day,' Doctor Horn told the *Baltimore Sun* after Agathe's death, aged 97, in December 2010. 'Even if it was to start drawing or painting, she always had a project. She had an extraordinary memory and in many ways lived in the genteel, civilized Old World.'

Maria von Trapp became a missionary in New Guinea, and remained there for thirty-two years before returning to Cor Unum, where she lived in a house in the grounds for a long time. She died in February 2014, aged 99. Werner and his wife Erika bought a dairy farm in Waitsfield, Vermont, which they worked along with their six children until they retired in 1979; Werner died in October 2007, aged 91. Many of their children and grandchildren have become musicians, with four of the grandchildren (Sofi, Melanie, Amanda and August) now performing as the von Trapps.

Hedwig became a teacher in Hawaii and then in the Tyrol. She suffered from asthma, and ended up living with her aunt in Zell am See; she died of complications from asthma in 1972. Johanna, one of the first to leave the singing group, married the son of a Vienna city official and brought up a family of seven children there, dying in Austria in 1994.

Georg and Maria's three children are still going strong. Rosmarie, by her own admission, went off the rails for a period after her father's death, but gave her life to God aged 40. She joined a religious community, the Community of the Crucified One, and helped to take care of her mother until her death in 1987; she has travelled extensively as a missionary. Like Johanna, Lorli raised a large family, while Johannes took over running the Lodge in 1969, passing responsibility to his own son Sam in recent years.

PART TWO: THE TRAPP FAMILY SINGERS ON STAGE

9

THE FIRST BIG SCREEN EXCURSIONS

Every generation has its icons, those people whose heroism or unusual deeds form the core of a good story, a tale which spreads among their contemporaries. In recent years, that dissemination has come through newspapers and magazine articles, but they are ephemeral, and, even now, it's still very much the case that unless the tales are collected into some larger, more permanent volume, they tend to disappear. Certainly in the pre-internet days of the immediate post-war period, had it not been for Maria von Trapp's 1949 book, chances are that the tale of the 'singing von Trapp family' would have been lost in the mists of time, occasionally to be disinterred by someone going through back issues of *Time* or *Life* magazine.

Of course, we know the story now because of *The Sound of Music*, but that was by no means the first time the tale was told. The road to *The Sound of Music* really begins with that

1949 book, *The Story of the Trapp Family Singers* – a title Maria herself realized in later life wasn't particularly inspired. There are various different versions of how she came to write it: an American publisher, J.B. Lippincott, was intrigued by the various pieces of the history revealed in interviews, and asked her to pen her life story. Alternatively, in the time after Georg's death, she sat down to put her tale in writing after apparently being pushed by a friend to do so. In the introduction (what she called 'The Chapter Before the First'), Maria recalls visiting the Tyrol around 1933, and ringing a bell while making the wish that she could become a writer 'after she was forty', but doesn't give any other indication as to why she began writing.

The book is written in a very conversational style, although it often sidetracks into discussions of God's love, and although its title would suggest that it's about the whole family, it is very much a tale told from Maria's perspective. It would be wrong to say that the book is a fictionalized account of the family's story, but certainly there are sections where events are conflated to present a better dramatic picture (ironically, something for which the musical and film would be attacked by the von Trapp family in later years). Some of the chronology does not fit documented history, and her eldest stepdaughter, Agathe, disputed the sequence of events in her own book.

The Story of the Trapp Family Singers was moderately well received on publication: religious publications praised the way in which it 'presents a real example of a family in which Christian traditions and Christian faith illumine and enliven every event', while the *San Francisco Chronicle* suggested that readers would be 'missing something if you don't get hold of it right away'. However, it did look as if it was a musical book rather than a biography, and it was often misplaced in bookstores in the music section. (Many people came to it through its availability in religious bookstores or collections.)

The book came out when the Trapp Family Singers were

still popular, and their Town Hall concerts a fixture of the New York social calendar. Perhaps not too surprisingly, Hollywood came calling quite quickly. According to the account she gave in *The Trapp Family on Wheels*, her second volume of autobiography published in 1959, which covered the family's peripatetic existence making music between 1948 and 1956, Maria received a phone call from Hollywood offering 'a large sum of money' for the rights to make the film. Almost in passing, Maria asked if they were planning on changing the story, and was not impressed when she was told that the producers didn't want the story within the book – they simply wanted the title. (It's been suggested that this story was referring to the title 'The Sound of Music', but Maria wrote the autobiography long before the musical came out.) The producers raised their offer, but insisted that they were only buying the title; despite this, Maria refused.

The Story of the Trapp Family Singers was translated into German, and became very popular; in 1955, agents for German film company Divina-Film made contact with Maria, and expressed an interest in buying the film rights. According to Maria's version in her 1972 autobiography, *Maria*, they offered $10,000 for the rights; her lawyer suggested that she should ask for royalties in addition. The agent, she claimed, then told her that unfortunately West German law at that time forbade companies from paying royalties to foreigners. Maria took this at face value, and, without checking with her lawyer, signed the contract without the royalties attached; the payment of the $10,000 was due within a year. Shortly afterwards, the agent contacted her again and offered $9,000 immediately for the rights. Needing the cash, Maria accepted, not realizing that she had signed away the entire rights to the story – not just the German language ones – to the company.

The film was made in 1956, and released in West Germany that October. In *The Trapp Family on Wheels*, Maria said that what she referred to as the 'Gloria Film' (the name of the

distributors) 'finally presented the screen version sympatheti-
cally'. Various members of the von Trapp family have gone on
record with their comments on *The Sound of Music* (as discussed later in chapter 11) but many of their criticisms could
equally be made of *Die Trapp-Familie*.

The film opens with a note before the credits that this is 'A
film from the memories of Baroness Maria Trapp who lives
with her family in America', before focusing on various
Salzburg landmarks over the titles. According to the English
subtitles, this is Salzburg in 1926 (although this doesn't really
fit with the way the rest of the movie works, and the dating
doesn't appear in the film), and we see a group of nuns walking through some cloisters. They go up to their room where
young Maria flings open the window and proclaims what a
glorious day it is. But she's running late for her lesson, and
arrives there with a smudge on her nose. She's just starting
to teach the youngsters when she's called to see the Reverend
Mother.

The venerable nun explains that it's God's will that Maria
should leave them. They have had a letter from war hero
Baron von Trapp, a widower with seven children. Multiple
governesses have run away from his employ. Maria will be
loaned to them for a few months. She's sent out in some quite
unworldly clothes with the reminder that when God closes a
door, he opens a window. Maria leaves the convent (filmed at
the real location) and descends into Salzburg.

Jump to her arrival at Villa Trapp where she's met at the
door by Franz, the butler. As she waits in the hall, she admires
the large Austrian flag over the fireplace. She's nervous when
she meets Georg von Trapp and surprised when he uses his
bosun's whistle to summon the children, with different notes
for each child. All seven children, dressed very smartly,
come downstairs in order, and he introduces them: Agathe,
Rupert, Werner, Hedwig, Maria, Rosemarie and the youngest, Martina. He tells them that Maria is in charge of them,

and also introduces her to Baroness Matilda, the housekeeper. He then uses his whistle to dismiss the children.

The Baroness shows Maria to her room, and explains she is the twenty-sixth governess they've had, and that the Baron insists on strong discipline. She also tells Maria about the Baron's interest in Princess Yvonne, and Maria prays that he will find a kind wife. She's late down to dinner, which is extremely formal. The Baron says he will leave tomorrow to see the princess.

The next day, the children are marching around in pristine white sailor suits, which they tell Maria they don't want to get dirty; they haven't got any other clothes. Maria runs to the seamstress and asks her to make play clothes for the children from some old drapes. Now dressed more appropriately, the children start having fun, rolling down the hill and getting muddy. However, Baroness Matilda is horrified by this and can't believe her eyes when she finds the children playing hide and seek in a tree. She gives Maria a dressing down but Maria stands up to her: she's on loan from the abbey, she explains, and she can't stand how the children are being treated. She will let them play. The Baroness determines to tell the Baron.

That evening, Georg von Trapp is at an elegant soirée where Princess Yvonne is entertaining at the piano. He's interrupted by a phone call from the Baroness, who says Maria is uncontrollable and leading 'unbelievable' activities. Georg agrees he will come home, and his banker friend, Rudi Grubier, points out that he has less trouble with his staff than Georg does with seven children. He also asks how Georg got on with the princess, but von Trapp reveals that she turned him down. When they re-enter the soirée, the princess tells Georg that the children's place is at boarding school, and although Georg was unhappy himself at boarding school, he is encouraged by the others present to consider it. Rudi drops the hint that if the children weren't around, Yvonne would look more favourably on him.

That night, Maria is in bed during a loud thunderstorm,

when Martina comes to the door saying she's frightened, but she's the only one who is. That turns out not to be true as first the other girls and then the boys (claiming that they're just checking if the others are afraid) arrive at Maria's room. To keep them cheerful, Maria gets her guitar and starts singing with them. Downstairs, the Baroness hears the singing, and Franz asks if he should stop them; the Baroness says no, since the Baron will be back the next day.

Waiting for the Baron's return, the children are back in their sailor suits (Maria has put the play clothes away), but they're bored. They know if they get dirty, it'll mean Maria has to leave. They decide to play U-boats and Martina knows just how to add to the realism of the experience: she gets the garden hose and starts spraying them all. What she doesn't realize is that her father has arrived back, and he and Franz are standing near enough to the hose to get wet. Maria comes to get them changed since they're now soaked, and the Baron is furious at what he's seen. Franz is delighted: it means the 'country bumpkin' will be leaving.

The Baron tries to find his sons, but they're not in their room and he is angry when the Baroness explains that the children have been spending a lot of time together. They hear Maria playing guitar and the children singing, and Georg is about to burst into the nursery – but then he stops and listens. He opens the door to see the children in their play clothes sitting at Maria's knee, singing. He tells the Baroness it's unbelievable – which she takes to mean them all on the floor together. When the song finishes, they spot their father and rush to him. He asks what they're wearing, and they tell him that Maria got them their new clothes, as well as some clogs. Georg sends the children out to the garden while he speaks to Maria on his own, and tells Martina to leave the hose alone.

Maria says he was only supposed to find out about the changes a bit at a time, and Georg asks if he is really so difficult. Yes, she says, he is, and his methods of upbringing are fundamentally wrong and old-fashioned. Maria's father was a teacher in a small village and the children loved him; she says that life with the von Trapps is like a boarding school. Children should be together in a family, not separated. Maria realizes she's gone too far, but Georg sees her point and also concedes that changes are needed. The children call for her to play and she goes – he says he'll follow to play too.

The children's bubbles merge with Christmas baubles, as Georg and Maria set up the tree. He tells her that the children love her, and she says it's mutual. They're now teasing each other, but they know Maria must return to the abbey in a month and eighteen days. She asks if he's getting remarried, and he says he is, which pleases her. The children sing 'Silent Night' together before opening their presents, and there are even a few things for Maria (even though she can't take possessions back to the abbey when she leaves). Her main present from Georg is a hundred pairs of clogs, which he has arranged to be given to each of the children who are given presents by the abbey every Christmas. As Maria and the children start to play their new musical instruments, Georg says to Rudi that Maria is a gift from heaven. His friend points out that she's an innocent, and sometimes a more practical head is needed. With the princess arriving the next day, Rudi suggests that he keep Maria hidden. Trapp can't see why . . .

For the princess's entertainment, the children and Maria put on a shadow play of the story of Briar Rose, but Yvonne can't help but notice the interaction between Georg and Maria – and Rudi sees her reaction. Yvonne takes Maria off for a talk, and tells her it's a shame she can't stay forever, but points out that when Maria leaves, she'll leave a broken heart behind unless she behaves in a more restrained way towards the Baron. He's in love with her.

Maria is horrified. All she knows of love is from stories like *Romeo and Juliet*: love leads to murder and manslaughter. She determines to leave straightaway. Yvonne asks where she'll go, and she says she'll return to the abbey. Yvonne says all Maria has to do is hold herself back for the final few weeks.

At that point, the children rush in to find Maria packing. She says they knew she was going at some point but they complain that it's not supposed to be for another month. Maria says things have changed. When Rupert asks if their father knows, Maria says no, and the oldest boy takes the other children out.

They tell their father, who says he'll talk to Maria – but then he sees Yvonne coming down, and asks her what she said to Maria. Yvonne claims she was joking with the girl, but asks Georg if he sees Maria as governess or mother to the children? Angered, Georg tells the children to go their rooms, and storms into Maria's room, as she is changing. She tells him what Yvonne said, and asks if he is in love with her. He denies it – it's not the truth, at least not the whole truth.

There's a commotion outside as the princess and her party depart. Georg returns to Maria and she agrees that it would be a great sin for him to marry Yvonne when he's in love with someone else. Georg knows she can no longer stay as governess, but could she as his wife? He knows it's not possible unless she likes him a little. If she does, she doesn't know it, she says, but she could ask someone.

That someone is the Reverend Mother. She tells Maria that God has put a decision in her path, which is critical to the lives of many people. Does she love Georg? She respects him and wants to help him – and, she finally admits with a huge beaming smile, he pleases her very much.

Georg anxiously waits at the villa for her return. 'She said I must marry you, sir,' Maria tells Georg and falls into his arms in tears. The children, who have been hiding on the balcony overlooking the hall, begin cheering.

The wedding takes place at the abbey, with the boys walking Maria up the aisle, and the girls all there accompanying either her or their father. Rudi, the Baroness, and the children all watch as they receive a blessing, as do the nuns from the balcony.

* * *

Cut to some time later: Maria has recently given birth to a baby boy. Georg jokes with her that he's jealous of all the attention she gives everyone else, but when she promises to keep him on a pedestal, he's mollified. A priest is arriving at the villa as Rudi drives in: it's Father Wasner, there to ask Maria about a donation for the church organ. He, Georg and Rudi all go up to the nursery where the children and Maria are practising the Scarlatti Hallelujah. Wasner tells Maria that she has a glorious organ there at home – the children. Maria asks if he will be their teacher, and Wasner (rightly) points out that he is a tough teacher and can be short-tempered. Rudi and Georg leave them rehearsing, as Wasner shows that he wasn't joking!

Rudi has bad news: he's near bankruptcy, but luckily he doesn't have much of Georg's money, since it's in England. The depression and the Nazis' trade boycott of Austria have hit hard. Georg believes in his country, and transfers his money to Rudi's bank. He explains that he couldn't stay if the Nazis arrived.

However, it's too little, too late. Bankrupted, Rudi commits suicide, and Franz brings the newspaper in to Georg at breakfast, where Father Wasner keeps some order by getting the children to sing, not hesitating to criticize them even at mealtimes. Georg tries not to react to the headline about Rudi, but Maria can read him, and follows him out. When he calls their bank in Vienna, he learns that they've lost everything – they are now poor people. Georg blames himself, but Maria says that helping a friend and his country can't be wrong. (Even so, Franz removes the gun cabinet key, in case the Baron has suicidal thoughts.)

When it becomes clear that they are in real financial trouble, Maria suggests taking in paying guests, particularly during the Salzburg Festival. Georg is aghast at the idea of a Trapp Castle Hotel, but she persuades him, even though she's never been in a hotel, just a hostel. The hotel duly opens with Italians and Americans (and a dog) flooding in.

Out in the town, Rupert and Werner see a poster for the 1937 Salzburg Festival, and decide to sign the family up for the singing contest. They know their father will be angry, but he'll get over it. However, when it comes to the festival, he is still cross, and wants to know how they got involved. His anger peaks when he learns that eight radio stations are broadcasting the contest: 'One may go broke but one mustn't beg on the streets,' he complains. Werner and Rupert admit it was their fault, and Georg starts to berate them. Just as they are about to go on stage and are being introduced as a family 'full of inner harmony', Georg leaves the hall as they go on.

Just before they start singing, Maria explains that they're not really singers, they just sing at home. However, as they begin a hunting song, the audience starts to become entranced. Even the Chancellor of Austria is listening to the broadcast, and considers that fortune has come war hero von Trapp's way. Regarding the singing as 'a slice of the best Austria has to offer', he tells an aide he wants the choir singing at the next major reception.

The family finish the song to rapturous applause, and they win first prize. An American agent, Mr Samish, tells Maria that they must come to America and he'll deal with everything. The Chancellor's representative passes on the request from the Chancellor, but Maria only wants to find Georg.

He's returned home, and is busy making model submarines. She tells him that they won first prize and got a lot of offers. Georg says his family will not be in the entertainment industry – even if one of his ancestors was a poet. Maria says she will refuse the offers and he tells her to cancel the one that she says she did accept. Casually, she asks if she can call the Chancellor on the phone, and explains that although everyone important was going to be at the reception, she'll write to cancel. Georg has a rapid change of heart: a request from the Chancellor is the equivalent of an order. They will have to go – and she'll need a new evening dress, which a young girl tries to deliver but can't amid the hubbub of the Hotel Trapp.

A little time later, there are no longer any visitors staying at the hotel, and Maria and Georg listen to the cheering on the radio as the Nazis enter Austria. Franz tells them he must put up the swastika, but Georg says they don't have and never will have one. But Franz has bought one – as he explains, he's been a Nazi for three years. At that point, a Nazi representative, Diener, arrives at the door, and asks why there's no flag flying. Georg tells him to get out, but it's clear that Diener has been briefed: he knows Georg gave money to Rudi, who used it to finance Nazi enemies, and he insinuates there's something suspicious about the relationship between Maria and Father Wasner. Georg thumps him and tells him to leave – but Diener tells him they'll see who has to leave. Franz is concerned by the turn of events. Maria says they must leave, but Georg welcomes being arrested – he thinks that the arrest of a national hero will open people's eyes, but Maria is adamant they need to go to America.

Shortly after, the family come downstairs, dressed for a day in the mountain – even taking the baby along. Georg says goodbye to his Austrian flag, and Maria tells Franz she wants to remember the good times they had before the Nazis changed their lives. Franz clearly knows what they're planning, and when the police arrive, he urges all of them, including Georg, to hide. Diener is back, with some troops. Franz says the von Trapps are away until the next evening and is about to get verbally abused when Diener spots Franz's Nazi pin. They agree to come back the next night – and that evening the von Trapps depart, with Franz closing the gate behind them.

The next thing we see is the Statue of Liberty through a window. God may have opened a window for them, Georg points out to Maria, but it is barred. They're locked in on Ellis Island, the US immigration terminal: Maria blames herself for being there, and Wasner explains to another immigrant that they only have visitors' visas, but Maria told the officer they wanted to stay in America forever. One man has been there for ten months, and Martina has gone round begging for food for them.

Father Wasner is called to the office, and is told that he, but not the family, has been given permission to stay. He refuses to leave them and asks what can be done. The officer isn't unsympathetic: they need sponsorship, or the help that was promised from the agent. They've tried telegrams, but got no response – and if there's no answer soon, they'll be sent back to Germany.

At the agents, Samish's superior, Petroff, is not pleased at getting the cables from the von Trapps. Why did Samish make the offer? Was it witnessed? He's not happy when Samish admits Father Wasner heard it, because it'll be their word against a priest. Petroff decides to go to Ellis Island to make it clear the von Trapps must be returned. He tells the immigration officer that they neither want to see them nor help them, but the officer forces him to tell the family himself.

Maria recognizes Samish who introduces Petroff, who says they will do nothing to help, particularly since Father Wasner isn't totally certain what he heard discussed between Samish and Maria. Petroff says Maria is deluded – which angers Georg – but she tries to persuade him to hear them sing. The agents can't leave without the immigration officer's help, as they are locked in, and as the officer goes to open the door for them, he urges Maria to sing! As he reaches for the key, the choir starts singing a song about sweet dreams and freedom.

Everyone in the room, including Petroff, the guards and the other immigrants, start to listen, and Samish watches as his colleague falls under the von Trapps' spell. When they conclude, Petroff says he wants to hear a whole evening of their singing, and agrees to pay for them to get out.

The von Trapps' first concert is a success, and Petroff is inundated with offers. Although the children are tired, Maria agrees to end the performance – and the film – with a lullaby, which concludes with her turning directly to the camera to wish all watching goodnight.

* * *

As the above synopsis makes clear, quite a number of alterations to the story were made for this film, which fed through to later versions: the portrayal of Georg von Trapp as a martinet, keen to exert discipline on his children with his bosun's whistle, derives from here, as is the idea that Maria was sent to look after all the children, rather than just little Maria. Oddly, Johanna's name is changed to Rosemarie (a variant of the name of Georg and Maria's first child), and the pair only have the one baby prior to departure (and it's a boy!).

Die Trapp-Familie and its sequel were part of the Heimat ('homeland') school of film-making, particularly popular in Germany in the 1950s, since it hearkened back to the days of plenty and beauty before the ravages of the Second World War, and focused on love, friendship and family life, as well as the idyll of country life. Its signature timeless quality is clear throughout: obviously a number of years go by, but there's no indication that the children grow up at all. Matilda, notably, is still the 'cute' youngster in the final scene as she was in her introduction, which at the very least is set two to three years earlier, and probably much more. The trip from Salzburg to America is glossed over – we see them leave the villa, but have no idea how they even got out of Austria, let alone across the Atlantic.

Ruth Leuwerik makes a screen-friendly Maria, although you can never quite believe that she ever really heard the call to serve God in the first place, or that she is a twenty-one-year-old innocent (she was thirty-one when she made the movie, and it shows). She was becoming recognized as a powerful actress when she was cast as Maria; she had already won the first of her seven Bambi awards, given by *Filmrevue* magazine to their favourite big-screen star (the name derives from a comment made by the daughter of the first prize winner, Marika Rökk: 'Oh my,' she said of the fawn-shaped award, 'That looks just like Bambi'). *Die Trapp-Familie* broke attendance records in West Germany, and saw Ruth

Leuwerik displace Maria Schell as the most popular actress in Germany.

Hans Holt, who played the Baron, was regarded as the epitome of Viennese charm, and brought those qualities to the role; he's clearly much happier once Georg von Trapp shows his human side than playing the strict father. The fifteen-year age gap between him and Leuwerik makes the relationship more believable.

Wolfgang Liebeneiner was an actor and director, who had been employed by the Nazi Ministry of Propaganda during the war to produce a film promoting the euthanasia of patients suffering from multiple sclerosis. He was prolific during the 1950s, directing over two-dozen movies that decade, and worked with Ruth Leuwerik on many of these.

Die Trapp-Familie was predominantly based on the first half of Maria's account, which concluded with the departure from Austria – the second half started with the family already on the ship heading for America for the first time. The final thirteen minutes of the film combine a number of events from their various arrivals in the United States: the incident that led to most of the family being incarcerated on Ellis Island happened when they returned in 1939, and its depiction of the agents is, to put it mildly, completely at odds with the reality of their dealings (although on that occasion, they did need to bring in help from outside in order to be released).

Given the box office success, a sequel was inevitable and *Die Trapp-Familie in Amerika* was released two years later. Liebeneiner reunited with Ruth Leuwerik and Hans Holt as well as the seven children (Michael Ande, Knut Mahlke, Ursula Wolff, Angelika Werth, Monika Wolf, Ursula Ettrich and Monika Ettrich) for the new movie, which once again mined Maria's reminiscences while making some changes for dramatic effect.

The poster for the original film had promised that it would show the von Trapps going 'From the cloister to global success', but in fact had only hinted in the final scene what would be in store for them. The second film showed them initially experience failure, then locate new agents; from there they embark on a tour, and only because they have to improvise on one occasion when they're late, do they discover the sort of programme that the audience wants. A classic montage shows them increasing audiences, and thus able to buy a lodge in Vermont, before they once again sing for the immigration office and Ruth Leuwerik directly bids the watching cinema audience goodbye, as she did at the end of the first film.

The core story remained faithful to history, and some of the most dramatic recollections retained (notably Maria's attempts to understand what 'sex appeal' has to do with a musical choir), but it didn't have the narrative strength of its predecessor. However, by the time that *Die Trapp-Familie in Amerika* was released in Germany on 17 October 1958, the von Trapp story was already starting to head in a different direction. The original German movie had done well enough that Paramount Pictures in Hollywood decided to take a look at it. Rather than simply redub it for an English audience (although this was done eventually by 20th Century Fox in the wake of the success of the stage show with the rather misleading strapline 'The story of a beautiful girl who gave her love to a man and her songs to the world'), bosses there wondered whether there might be potential for an English-language remake of the story, maybe as a vehicle for Audrey Hepburn?

10

CREATING THE MUSICAL

The idea of taking a foreign-language movie and reworking it for an English-speaking audience is nothing new; we're used to the idea nowadays, with projects for both the large and small screen taking their inspiration from other countries' output. The major Hollywood studios have always kept an eye on what's being released abroad, but sometimes, as was the case with *Die Trapp-Familie*, the project may not move forward in quite the way that its original creators would expect.

A number of sources claim that both *Die Trapp-Familie* and its sequel were the subject of Paramount Pictures' interest, but it's clear from an examination of the dates that only the first film can have been under consideration: *Die Trapp-Familie in Amerika* wasn't released until the autumn of 1958 in West Germany, by which point work on an American version of the story was well under way. This also explains why both stage and film incarnations of *The Sound of Music* conclude with the uncertainty of the escape from Austria, rather than the family's eventual triumph in the United States.

The man responsible for bringing the von Trapp story to a wider audience was stage and screen director Vincent J. Donehue. On Broadway, he had helmed *The Trip to Bountiful* in 1953, with Lillian Gish, Jo Van Fleet and Eva Marie Saint, as well as Tennessee Williams' one-act play *27 Wagons Full of Cotton* with Maureen Stapleton. On television, he was responsible for the televising of many plays including Thornton Wilder's *The Skin of Our Teeth*, with Mary Martin; the star credited Donehue with saving what seemed like a disaster and the pair agreed to work together again on a future project.

Donehue began working at Paramount Pictures in Hollywood in late 1956, and the following year he was asked to take a look at *Die Trapp-Familie*. Although he thought the film in many ways was 'amateurish', he later admitted he was 'terribly moved by the whole idea of it, almost sobbing'. He wasn't sure that it was something that could work for Audrey Hepburn in the movies, but as a stage show, with Mary Martin in the lead as Maria, he thought the idea could be viable. Once Paramount passed on taking the project any further, he sent a copy of the movie to Martin and her husband, Richard Halliday.

Mary Martin had shot to fame nearly twenty years earlier when she appeared in the Broadway run of Cole Porter's *Leave It to Me!* in November 1938, particularly for the song 'My Heart Belongs to Daddy' (whose title she appropriated for her 1976 autobiography). Her most famous role was as Nellie Forbush in Rodgers and Hammerstein's *South Pacific*, a part she played both on Broadway and in London's West End, and she followed that with the lead in *Peter Pan*, which she reprised on television three times (the last in 1960 with Vincent Donehue as director). However, the stage version of *The Skin of Our Teeth* hadn't been her finest hour, and she was keen to find another vehicle for her talents. When she and her husband received the copy of *Die Trapp-Familie*, they too thought it was a strong basis for a stage production: 'The idea was just irresistible,' Mary Martin explained, 'a semi-Cinderella story but true.' She later pointed out that she could see elements of herself in Maria: 'We both have the same drive, utter determination'.

Although the film rights, at least in German, clearly belonged to someone else, Halliday, Martin and Donehue assumed that they would simply need to get the stage rights from Maria herself, and probably from the other children. The von Trapp family had ceased performing as a choir the previous year, and the children had spread far around the world. Maria had joined three of them working in Papua New Guinea, and was far from easy to contact.

Undaunted, Martin and Halliday wrote to Maria, hoping that the letter would eventually make its way to whatever outpost she contacted. Maria did indeed find the letter, among stacks of other correspondence, and briefly skimmed through it; apparently someone called Mary Martin, whom she hadn't heard of, wanted to star in a musical based on her life. With 'much more interesting and worthwhile work' to consider, Maria tore up the letter without even finishing reading it properly.

However, Martin and Halliday hadn't just sent one letter. When Maria reached first Rabaul, and then Port Moresby on New Guinea, variants of the missive were waiting for her. Regarding the whole thing as a 'silly idea', Maria tore up the other copies, not even bothering to read the third one before boarding the ship that would take her and Father Wasner back to the United States.

Maria began to realize that this simply wasn't going to go away when they arrived back in San Francisco in August 1957. Waiting for them on the quayside was Richard Halliday, who told them that his wife was performing in *Annie Get Your Gun* at the Curran Theatre in town, and she would be delighted if Maria and Father Wasner would be her guests of honour at a performance that evening. Maria was delighted by the performance – even if she couldn't see for one second how the vivacious Mary Martin could possibly play her.

There was a major sticking point, to which Maria had to confess when she spoke with the Hallidays. She no longer owned the rights to her story. Everything had been taken by the German film company when they were preparing *Die Trapp-Familie*. She could give them her blessing, but not the legal permissions they needed. She herself had more important work to get on with at the family lodge in Vermont.

(There's an odd alternative version of this story in Frederick Nolan's biography of Rodgers and Hammerstein, which suggests that Richard Halliday's lawyer, Bill Fitelson, chased around Europe looking for 'hints and clues as to the whereabouts of the Trapp children' and finally gained Maria's signature on the contract in a 'hospital ward in Innsbruck, where she was recuperating from malaria contracted in New Guinea'. It's a nice theatrical anecdote, but doesn't seem to bear much resemblance to the facts; certainly Agathe's autobiography doesn't suggest that there was any contact made with her or her siblings by the producers prior to work beginning on the musical.)

The Hallidays were close to Broadway producer Leland Hayward, who had been a co-producer on *South Pacific* and *Peter Pan*, and brought him on board the von Trapp project. With his connections, he might be able to sort through the tangled legal morass and make the necessary arrangements with the German film producers. Protracted negotiations followed with the Europeans; according to some sources, the final discussions needed to be held in Yiddish, since Hayward didn't speak German and the producers spoke no English. Finally, though, the rights belonged to the Hallidays – and with what most people at the time would have regarded as astonishing generosity, Hayward arranged for Maria von Trapp to receive three-eighths of 1 per cent of the eventual royalties (according to Maria, this wasn't something about which the German film producers cared either way). She was also given an extra fee for some script suggestions – whether they were taken notice of or not – and for teaching Mary Martin the Laendler dance.

At this point what Martin, Halliday and Hayward had in mind was a straight play with some musical numbers, probably taken from the von Trapps' own repertoire, as listed in the book and familiar to audiences around the United States from the family's tours over the years and their LPs. Hayward approached Howard Lindsay and Russel Crouse to pen the adaptation.

Lindsay and Crouse were Pulitzer Prize-winning writers, with Lindsay also an accomplished actor. They had been responsible for rewriting Guy Bolton and P.G. Wodehouse's book for the Cole Porter show *Anything Goes* back in 1935, leading to its great success. They had worked with Hayward on a number of other projects, and he presented them with three possible options: a version of *Gone with the Wind*, the great Civil War epic; the memoirs of burlesque performer Gypsy Rose Lee (which eventually became the basis for Stephen Sondheim's *Gypsy*); or the von Trapp story. The pair chose Maria's tale, agreeing to write a sixty-page outline for Mary Martin's approval. Mary Martin did indeed approve, but wanted input from Richard Rodgers and Oscar Hammerstein II, her friends from *South Pacific*. 'Ever since I first worked for them,' she explained, 'I've always asked their opinions about scripts I was thinking of doing.'

The legendary show creators had been working together for fifteen years at this point. Both had achieved success independently prior to their collaboration – composer Rodgers had worked with Lorenz Hart on hit shows including *A Connecticut Yankee*, *Babes in Arms* and *Pal Joey*; book writer and lyricist Hammerstein was Jerome Kern's collaborator on *Sunny* and *Show Boat*, among many others. They were brought together for *Oklahoma!* in 1943 and followed this with *Carousel*, *South Pacific* and *The King and I*. At the time Mary Martin got in touch, they were committed to the production of *Flower Drum Song* with Gene Kelly, which was due to start rehearsals in September 1958.

Lindsay and Crouse's initial draft, under the working title 'The Singing Heart', incorporated various von Trapp songs, and both they and Mary Martin thought there could be room for a couple of new songs, perhaps to be written by 'Dick and Oscar'. Rodgers and Hammerstein read through the outline and liked the idea, but they both felt that the mishmash of classical pieces and their own compositions wouldn't work. Rodgers told *The New York Times* that the idea 'seemed to me most impractical. Either you do it authentically – all actual Trapp music – or you get a complete new score for it.' Lindsay's reaction was to say it would be great if they were to write it, but Rodgers pointed out they hadn't been asked. Even if they were, there would have to be a hiatus in production, since the pair had to complete work on *Flower Drum Song*. Rodgers noted later that the producers said 'the most flattering thing in the world' at that point: 'If you and Oscar will write the music and lyrics, we will wait.'

'The Singing Heart' in its original form was much closer to the story as related in *Die Trapp-Familie*. Lindsay and Crouse adopted the approach taken by George Hurdalek and Herbert Reinecker for the German movie, and ended the story with the family on Ellis Island. They too had a fictional agent come to assist with the family's release from detention, and concluded with the promise of the fortune to come in the States.

The writers were determined to make sure that the show was never allowed to 'get into the never-never land operetta lives in', but certain concessions to the stage had to be made, in particular a condensation of the timeline. Rodgers and Hammerstein started working on the project in spring 1959, by which point the script had reached its third draft (now entitled 'Trapp Family'). Lindsay and Crouse had already begun to make further changes to the story, beyond those in the German film. The von Trapps' financial problems, which led to their letting their home to the public during the festival, were not mentioned, since the story jumped straight from the von Trapps' honeymoon to the Anschluss, and they were placed pretty much consecutively. That meant there was no room for the additions to the von Trapp family: there were seven children when Maria arrived at the villa, and they departed with the same septet. Whereas the German movie altered one of the girls' names (although not the one you might expect), Lindsay and Crouse went for a wholesale rebaptism, and reordering, of the family. Rupert, the oldest boy, was demoted in age and rechristened Friedrich; Agathe became the oldest child as Liesl; Maria became Louisa; Werner was now Kurt; Hedwig, Brigitta; Johanna was Marta; and baby Martina was Gretl. Even Maria herself was no longer Maria Kutschera before her wedding: the stage Maria's surname is Rainer. There were other alterations: Princess Yvonne, who calls off her wedding to the Captain, became Elsa Schraeder; while a new character, Max Detweiler, was created to explain how the family became involved with the Salzburg Festival (the movie's idea of the two boys seeing a poster was dropped early on).

Lindsay and Crouse, and Rodgers and Hammerstein then worked together to produce the core of the musical, adapting some of the dialogue into songs and devising a list of musical 'beats' which would keep the show flowing freely. Their early list has been retained for posterity, and while it includes such notations as 'Sad Song/Happy Song' for Maria early on and 'First Singing Lesson' for Maria and the children, it's extremely close to the final breakdown. (The order would be tweaked considerably when the movie script was written: the considerations of a stage show and a film screenplay are very different.) This sometimes meant altering the structure of the whole piece: Lindsay and Crouse had ended the first act with Maria departing the villa and returning to the abbey, her heart broken. Rodgers and Hammerstein felt it would be better to conclude on a more uplifting note, and asked the writers to move the first scene of the second half back – where Maria discusses her problem with the Reverend Mother. This

allowed Rodgers and Hammerstein to add a song which
would complement Lindsay and Crouse's dialogue line: 'You
have to face life, wherever you are.' (The writers' own script
for this scene has a handwritten addition: 'At this point she
also has to face Rodgers and Hammerstein'.)

This was an unusual show for the experienced writing team
of Rodgers and Hammerstein, particularly since they weren't
penning the whole musical. Hammerstein, whose health was
beginning to fail during the writing of the score following
an operation on his stomach the previous July, began a correspondence with Sister Gregory of Rosary College in River
Forest, Illinois, who was able to act as an unofficial advisor
on all things Catholic, and many commentators have noticed
an increased spirituality to his lyrics as a result of their discussions. Sister Gregory had been a friend of Mary Martin
for some years, and she gave hints to every department on the
musical – showing the designer how nuns' habits had inner
sleeves which could be detached, and how the outer sleeves
rolled up when they needed to scrub the floors. One thing she
was adamant about: 'Don't make nuns sanctimonious!'

Rodgers found himself in an unaccustomed musical situation, having to write liturgical music, particularly for the
scenes where Maria is at the convent. He was introduced to
Mother Morgan of Manhattanville College in Purchase, New
York, who staged a concert which included some of the key
elements of this style of music – from Fauré's Requiem to
Gregorian chants – and was available to answer any of the
more technical questions which the composer might have.

Maria von Trapp may only have had a small financial interest in the show, but she was very invested in seeing how
her family's story was portrayed on stage in what was now
known as 'Love Song'. In the summer of 1959, two weeks
before rehearsals started, Mary Martin came up to the family
lodge in Vermont to stay with her for ten days; Maria gave
her the one room with its own bathroom! The two women
bonded, with Maria also teaching the actress how to cross

herself, kneel properly and play the guitar; they stayed in touch for many years. In her autobiography, Mary Martin recalled the Baroness telling her: 'Mary, you were born in Texas, and I was born in Austria, but underneath we are the same Maria.' Maria later told Mary that in order to get on a plane which was full, she originally said she was Baroness Maria von Trapp, but was refused a seat; however, when she claimed to be Mary Martin from *The Sound of Music*, she got one instantly. (Mary notes that she didn't believe a word of it.)

The von Trapp matriarch also had some queries about the script: she wanted Maria to be a bit more of a tomboy than Lindsay and Crouse had made her, so the change in her was more apparent, and she hoped that the portrayal of Georg von Trapp might be a little less humourless. (While the character in the German movie starts off that way, he does mellow by the time of the wedding, which occurs comparatively early in that version of the story.)

Her largest concern, though, was the removal of Father Wasner from the plot. Right from the outset, Lindsay and Crouse made it clear that 'The Singing Heart' was going to be a starring vehicle for Mary Martin, and so it needed to be her character who was the catalyst for the family singing, rather than Father Wasner. This element (and the exaggerated role which Maria played in the children's musical education) formed the basis of a lot of the von Trapp children's complaints about *The Sound of Music* in years to come.

It only took Rodgers and Hammerstein six months to create the musical, in collaboration with Lindsay, Crouse, Mary Martin, Richard Halliday and director Vincent Donehue. This was unusually fast for them: Rodgers noted that they usually took two years, although of course Hammerstein didn't have to work on the libretto from scratch as he normally would do. It meant that by August 1959, rehearsals could begin. By now, the show was known as *The Sound of Music*; there were numerous other works by the title of 'Love Song' out there already.

Casting for the opening run had gone smoothly. Viennese-born Theodore Bikel was a shoe-in for the role of Captain von Trapp: ironically, he had fled Austria aged fourteen after the Anschluss, although he had been taken to Palestine, rather than America. He had moved to America in 1954, and had produced and sung on various albums of folk songs, and in 1959, around the time he was cast as von Trapp, he helped to co-found the Newport Folk Festival. When he started playing the guitar in his audition and accompanied himself singing folk songs, Mary Martin was certain they had found their leading man. Marion Marlowe was cast as Elsa, with Austrian actor Kurt Kasznar, who had played Pozzo in the original production of Samuel Beckett's *Waiting for Godot*, as Max. The operatic soprano Patricia Neway donned the robes to play the Reverend Mother. Lauri Peters, William Snowden, Kathy Dunn, Joseph Stewart, Marilyn Rogers, Mary Susan Locke and Evanna Lien completed the main cast as the seven von Trapp children.

Try-outs for the show were booked for the Shubert theatres in both New Haven and Boston in October, with the grand opening set for November. No expense was spared – experts from the navy were brought in to ensure that Theodore Bikel was using his whistle properly (they told him that he wasn't doing it correctly, but the sounds he was producing were fine). An extra song was added during the rehearsals for the Captain and Maria to sing together, since oddly there was no place in the original version for the two lovers to declare their affection for each other. However, 'An Ordinary Couple' was never particularly popular with either Bikel or Martin: Mary said, 'I never was happy singing it. It went downhill. I liked the lyrics but I never did like the music.' The try-outs allowed the production team – minus Oscar Hammerstein, who had been diagnosed with cancer of the stomach, and had under-gone a strenuous operation in September, which removed most of his stomach – to make further changes.

Not many were required, although everyone felt that

the threat of the Nazis needed to be strengthened, without necessarily giving them more to do. The idea of Nazis in a Broadway musical was still potentially shocking, so the subject had to be treated carefully. One critic in Boston called the ending, in which the Nazis were seen on stage pursuing the von Trapp family, melodramatic. As Rodgers told *The New York Times*: 'The end result is that there's more menace without seeing them than there was on stage in those musical comedy uniforms – after all, who are we going to offend, people who like Nazis?'

The other big change was during the preceding festival sequence. Rodgers wanted to give Theodore Bikel's von Trapp a solo moment before the children began to leave the stage, and penned a piece for guitar, which the actor learned to play even before Hammerstein came up with the lyrics. As it transpired, it was the last lyrics he wrote before his death on 23 August 1960.

It often happens that a song or scene that becomes most associated with a particular piece in the public perception is a last-minute addition. It definitely was the case with *The Sound of Music*: the song in question was 'Edelweiss'.

II

THE SOUND OF BROADWAY

The Sound of Music opened on 16 November 1959 at
Broadway's Lunt-Fontanne Theater, with advance sales of
$2,3235,000 amounting to four times the cost of produc-
tion. One of the key guests at the premiere was Maria von
Trapp, dressed in a pale green gown with matching slippers
that Mary Martin had bought for her from Saks Fifth Avenue,
and which Maria had worn to each of the opening nights for
the previews as well. Martin bowed specifically to Maria and
blew her a kiss.

The critics weren't as kind to the show as the producers had
hoped. Some were positive. *The New York Journal-American*'s
reviewer said that *The Sound of Music* was 'the most mature
product of the team . . . it seemed to me to be the full ripening
of these two extraordinary talents' and *The New York World-
Telegram and Sun* called it 'the loveliest musical imaginable
[which] places Rodgers and Hammerstein back in top form as
melodist and lyricist'.

However, Brook Atkinson, writing for *The New York Times*, noted that 'the scenario of *The Sound of Music* has the hackneyed look of musical theatre that Richard Rodgers and Oscar Hammerstein 2d replaced with *Oklahoma!* in 1943'. He occasionally damned with faint praise: 'The best of *The Sound of Music* is Rodgers and Hammerstein in good form', but he noted that 'the direction has the stereotyped quality of the libretto'. Perhaps as far as Lindsay and Crouse were concerned, his final paragraph was the most worrying: 'It is disappointing to see the American musical stage succumbing to the clichés of operetta. The revolution of the Forties and Fifties has lost its fire'. However, Atkinson noted, '*The Sound of Music* retains some of the treasures of those golden days – melodies, rapturous singing and Miss Martin. The sound of music [*sic*] is always moving. Occasionally it is also glorious.'

Pacifica Radio commented on the high cost of the musical; with that money, a new hospital wing or several new school buildings could have been built. *Time* magazine noted that 'as musicomedy, *The Sound of Music* combines the cloister and the kindergarten, nursery rhymes and Nazi salutes . . . The show's pervasive fault is that, instead of offsetting sweetness with lightness, it turns sticky with sweetness and light . . . It insists on the syrup, till even the Nazis seem mere bad goblins in a fairy tale.'

Neither Rodgers nor Hammerstein was able to let this rest. 'Sentiment,' Hammerstein noted, 'has never been unpopular except with a few sick persons who are made sicker by the sight of a child, a glimpse of a wedding, or the thought of a happy home.' Noting that the book was based on Maria von Trapp's autobiography, he claimed that 'no incidents were dragged in or invented to play on the sentimental susceptibilities of the audience as some critics seem to feel'.

It's perhaps a good thing that no one put Hammerstein's comment to the test: as the synopsis of the stage musical below shows, the story had begun to stray quite a considerable way from Maria Kutschera's life. Where the German

film was described as being from her 'memories', the credit
on the stage show divorces it one degree further: the musical is 'Suggested by "The Trapp Family Singers" by Maria
Augusta Trapp', and 'is laid in Austria early in 1938' – the
libretto makes clear exactly how long there is between scenes
(indeed it's so precise you can actually work out the exact
dates if you choose, as the Anschluss on Sunday 13 March is
stated as being four days before the penultimate scenes).

The musical opens in the evening at Nonnberg Abbey as
the nuns chant, but there's someone missing – Maria isn't
back yet. On a mountainside near the abbey, Maria is singing 'The Sound of Music'; she's out with permission from the
Mother Abbess but has lost track of time. The next morning, she's called before the Mother Abbess, who has been told
by Sisters Sophia and Berthe that Maria isn't a credit to the
abbey ('Maria') although Sister Margaretta defends her. Maria
is full of apologies for her behaviour, but the Mother Abbess
is interested in one of the songs she was singing, which
Maria duly repeats ('My Favourite Things') and, by singing
together, the two women reach a degree of communication
that they've not had before. The Mother Abbess knows that
although Maria wants to be a nun, she's not ready for their
way of life (with which Maria agrees), and the older nun tells
her it is the Will of God that she leaves for a time, and that
when she returns, maybe she'll be ready for the religious life.
War hero Captain von Trapp needs a governess for his seven
children until September. Singing 'My Favourite Things' to
keep her spirits up, Maria leaves.

   That afternoon, at the Trapp villa, Captain Georg von
Trapp summons his butler, Franz (who was previously the
Captain's orderly in the Austrian Imperial Navy), and the
housekeeper, Frau Schmidt, using his bosun's whistle. He
tells them of Maria's impending arrival and that he will be
away for a month, then returning with some guests. Franz
has Nazi sympathies but Frau Schmidt warns him not to say

such things in front of von Trapp; neither of them is keen on the Captain's recently adopted military ways.

Maria arrives, bearing her guitar and little else, and meets the Captain who emphasizes that the first rule of the house is discipline. The children are to have lessons in the morning, and march in the afternoon. He gives various blasts on his whistle, which bring the seven children down, and then introduces them, demonstrating their individual signals, and asking Maria to repeat them back to him. She is surprised by this, and even more shocked when von Trapp indicates the signal he'll use for her. Maria only uses the whistle once – to stop the Captain in his tracks and allow her to return it to him. She then starts to break the ice with the children, but is surprised that they don't know any songs, so she starts by teaching them the basics ('Do-Re-Mi').

That evening, Liesl, the oldest of the girls, is outside in the grounds, saying goodnight to Rolf, the local lad who delivers telegrams. Rolf also has some Nazi sympathies, but he knows that Liesl's father doesn't, and he doesn't want the Captain to get in trouble with the Nazis, should something happen. Liesl doesn't want to be thought of as a youngster, and wants someone older and wiser (i.e. Rolf) to be her guide ('Sixteen Going on Seventeen'). At the end of their song and brief waltz, they kiss, much to Liesl's delight.

As Liesl runs back to the house, Frau Schmidt fills in some of the Captain's story for Maria as she provides some cloth for her to make a new dress, and tells her there will be new curtains in her room the next day. When Maria says the children should be able to play, the housekeeper makes it clear that the Captain won't have it, and that she suspects the children play up with the governesses to get their father to come home so they can see him. The problem is, she thinks, they remind him too much of his late wife. That's also why he won't have music in the house, even though he and his wife used to sing and make music. She leaves Maria, telling her that the Captain may remarry before the summer.

Maria is saying her prayers when Liesl comes through the window, soaked from the storm that's started up outside. Maria tells her to wash out her dress and they'll keep her unusual entrance a secret between them. As the storm rages, the other children gradually come in as they're scared of the thunder and lightning – first Gretl, then the other three girls, and finally the boys (who want to check the others aren't frightened). To keep them calm, Maria sings them 'The Lonely Goatherd'.

Six weeks later, the Captain has returned with two guests: the cosmopolitan Elsa Schraeder and the charming politician, Max Detweiler. Georg is having coffee on the balcony with Elsa, who is enjoying flirting with him, noting she's getting glimpses of the fascinating and exciting man inside the Captain. She likes his home in Salzburg, although she knows she has to spend some time in Vienna looking after her late husband's corporation. Detweiler has been on the phone trying to book acts for the Kaltzberg Festival without much luck; he's obviously a bit of a chancer who likes spending time with rich people. Max wants the Captain to introduce him to everyone important locally. As Georg goes off to find the children, Max asks Elsa if she's made up Georg's mind for him to marry her. They jokingly sing about the problems of a love affair between Georg and Elsa – they both have too much money for love to survive ('How Can Love Survive?'). Rolf arrives with a telegram for Max and gives the Captain a 'heil' salute, which annoys Georg no end. Max is more laissez-faire about such things and goes in to take a phone call.

The children bound in, dressed in their play clothes, made from the old curtains in Maria's room. They're delighted to see their father, but he coldly blows the whistle to get them lined up. He orders them to get cleaned up, and changed. He asks Maria what's going on and she tells him that they've been having fun. When she tells them they were just unhappy marching machines before, he doesn't want to hear – and gets increasingly angry as Maria tells him exactly what his children are like. Furious, he orders her back to the abbey.

Maria apologizes, but any further discussion is halted when they both hear the children singing 'The Sound of Music', which they were preparing for Elsa's arrival. They come back down and sing the song, with Georg joining in. When it's finished, he's overcome with emotion but asks the children to show Elsa the garden. He tells Maria she was right – he doesn't know his own children – and asks her to stay. As they sing 'The Sound of Music' together, he gets rid of the whistle. Elsa comes back to congratulate her, since the Captain was clearly moved by what she'd done; Maria tells her she will stay till September, and will pray for Elsa when she returns to the abbey.

A week later, there's a party at the von Trapp villa. Not everyone is having a good time, though: political tensions are rising, and there's talk of Anschluss – the reunification of Austria and Germany – notably from Herr Zeller. Georg is about to fetch Elsa, who has been suffering from a headache, but Frau Schmidt says she'll be down shortly. He therefore stands on the stairs and watches as Maria shows Kurt how to dance the Laendler, an Austrian folk dance. When Kurt makes a mess of it, his father steps in, bringing him and Maria in close physical proximity – something the young woman has never experienced before in quite that way. As both part, a little flustered, Elsa arrives, noticing the byplay.

Max arrives for the party, but since that gives them an extra man for dinner, Georg decides to ask Maria to join them. Brigitta tells Maria that the Captain is in love with her – and that she is in love with him. The young girl can tell from the way her father watched Maria when they were singing the previous week, and from how Maria looked at Georg when they were dancing. Maria can't believe it, but before she can take it in, she is asked to join the dinner party. She heads upstairs, as Elsa asks Georg for the children to sing 'So Long, Farewell' before they go to bed. Seeing this, Max realizes that he's found the act he's been seeking for the festival right under his nose.

But Maria doesn't join them for dinner. She's put on the clothes she was wearing when she arrived at the villa, and is carrying her guitar case and bag. The adults are at dinner and the children upstairs in their rooms as she slowly and sadly walks out of the house.

Three days later, Maria has finally decided to talk to the Mother Abbess. She's said nothing to anyone since her return from the villa. When the older nun asks her why she was sent back, she explains that she left because she was frightened. The Abbess asks her bluntly if she's in love with Captain von Trapp, and Maria admits she doesn't know. She feels torn because she was there on God's errand, so she could not ask for the Captain's love. The Abbess points out that the love of a man and a woman is holy, like the love of Maria's parents was, and if she loves the Captain, it doesn't mean she loves God less. She has to find the life she was born to live – 'Climb Ev'ry Mountain'. As the Abbess finishes her song, Maria removes her veil . . .

Act two begins the same day at the Trapp villa with Max trying to get the children to sing. They say they can't without Maria, which their father says is nonsense, but then, once Elsa and Max have departed, he tries to find out why she left. He then tells them they are going to have a new mother: Fräulein Schraeder; everything was settled the previous evening. The children aren't pleased by this and sing 'My Favourite Things' listlessly – only to have Maria arrive back. They tell her that their father is getting married, so when he asks why she left, she says only that the reason no longer exists, and that she'll stay till they find a new governess.

Max has been getting calls from Berlin: he wants to be sure that if the Germans don't keep their promise not to invade Austria, he has some friends there. Elsa asks Georg if he would defy the Nazis if they do invade, and after a few moments' thought, he says he would. Max and Elsa both think he should be a realist ('No Way to Stop It') but Georg will not bow to men he despises. Elsa realizes that Georg will never betray his principles, and that their paths must go in separate directions: she's delighted to see that Maria is back, and says that she must return to Vienna. When she leaves Georg and Maria alone, they admit their love ('An Ordinary Couple') and Georg enquires whom who he needs to ask permission for her hand in marriage – and she says it must be the children.

Two weeks later, Maria and Georg are married at Nonnberg ('Maria' reprise and 'Processional') with the girls attending Maria, and the boys their father. The nuns watch from behind the grille of the convent.

A month goes by, and Max has brought the printed programmes showing The Trapp Family Singers' appearance at the Kaltzberg Festival 1938. It's four days since the Anschluss, and Herr Zeller, formerly one of Georg's friends, arrives at the villa demanding to know why it's the only house not flying the flag of the Third Reich (or the one with the black spider on it, according to Brigitta). Max has been promoted to First Secretary of the Ministry of Education and Culture, which impresses Zeller not one bit – but it does mean Max can order the von Trapps to fly the swastika. He exits, sure that his orders will be obeyed.

Brigitta isn't sure that her father is going to be happy about Uncle Max's plan for them to sing at the festival – and she's absolutely right. Georg and Maria arrive back from their honeymoon a week early, and Georg is adamant: the von Trapp Family will not sing in public, even if, as Max claims, it's for Austria. It can't be, Georg points out, since there is no Austria any more.

Hearing the way Maria talks about her father, Liesl realizes how much his new wife loves him (a reprise of 'Sixteen Going on Seventeen'), just as Rolf arrives with a telegram to be handed to Captain von Trapp personally. He's now very much the good little Nazi – as is, he points out to Liesl, everyone in Nonnberg (*sic*) except the great Captain von Trapp. Even Franz admits his Nazi leanings.

The telegram is bad news: Georg has been offered a commission in the German Navy. Much as the prospect both of going to sea again delights him, and knowing his family will be safe if he does so, Georg can't do it, and they decide they have to get out of Austria straightaway. Zeller arrives back accompanied by Admiral von Schreiber of the Navy of the Third Reich, who has been sent in person since there was no response to the telegram (which should have been delivered three days earlier) to reactivate the Captain's commission and to order him to report to Bremerhaven immediately. Maria thinks quickly and says it's impossible, since the family are singing at the festival in two days' time, on Friday; the Admiral concedes that Georg could arrive on Monday. Zeller tries to protest that the Captain's name isn't on the programme, but Georg points out he is the head of the von Trapp family – and even gives a brief demonstration of his singing prowess ('Do-Re-Mi').

Friday night (18 March), and at the Concert Hall in Kaltzberg, the von Trapp Family are performing 'Do-Re-Mi', before the Captain gives a solo rendition of 'Edelweiss' with its blessing of his homeland forever. Max, acting as compere, announces that a guard of honour has been prepared to escort Captain von Trapp to his new duties at Bremerhaven, and as the family depart, they sing 'So Long, Farewell'. Max stalls for time as long as he can, announcing the winners of the festival in reverse order. When he gets to the first prize for the von Trapps, there is no response – the family are no longer there.

The family have gone to the abbey at Nonnberg, but there's no sanctuary there – the Nazis are searching the building, but the nuns believe the von Trapps will be safe in the garden. Once the stormtroopers have departed, the plan is to drive away as far as possible. Rolf comes out, now in his full SS uniform, and shines a flashlight around the garden, spotting first the Captain and then Liesl. He calls for his lieutenant, but after an agonizing few moments, Rolf turns and tells him there is no one there. The Nazis drive off, leaving a guard in front of the gate – and the borders and roads are now all blocked too.

There is only one option: to go over the mountain above Salzburg into Switzerland. The Mother Abbess notes that they will have help from God in their journey, and as she sings 'Climb Ev'ry Mountain' the von Trapps head off into the mountains . . .

Lindsay and Crouse had managed to incorporate elements of the real story that had been overlooked or rewritten for the German film – notably Georg von Trapp's commission into the Navy of the Third Reich being the last straw for the loyal Austrian – with their own characters Elsa and Max stepping in for the roles that Princess Yvonne and Lotte Lehmann played in real life, as well as representing the varying responses of the Austrians to the impending Anschluss. It wasn't enough for some of the von Trapp children: Agathe recalled that when she saw the musical for the first time she cried: the man in naval uniform on stage wasn't her beloved Papá, with his strict ways and distant attitude. The reason that the normally intensely private family stood on stage to sing was through sheer necessity. And they did not cross over the Alps from Salzburg into Switzerland – as Agathe, and anyone with a basic knowledge of geography, was aware, if you go over the big Alp behind Salzburg, you end up in Germany . . .

Maria had her own travails connected to the show. According to her 1972 autobiography, she attended the first night and the celebrations with the cast afterwards, but as she was leaving, a young man asked if she was Mrs von Trapp, and when she said yes, he handed her a piece of paper. Maria put it in her bag and didn't look at it for some time, but when she found it and handed it to Father Wasner, he was horrified. She had been served with a subpoena on behalf of a man who claimed that he was her agent, and that she owed him $35,000 for the work he had done putting *The Sound of Music* on stage.

The case carried on for some years before finally arriving in court, and when it did so, Maria found it hard to believe that what she regarded as blatant lies that were being said were not challenged by her lawyer when the case was being presented. During a recess, the judge summoned Maria to his chambers, and told her that he suggested offering $3,000 to settle the case, explaining to her gently that she could end up spending considerably more if the court proceedings continued. When the court resumed, her lawyer started to cross-examine the petitioner, establishing that in his various affidavits he had stated he had met Maria for the first time in different places and on different dates. When the judge interrupted to say he was empowered to offer a settlement, the petitioner's attorney, perhaps not surprisingly, jumped at it.

By the time it was settled, the stage show had long departed from Broadway, but it had a very successful run there – Mary Martin noted that she eventually had to sell her shares in the original stage production because they were attracting so much tax. There was rarely an empty seat in the theatre, Martin recalled, with parties block booking to see the show multiple times – and they weren't going to be disappointed if there were technical problems, as occurred during a blackout in the show's first summer, 1960.

The blackout was on nothing like the scale of the one that took place on 9 November 1965, when a pilot overflying the city thought there must have been another Pearl Harbor given how dark the metropolis looked. The power in the theatre went off shortly before curtain time, but the crowds lined up to see the show refused to depart, even after being told that the cast couldn't see to get made up or into their costumes, and that the stage was bare of scenery. The cast, crew and musicians all agreed to go ahead with the performance (something which Health and Safety regulations simply wouldn't

allow nowadays), and producer Richard Halliday sent out
for as many flashlights as could be found. The audience were
shown to their seats, and Mary Martin came out to explain
the situation: this would be a performance of *The Sound of
Music* like no other.

After the initial number with the nuns, the show should
have begun with Maria in a tree (the script says she's underneath it, but it was felt that it would be more fun for her to
actually be up the tree). That night, she wasn't. She was on a
stepladder, and Mary Martin sang her opening number point-
ing a flashlight at her face so the audience could see her. There
hadn't been time to brief the children playing the von Trapps,
but they had all been watching Mary from the wings and did
the same thing for their cues. There was almost an air of disappointment after the lights came on half an hour into the
show, and the cast went off to get changed.

Reminiscing with her co-star Theodore Bikel in 1986
for a television special celebrating the work of Rodgers and
Hammerstein, Mary Martin also recalled another incident
which showed the children at their best. A pigeon decided
to join in the proceedings at the matinee, and she encouraged them quickly to ignore it – which, thankfully, they all
did. She reassured them before they went on in the evening
that the stage hands would have dealt with it in the interval
between shows; they hadn't – their avian friend participated
in both houses that day.

The show received many religious attendees, and Mary
Martin recalled that one particular group of nuns who
came to visit her backstage were rather shocked to be told
to get their costumes off by the show's staging director, Joe
Layton. 'You girls know you're not supposed to stand out
here in the hall in your goddamned costumes,' he expostu-
lated, and didn't listen to their protests until the actors came
out of their dressing rooms, ready to go to dinner – at which
point the real nuns departed, giggling. On another occasion,
during the show's try-outs, the chorus went out for a break

during rehearsals still dressed in their habits – and shocked the Bostonians who saw them with their highly un-nun-like anecdotes, language and behaviour.

Maria's entrance at the beginning could have played to Mary Martin's natural comedic talents, if Richard Halliday had had his way. According to Ethan Mordden's biography of Rodgers and Hammerstein, at one early production meeting, Halliday suggested that Mary should catch her bloomers on a branch as she climbed down. The writers told Halliday that they didn't think such underpants humour had any relevance to the story or the character, and Halliday's reply was classic: 'You know what's wrong with you guys?' he asked. 'All you care about is the show!'

And they did care about the show. Even though he was terminally ill, Oscar Hammerstein worked on it for as long as possible, auditioning for cast replacements until he simply wasn't able to go on. He defended it vigorously when he and Rodgers were accused of simply trying to create a 'sure-fire' hit for Mary Martin, noting that Martin had brought the property to them, and they had joined it because 'we liked the story very much'. The scene which closes the first act, in which the Mother Abbess tells Maria to go back to the man rather than choose the veil of the postulant, was 'a very original situation . . . We, in our innocence, considered this a very original turn of plot and a situation of great human interest.'

Oscar Hammerstein died at his farm on 23 August 1960, a matinee day, so the cast had to perform the show twice. Martin recalled that Hammerstein's widow Dorothy called to tell her to do the shows, 'and do them well, because that's what Oscar would want'. Like her colleagues, Martin found it hard not to choke up during the shows. The words of 'Climb Ev'ry Mountain' were read at his funeral; that night, the lights of every theatre on Broadway and in London's West End were dimmed for three minutes in homage, and even the lights of Times Square went dark for one minute at 9 p.m.

Before he died, Oscar Hammerstein knew how much his

final show was appreciated. At the fourteenth Tony Awards (or The Antoinette Perry Awards for Excellence in Theatre to give them their proper title), held on 24 April 1960 at the Astor Hotel Grand Ballroom, *The Sound of Music* was nominated in nine categories. Neither Theodore Bikel or Kurt Kasznar triumphed for Best Performance by a Featured Actor in a Musical (that went to future *Happy Days* star Tom Bosley for his role as New York Mayor Fiorello La Guardia in Jerome Weidman and George Abbott's *Fiorello!*); Vincent Donehue's work as Best Director (Musical) wasn't recognized. Lauri Peters 'and the Children (Kathy Dunn, Evanna Lien, Mary Susan Locke, Marilyn Rogers, William Snowden, Joseph Stewart)' were unsuccessful for the female equivalent (an unusual nomination for a group, particularly one including two boys!). However, Patricia Neway did win that award, with Mary Martin heralded for Best Performance by a Leading Actress in a Musical. The show tied for Best Musical with *Fiorello!*, and conductor Frederick Dvonch was given Best Conductor and Musical Director, with Oliver Smith wining Best Scenic Design (Musical), giving them a total of five awards (not the six or seven that many books claim). One of the presenters that year was Canadian actor Christopher Plummer, whose own date with *The Sound of Music* was approaching.

Changes occurred during the Broadway run of 1,443 performances: a young actor named Jon Voight, later to star in *Midnight Cowboy* and marry his Liesl (Lauri Peters), joined as Rolf. Martha Wright took over as Maria from Mary Martin in October 1961 – the second time she had succeeded her in a role, after stepping up in *South Pacific* a decade earlier – with Karen Gantz and Nancy Dussault as her replacements in July and September 1962 respectively. The show closed on 15 June 1963, with Bikel, who had left alongside Martin, promising to himself that he would never take on as long a run again, if he could afford it. The cast album, recorded a week after the opening, was a major money-spinner for Columbia

The von Trapp family during their 1940 tour of the United States.
(Imagno/Getty Images)

The Trapp Family Singers examining a new piece of music c. 1941.
(Popperfoto/Getty Images)

Hans Holt as Baron von Trapp and Ruth Leuwerik as Maria are watched by Josef
Meinrad as Dr Wasner, together with the children in the first filmed version of
the story, *Die Trapp-Familie* (1956). (20th Century Fox/The Kobal Collection)

Julie Andrews with the children from *The Sound of Music* on location at Leopoldskron Castle for the scenes on the lake.
(20th Century Fox/The Kobal Collection)

Christopher Plummer poses with Captain von Trapp's guitar on location for *The Sound of Music*. (20th Century Fox/The Kobal Collection)

A portrait of Julie Andrews as Fraulein Maria from *The Sound of Music*, taken by the lake at Leopoldskron Castle.
(20th Century Fox/The Kobal Collection)

Christopher Plummer as Captain von Trapp demonstrates how he uses his bosun's whistle to summon each of his children as their new governess, Fraulein Maria (just visible at the left of the picture) looks on in amazement.
(20th Century Fox/The Kobal Collection)

Julie Andrews admires a present from Angela Cartwright as Anna Lee (playing Sister Margaretta) looks on during a break from filming *The Sound of Music* in Salzburg.
(20th Century Fox/The Kobal Collection)

Captain von Trapp leads his wife and children to safety over the Alps at the end of *The Sound of Music* – although in reality the route he's taking them on would lead them to Hitler's Berchtesgaden!
(20th Century Fox/The Kobal Collection)

Director Robert Wise (third from left) and the crew look on as Julie Andrews leans against a wall near Nonnberg Abbey during preparations for a scene from the song 'I Have Confidence'.
(20th Century Fox/The Kobal Collection)

Julie Andrews and the children filming a scene from the montage sequence for 'Do-Re-Mi' not far from Nonnberg Abbey, high above the Salzburg rooftops.
(20th Century Fox/The Kobal Collection)

Masterworks, selling over three million copies, and spending sixteen weeks in the top slot on Billboard's best-selling albums in 1960. A recording of songs from the show by vibraphonist Gary Burton was released in 1965 with some unusual jazz arrangements of Rodgers and Hammerstein's songs; John Coltrane had produced an idiosyncratic version of 'My Favourite Things'.

A US national tour began with Florence Henderson getting in practice for dealing with a large group of children in *The Brady Bunch* by playing Maria from the start of the tour in Detroit on 27 February 1961 until June 1962, when Barbara Meister took over. The tour came to an end on 23 November 1963, the day after President John F. Kennedy's assassination.

The show crossed the Atlantic, opening at the Palace Theatre in London's Charing Cross Road on 18 May 1961. It was the most successful of the original runs of the show, completing 2,385 performances before closing in January 1967. Audiences lapped it up, despite an even more critical pasting by the press than the show had received on Broadway. Star Jean Bayless (who years earlier had shared a flat with another future Maria, Julie Andrews) recalled: 'On my opening night at the Palace Richard Rodgers held my hand at the side of the stage and he said: "Good luck and don't worry. I haven't had a good review since *Oklahoma*" and on I went with a dry mouth and started to sing on the rock.'

The notoriously acerbic Bernard Levin noted that Rodgers' ear for a tune 'saves the evening from foundering in a marsh of treacle, bathed in a dim religious light'. W.A. Darlington thought the show was made to a recipe: 'Take the basic story of *The King & I*, scrape the oriental spicing, and substitute Austrian sugar-icing an inch thick. Add a little bit of drama at the end. Serve – and sit back and listen to the praises of the flavour'. Andrew Lloyd Webber, later responsible for one of the show's periodic revivals, recalled that one review said: 'If you are a diabetic who craves sweet things, take along some extra insulin and you will not fail to thrill to *The Sound of*

Music' – the producers quite rightly chose to quote only the last eleven words!

'The critics were not too kind but it ran for six years and everyone loved it,' Bayless recalled in 2007. 'I was in just over two years. I did eight shows a week. We didn't have mics, we had foot mics, but not as they have now. We did matinees and evening shows and you just got on with it. And we didn't get paid what they get now, now it is a different wonderful world.' Sonia Rees succeeded Bayless, with Roger Dann playing Georg von Trapp, and Eunice Gayson, who went on to play James Bond's occasional girlfriend in the early 007 films, as Elsa Schraeder. It was the longest-running American musical in West End history to that point, only losing its title to Kander and Ebb's *Chicago* in 2004.

There were other international productions: *The Sound of Music* opened in Melbourne, Australia, in October 1961 with opera singer June Bronhill as Maria, and Peter Graves as Captain von Trapp (although contrary to some sources, this wasn't the actor who went on to play Jim Phelps in *Mission: Impossible* – although he would no doubt have made an excellent choice). There was also a long-running South African version.

The show started to make its presence felt in other areas. Satirist Noël Coward set his sights on the perceived saccharinity of the story in his Broadway show *Sail Away*, for which he wrote both book and music. It starred Elaine Stritch as Mimi Paragon, an American cruise director on a British luxury cruise ship, and the choreography was created by Joe Layton who had worked on *The Sound of Music* both sides of the Atlantic. *Sail Away* ran on Broadway from 2 October 1961 to 24 February 1962, and then in London opening on 21 June for 252 performances. Coward skewered 'Do-Re-Mi' with 'The Little Ones' ABC' (in this A stands for 'Absolutely Anything' or 'Artichokes and Adenoids' while G 'of course stands for getting a divorce').

Julie Andrews and Carol Burnett gave a televised concert

at Carnegie Hall in June 1962, which included the adventures of the happy 'Swiss Family Pratt' (included on the 45th anniversary Blu-ray edition of the movie). Andrews was starring as Guinevere in *Camelot* at the time and had no thought of ever playing Maria seriously; Walt Disney, however, was in the audience and approached Andrews to appear as Mary Poppins in his film of P.L. Travers' stories – and that was a key role in convincing the powers that be that she was suitable casting for the movie of *The Sound of Music*.

12

THE SONGS OF THE SOUND

Each of the songs that forms the musical score to *The Sound of Music* has an important part to play in moving forward the story of Maria von Trapp, her husband and his seven children, with all of them going through various permutations before they reached the stage. Examination of them also occasionally provides clues to the story which were concealed by the composers. (The songs are discussed below in the order they appear in the original Broadway and West End productions; changes for the movie and later stage shows are mentioned at the relevant places – the additional songs written for the film are discussed in chapter 15.)

'Preludium'
The stage show opens with the nuns singing Richard Rodgers' setting of the Dixit Dominus, which is made up of verses 1, 5 and 7 of Psalm 110 followed by the Gloria. It's sung as solo and response – the solo chants 'The Lord said to my Lord: sit at my

right hand', to which the choir replies, 'Until I make thy enemies thy footstool' (the Latin uses the singular form, to make
it more personal). The solo then notes that 'The Lord at thy
right hand hath broken kings in the day of his wrath', and the
chorus skips the verse which refers to the Lord crushing heads
in the land of the many, and replies, 'He shall drink of the
torrent in the way: therefore shall he lift up the head.' The section concludes with the standard doxology added to psalms:
'Glory be to the Father and to the Son, and to the Holy Spirit'
to which the reply is, 'As it was in the beginning, and is now,
and is forever, and for ages of ages (world without end). Amen.'

This moves into a four-part harmonic setting of 'Rex
admirabilis', part of a hymn *Iesu, Dulcis Memoria*, which
was written by the twelfth-century monk St Bernard of
Clairvaux. In the Catholic Church, it was sung at Matins (the
first morning service) on the Sunday between the Feast of the
Circumcision (1 January) and Epiphany (6 January), or on 2
January if there's no Sunday. Rather cleverly, this provides a
clue to the date on which this is set: such a hymn would not
normally be sung by the sisters outside these dates – and in
1938, 2 January was a Sunday – but the timing's off: the nuns
are singing this at the close of the day, perhaps as a reminder
of the day's events? The words mean 'O Jesus, King most
wonderful!/Thou Conqueror renowned!/Thou Sweetness
most ineffable!/in whom all joys are found!'

The Angelus bell (it's given as a plural in the score, but there
was usually just the one) is then rung, to mark the curfew at
Nonnberg. This is followed by a final Alleluia sung by the
nuns, marked to be sung 'Allegro giubiloso' – fast and joyfully.

'The Sound of Music'

The show's title number is first performed by Maria when
we discover her in (or beneath) a tree. Oscar Hammerstein's
lyrics went through many variations: the early draft – which
begins with Maria hearing the echo of a far-off chime from a
church, a line which eventually turned up in the second verse

– talks far more about 'summer music', which doesn't fit with the eventual timeframe of the story, and the sound of silence, which is filled with the beat of a few million hearts. There are more prosaic images in there as well, showing Maria's love of life in general – a dog barking and a schoolboy shouting – and even in later versions, the avian analogy is different: it's not a lark learning to pray (whatever that might mean), it's a nightingale playing in the dark.

The earlier version also addresses Maria's yearning for faith – as the dialogue between her and the Mother Abbess in the next scene suggests, life in Nonnberg is not at all what she was anticipating. It doesn't connect Maria as firmly with the hills around Salzburg, which of course becomes relevant at the end of the musical when it's her knowledge of the hills that saves her life and those of her family. The addition of the hills thematically also harks back to the true Maria Kutschera, who had her own epiphany in the hills that led her to head to Nonnberg in the first place.

The song reprises in the stage version as the piece which Maria has prepared for the children to sing for Elsa when she arrives to visit the villa, and the Captain is able to join in very easily (a little oddly, since he hasn't heard it before).

'Maria'

Every version of the Maria von Trapp story has to include the complaints of the other nuns in Nonnberg about her behaviour. In the original book and in the German film, she's sliding down banisters and doing all sorts of distinctly un-nun-like things. For the lyrics for this chorus of (mainly) disapproval, Oscar Hammerstein took elements of Lindsay and Crouse's dialogue for the scene and reworked them; he was also very intrigued by the detail they provided – Maria wore curlers under her wimple, and that gave him one of the more unusual lines of verse. Sister Sophia's line about singing in the abbey was one of the changes made to the lyrics following the Boston try-out in the run-up to the opening on Broadway.

Joe Layton's notes, contained in the libretto, remind directors that this number should not 'look choreographed'. Only the movement of the nuns' hands to make a point should be used to enhance the song.

'Maria' reappears as part of the wedding music, as the nuns realize that they now have the answer to their question. What to do about Maria? Find her the man with whom she will be happy.

'My Favourite Things'

Those coming to the stage show only knowing the movie are always surprised to hear this sung so early in proceedings. Layton noted that its purpose in the plot was to 'help the Mother Abbess break the bad news of Maria's having to leave the abbey as quickly as possible', and so the Mother Abbess has more freedom to move than she normally would allow herself as she attempts to break the ice between the pair and enable them to bond. (Maria then sings it later to boost her spirits, perhaps the inspiration for its repositioning in the movie.)

In Rodgers and Hammerstein's original 'tentative routine of songs', this is just called 'Sad Song, Happy Song'; some analysts have suggested that it's meant to be sung by someone who is frightened of the new responsibilities being thrust on her, and while that certainly applies to the short reprise as Maria leaves the convent, it's important to remember that the original rendition is a song that the Mother Abbess and Maria both knew from their respective youth – and that it appears before the Mother Abbess mentions to Maria that she is going to be leaving.

'Do-Re-Mi'

Known in Rodgers and Hammerstein's 'tentative routine' (their initial breakdown of the musical numbers) as 'First Singing Lesson', this is the equivalent to the number 'Getting to Know You' in their previous hit, *The King and I*. In the stage show, this is how Maria starts to learn about each of the children, and show them that learning can be fun, not just boring rote. Mary Martin used the children like a human piano for the song, but because her eyesight originally was poor (she started to use contact lenses midway through her run as Maria), she memorized the colour of the children's hair, and woe betide the replacement child who had the wrong shade! Joe Layton's notes emphasize that the younger von Trapps shouldn't be used as 'musical comedy children' – they need to learn what they're doing, not be perfect from the start – and that they have been 'trained by their father as a battalion of soldiers' (or, more likely, sailors), which means they can march with some precision.

'Sixteen Going on Seventeen'
The romance between Rolf, the telegram boy, and the oldest von Trapp girl, Liesl, was a complete addition to both Maria von Trapp's memoir and the German film, by Lindsay and Crouse, and gave them a way to demonstrate how ordinary Austrians were affected by the growing rise of Nazism. The song also showed how Liesl, an ordinary sixteen-year-old, wants to get the attentions of a local boy, and the notes once again emphasize the simplicity necessary: Liesl hasn't been trained as a dancer, so 'more pantomime and gesturing than dance' is recommended. Known simply as 'Duet (Young lovers)' it has the word 'Balkans?' against it in the composers' original notes, perhaps hinting at the style of music they intended to use.

The song makes a reappearance later in the show, when Liesl has been spurned by Rolf after the Nazis arrive, and Maria explains how changes will come, but that she has to wait. This was inserted during rehearsals, and the introduction was written shortly after Oscar Hammerstein learned that his cancer was inoperable.

'The Lonely Goatherd'
Another song whose position in the stage play (if it's done per the original version) surprises film-familiar audiences, this

was known initially as the 'Yodelling Song' whose purpose was 'to drown out thunder', and, according to Jim Layton's notes, directors should ensure therefore that 'a great time is had by all'.

Although his notes have sadly not been transcribed into the libretto, Oscar Hammerstein's original document reads more like a film script than a set of lyrics: he suggests there should be a flash of lightning after the third verse, which freezes the children to silence, but then when there's no thunder, they smile and start the refrain. However, when the thunder crash does come, Liesl runs for cover, and Maria hastily starts a new verse. After that chorus, comes 'THE BIGGEST CRASH OF ALL!' (Hammerstein wrote this in his distinctive green pen in block capitals) 'MUST BE A TREE NEAR THE HOUSE!' which means that they all – Maria included – dive beneath the covers. When the thunder stops, Brigitta's head pops up and sings the last couple of notes, followed by 'a big chord in the orchestra. Blackout.' (That became 'Thunder and Blackout' in the final script.)

'How Can Love Survive?'

'My Favourite Things' and 'The Lonely Goatherd' transpose positions between stage show and film, but some numbers were dropped altogether, starting with this rather cynical number between Elsa Schraeder and Max Detweiler. Seen by some as a comment on the growing rise of Nazism, this song serves to demonstrate the differing priorities that the two have, compared with the upright and principled Captain von Trapp. The tune is jolly, contrasting with the lyrics, which have rightly been described as acrid (as well as acid) – trapped by their money, they simply have no time for love, whereas poor people, who can go for rides on the top of a bus in a freezing breeze, can feel love more easily. It also provides some foreshadowing: the person the Captain will eventually marry is neither rich nor his social equal.

In their assessment of the music from *The Sound of Music*

in 2013, *Entertainment Weekly* placed this seventh overall, noting that it's 'wry, clever, and surprisingly mature — an oasis of adult-friendly material in a show dominated by kid-friendly tunes'.

'So Long, Farewell'

The children's party piece (at least within the context of the fiction) serves a dual purpose in the show, since, of course, it is used to disguise the von Trapps' departure from the stage of the festival at the end of the musical. It's a choral version of the idea that Joseph Haydn used in his symphony no. 45, known as the Farewell: in that, as each instrument comes to the end of its allotted music, the player packs up and leaves the stage. The conceit of this song is that the children are like a Swiss clock winding up to strike the hour; on such clocks, only the last figure hits the chime denoting the time, and so the last child in line becomes the chime, and, according to Layton's suggested notes, 'gets hit on the head and staggers out of the room'.

'Climb Ev'ry Mountain'

Known as 'Face Life' in the original tentative routine of songs (and to be sung by the Abbess 'to and with Maria'), this is one of Rodgers and Hammerstein's tours de force in the show, and worthy to stand with some of their other best-known inspirational anthems, including 'You'll Never Walk Alone'.

As with many of the songs for the show, it went through various permutations, with the original intent that it was sung by Maria rather than the Abbess. Hammerstein's earliest lyrics are all about Maria realizing that she needs to constantly strive until she learns to live the life she was born to live, and how she must learn to play her part. Those ideas were appropriate for a lyric about sacrifice, and how Maria might be making the greater sacrifice not by giving her life to God, but by living it out in the world. When it became the Abbess's song, it took on the bolder approach – which Rodgers matched by not using a verse before jumping straight into the chorus – and hearkened back to one of Hammerstein's earlier works with Jerome Kern, 'There's a Hill beyond a Hill', for the show *Music in the Air* in 1933. It is also the song probably most influenced by Hammerstein's correspondence with Sister Gregory, and their discussions about the choices that nuns face when they give their lives to God.

The lines about love not being love until you give it away, which turn up in 'Sixteen Going on Seventeen', were originally written for this scene, and effectively acted as a 'verse', although they were intended to be sung 'softly and lightly' to Maria by the Abbess before she tells Maria that it doesn't mean she loves God less because she loves the Captain.

The song reprises at the end as its words are taken literally, and the von Trapps have to climb every mountain (including the ones that magically stand between Salzburg and Switzerland) in order to escape with their lives.

'No Way to Stop It'

Another of the songs that didn't make it beyond the stage show, this number dramatizes the reasons given in this variant of the story for the Captain and Elsa Schraeder to part. Elsa isn't going because she realizes that Maria and Georg von Trapp are in love: they separate because of the impending Anschluss and the devastation that it will bring on Austrians. Elsa and Max are going to look after number one – themselves; Georg can't believe that that is a proper way to live. The music is deliberately scored to emphasize the isolation of the Captain as the song progresses, and the fury that builds between him and Elsa. (Joe Layton suggests that 'All of the Captain's flirtations and fury are to be taken out on the Guitar'.) The dialogue which follows, with Elsa asking if the Captain can't see things her way, and him explaining that he can't do so if she's willing to see things the Nazi way, simply underlines the huge rift that has grown between them.

In Rodgers and Hammerstein's tentative schedule of songs, the song is known as 'Why Buck The Tide?' and was placed before Maria returned to the villa. Lindsay and Crouse's notes on the show point out that it is a 'play with music' at times, which means some scenes need a 'somewhat realistic treatment', and for this scene, their comment is: 'In this scene we go into twilight, and on the mountains on the backdrop we want the effect of one or more bonfires in the shape of swastikas'. Bearing in mind that Nazi Stormtroopers were eventually written out of the show, the chances of background swastikas making it were minimal, but it shows their intent for the scene: the Nazis are close, and time is running out.

'An Ordinary Couple'

The final song unique to the stage show, this was penned when Rodgers and Hammerstein realized during rehearsals that they had built up the relationship between Georg von Trapp and Maria – and not given them a love song to go with it. This may have been because they were having problems with their proposed song 'I've Been in Love Before (So I know what I'm saying)', which they placed at this point in the tentative schedule. Neither of the stars particularly liked it even when an extra verse was added. Rodgers would later explain to the producers of the movie that he and Hammerstein were planning to replace 'An Ordinary Couple' with a better love song, but they never had the chance to do so.

Lyrically, 'An Ordinary Couple' is a contrast to both of the other stage-only songs: Maria and Georg will be the titular ordinary couple, not suffering the problems of being too rich (as discussed in 'How Can Love Survive'), nor self-obsessed ('No Way to Stop It').

'*Gaudeamus Domino/Confitemi Domino*'

Prior to the wedding, the nuns sing the chorus '*Gaudeamus omnes in Domino, diem festum celebrantes*', which means 'Let us all rejoice in the Lord, celebrating a festival day' – of which a wedding is of course an example. The words are most commonly sung on saints' days, and in particular on the Feast of All Saints (1 November).

The second chant is taken from Psalm 117. '*Confitemini Domino quoniam bonus, quoniam in saeculum misericordia ejus*' is usually translated as 'Give praise to the Lord, for he is good: for his mercy endureth for ever'. It also appears in the Books of the Apocrypha, but it would seem highly unlikely that that was Hammerstein's source, since it's traditionally used in the Catholic Church after the blessing at the Benediction of the Blessed Sacrament. This is another often overlooked clever piece of writing by Hammerstein: the normal Blessed Sacrament to which this refers is the blessed Host, but here it's the sacrament of marriage which has been blessed.

'Edelweiss'

The last piece which Rodgers and Hammerstein wrote together was written in an unusual way for the duo – Rodgers came up with the tune for Theodore Bikel to learn to play on the guitar before Hammerstein devised the very simple words. This was from necessity: Hammerstein's developing cancer meant that he couldn't be at the try-outs when the idea was thought of.

His working process can be observed through the notes which are reprinted in *The Sound of Music Companion*: on 15 October, he did some research into the edelweiss flower itself, *Leontopodium alpinum*, noting its shape and the places in which it is found. He must also have been aware of its symbolic significance: in the preface to the 1869 English-language translation of Berthold Auerbach's 1861 novel, called simply *Edelweiss*, Ralph Waldo Emerson wrote that the flower 'grows on the most inaccessible cliffs of the Tyrolese mountains' and is 'immensely valued by the Swiss maidens'. Its name, Emerson claimed, signified 'noble purity'. In 1907, the edelweiss became the sign of the Austro-Hungarian Alpine troops and remains the insignia of the Austrian, Polish, Romanian and German Alpine troops today.

In some ways, it was an appropriate emblem to use for an anti-Nazi piece: the Edelweiss Pirates (*Edelweißpiraten*) in Nazi Germany were young people who objected to the paramilitary ways of the Hitler Youth (Himmler finally lost patience with them in 1944; ironically he may have given the order to have the group's leaders caught and hanged from the former von Trapp villa, which was his headquarters during the war). However, according to a 1934 song, '*Adolf Hitlers Lieblingsblume ist das schlichte Edelweiß*' – 'Adolf Hitler's favourite flower is an edelweiss!' – and one of the Wehrmacht marching songs during the war was '*Es war ein Edelweiss*' ('It was an edelweiss'), written in 1941 by Herms Niehl.

Hammerstein's first draft, dated 20 October, is a little more specific than the final version: rather than 'blossom of snow' it specifically calls the edelweiss the 'flower of Austria', and it talks of the singer coming back to find it, rather than it greeting him each morning. The latter change may have been made since it would otherwise have been a very obvious piece of foreshadowing when sung by the Captain – in the stage show, the song only appears this one time, just before the von Trapps make their break for the border, although Brigitta reminds Maria at the gala party that her father has sung it with the children and her a few days earlier. The final version was completed on 21 October.

Contrary to popular opinion – and that of US President Ronald Reagan – 'Edelweiss' isn't the Austrian national anthem: that's '*Land der Berge, Land am Strome*' ('Land of the Mountains, Land on the River'). Before the Anschluss, it was '*Sei gesegnet ohne Ende*' ('Be Blessed Without End'), which was sung to the same tune as the German national anthem, and therefore banned after the Second World War (the tune is called 'Austria' in hymn books).

PART THREE: THE TRAPP FAMILY GET WISE

13

COUNTDOWN TO ACTION

The Sound of Music opened on Broadway in November 1959, and seven months later, the entertainment industry bible *Variety* announced that the rights had been sold to 20th Century Fox. However, it would be a full five years before the big-screen version of the musical was released, during which the project – not to mention the studio that produced it – went through many permutations.

Although the professional critics went to town about the musical's perceived saccharine qualities, there were some in the audience on the Broadway first night who saw the potential for the von Trapp story to become a hit in other media. Among them was Spyros Skouras, then president of 20th Century Fox, who apparently cried like a baby watching the denouement. His opinion of the musical's viability was shared by scriptwriter Ernest Lehman, who saw the show along with his wife a couple of weeks into the run. Although he was aware of the mauling the musical had received from the critics, Lehman confidently predicted to his wife during the interval that he wasn't worried about what other people thought of *The Sound of Music*: 'someday it's going to make a very successful movie'. Lehman knew quite a bit about adapting musicals for the big screen – he had written the screenplay for the large-scale version of Rodgers and Hammerstein's *The King and I*, and was working on Robert Wise's adaptation of *West Side Story*, which eventually came out in October 1961. When he was visiting the Fox lot sometime later, he chatted with David Brown, the head of the studio's story department, and told him what he thought, asking Brown to make sure that Richard D. Zanuck (known as Dick), the son of the studio chief Darryl F. Zanuck, was made aware of his opinion.

20th Century Fox had scored a success with their versions of Rodgers and Hammerstein's previous stage musicals *Carousel* and *The King and I* in 1956 and *South Pacific* a couple of years later, so Skouras had already secured 'first refusal' rights on any other projects that the pair came up with. While *The Flower Drum Song*, Rodgers and Hammerstein's 1958 show, didn't spark his imagination, *The Sound of Music* did, and negotiations with the legendary Hollywood agent Irving 'Swifty' Lazar began, resulting in the studio deciding to 'plunk down over $1M for a fifteen-year lease on the property', as Variety explained in June 1960.

As many people have learned the hard way over the years, just because a Hollywood studio negotiates rights of varying degrees over a property – whether it's a book, film, play or board game that takes their fancy – that doesn't mean it's inevitable that there will be a motion picture at the end of the process. Sometimes deals are reached in order to keep something off the market that will potentially harm the success of a project already under way; other times, the terms and conditions of the deal mean that everything has to go on hold for a time. That was the case with *The Sound of Music*. Much as they might have wanted to capitalize on the hit status of the musical on Broadway and around the world, Fox couldn't.

A clause within the agreement meant that the film couldn't open until after the first run of the musical had stopped playing, and there was no sign of that happening any time soon. It therefore joined a number of such projects with a nebulous future.

However, when Fox needed a hit soon after, it was to *The Sound of Music* that they turned. Things went seriously wrong for the studio in the early 1960s as a direct consequence of the massive overspending on various projects, most notably the epic retelling of the story of Cleopatra, featuring Elizabeth Taylor as the Egyptian queen and Richard Burton as her lover Mark Antony. The film began shooting in 1960 in London, and then production was moved to Rome where everything had to be constructed afresh; its original $2 million budget didn't so much balloon, as explode up to $44 million.

Although *Cleopatra* would end up more successful than hoped – but still made a huge loss – Darryl F. Zanuck had no option but to make major changes in an effort to restore the financial viability and prestige of his business. His son Dick stepped up to take a key role at the studio as vice president of production in California. As well as carrying out stringent cost-cutting across the board, Dick Zanuck looked for something to which Fox already owned the rights to get into production.

The Sound of Music was the answer. To Zanuck, it was an obvious solution: the musical was a wonderful piece of family entertainment which had been hugely successful, and even if they couldn't get on with actually making the film, at the very least – particularly given that it was a historical subject – they could put a writer to work, so they were ready when the time came.

Ernest Lehman's affinity for the subject and his recommendation of the property two years earlier made him the obvious candidate, and by this point in 1962, he had been responsible for the screenplay for Robert Wise's adaptation of Leonard Bernstein's *West Side Story*, which had triumphed at the Academy Awards with eleven nominations and ten wins. Ironically, Lehman himself wasn't honoured: during his career he was nominated six times for an Academy Award for Best Writer, but never won; he was eventually the first ever recipient of an Honorary Oscar in 2001 to mark his career.

Despite his agent advising strongly against him taking the job, Lehman was officially signed up to pen the screenplay for *The Sound of Music* in December 1962, one of the very few people at that time to be working on the 20th Century Fox lot – he was offered the choice of any office he desired, even Darryl Zanuck's old one, by the studio manager, since the place was so deserted. Even before he had started work – according to legend, on the very first day when he and his boss were due to discuss the project over lunch at Romanoff's (the popular restaurant on South Rodeo Drive) – Swifty Lazar approached Dick Zanuck offering to buy the rights back for two million dollars. This was supposedly because Warner Bros.' Jack Warner was interested in buying them from him in order to keep *The Sound of Music* away from competing with his studio's production of *My Fair Lady*. Although the quick fix of money was no doubt tempting, Zanuck had faith in *The Sound of Music*'s money-making potential, and refused the offer of a $750,000 payday. (Lazar didn't give up easily – later that afternoon he rang Lehman and tried to get him to pull out of the project, ignoring the writer when he told him that he was aware of Zanuck refusing to take the quick buck.)

The project had a bad reputation in Hollywood, and not just because of Fox's financial problems. At a party at Jack Lemmon's house, director Billy Wilder counselled Lehman against *The Sound of Music*, claiming that no musical with swastikas in it could be a success (Lehman noted later that Wilder was quite prepared to admit that he was wrong after the film's extraordinary reception). During a chance encounter in the studio commissary, Burt Lancaster told Lehman that he must really need the money to be working on the film. Even Gene Kelly described *The Sound of Music* as 'that piece of shit' when he was approached to be part of it. (Christopher Plummer's often quoted mistitling *The Sound of Mucus* seems mild by comparison, although he also would call it 'S & M'.)

Normally when a film enters the pre-production phase, there are multiple people involved, but because of the pared-back environment at Fox, Ernest Lehman was something of a one-man band. Very unusually, that meant that not only was he scripting the film, but he was also looking for a director on Zanuck's behalf. Zanuck had approached Robert Wise, who had directed Lehman's first ever produced screenplay, hoping to capitalize on his experience on *West Side Story*. However, Wise flatly turned down the project. He wasn't enthused by the subject matter, feeling that Rodgers and Hammerstein's treatment of the material rendered it 'saccharine'; he preferred to start work on *The Sand Pebbles*, a film based on science fiction writer Richard McKenna's novel about a rebel American sailor in the 1920s, which would see him team up with Steve McQueen.

Lehman approached *Singin' in the Rain* and *Seven Brides for Seven Brothers* director Stanley Donen, who was one of the backers of the Broadway version of *The Sound of Music*. Donen didn't want to have anything more to do with the von Trapp family story. Vincent Donehue, the stage musical's director, turned down the chance to immortalize it on celluloid. Future *Butch Cassidy and the Sundance Kid* director George Roy Hill wasn't interested. Gene Kelly bluntly told Lehman his opinion of the musical as he ushered the writer out of his house.

Running out of ideas, Lehman and Richard Zanuck flew to New York to discuss the situation with Darryl F. Zanuck, who was unable to visit his studio in Hollywood because of the threat of divorce proceedings hanging over him if he entered California. During the conversation in Zanuck's suite in the St Regis Hotel, Lehman threw out the name of William Wyler as a potential director. The veteran Wyler had been directing films since 1925, and won three Academy Awards, most recently for the epic *Ben Hur*. He would certainly be able to bring scope to the motion picture of *The Sound of Music*, even if he had never directed a musical before. What neither Zanuck nor Lehman knew was whether he had any interest in adding such a different type of film to his resumé.

When Lehman rang him from New York, Wyler admitted that he had not seen the stage version; he also pointed out that he had concerns about taking on the project because of his loss of hearing, which meant he wouldn't be able to appreciate the music fully – he was deaf in one ear as a result of a bombing raid when he was in the US Army Air Force during the war. However, if he didn't have to worry about the musical side of production he might be interested, so he agreed to fly from California to see the Broadway show with Lehman.

The collaboration between Wyler and Lehman didn't get off to a good start. The two men went to the Mark Hellinger Theatre (where the stage show had moved in November 1962) and Wyler came out complaining how much he had hated the show. Darryl Zanuck was waiting for them at the 21 Club, but Wyler didn't want to meet the studio boss, given his depth of antagonism towards the musical. Instead, Lehman and Wyler went for a walk around the Manhattan streets. Eventually, the writer asked Wyler how he had felt during the scene where the Baron returns to the house, hears the children singing 'The Sound of Music' and eventually joins in. Wyler admitted that that particular moment had made him feel as if he wanted to cry. Lehman pounced, and explained that that was why the film would be successful. Wyler saw his point – and the scene is one of those which powers the movie forward into its second act.

Before signing up with Darryl Zanuck – eventually setting up a situation where he and his brother had use of their own separate building on the 20th Century Fox lot – Wyler sought advice from various colleagues. He understood why in operas people would burst into song, but he didn't feel that there was sufficient justification in the stage show for the outbreaks of music – it seemed as if the von Trapps sang simply because they enjoyed singing. (Bearing in mind the true story of the family, Wyler had actually hit on a good point, one that Lehman's screenplay would eventually tackle). Although he relished the challenge of something different now he was in his seventh decade, he was concerned about the prospect of failure, so he wrote to the producer of the 1956 German film. On hearing that the producer felt that the project couldn't fail, Wyler's fears were assuaged.

However, according to Ernest Lehman, Wyler had a reputation in the film industry for blowing hot and cold on different projects, and effectively pitting one studio against another until he found a project which he really wanted to do, even after he had signed on the dotted line. Certainly during the early stages of preparation on *The Sound of Music*, Lehman found himself acting as a go-between for Wyler with MGM's Martin Ransohoff, discussing their movie *The Americanization of Emily*. Lehman warned Richard Zanuck that he had his doubts about Wyler's commitment to *The Sound of Music*, and the studio boss told him to get his first draft screenplay completed quickly, hoping that that would help to lock Wyler into the project.

When his attention was focused on *The Sound of Music*, Wyler did move the film forward. He hired Roger Edens as an associate producer, who had worked extensively at MGM and had been involved in the promotion of Judy Garland's career. Wyler, Edens and Lehman made a list of possible locations for the film, and in May they took a trip to Salzburg, where they found many of the shooting spots which were finally used in the movie. According to Wyler's biography, the director visited Nonnberg Abbey and discussed the possibility of filming some of the critical scenes there with the Mother Superior – Wyler's wife Talli recalled that the venerable nun seemed amazed at the idea. He also sounded out the Mayor of Salzburg about the scenes which reconstructed the Anschluss. How would his electorate feel about Nazi soldiers once more parading through the streets of Salzburg? The answer was simple: they'd survived it once; they would survive it again. The team also visited Hitler's Berchtesgaden twenty-five miles south of the town, but that was 'purely a tourist call' according to Edens' notes.

Both Lehman and Wyler were well aware that the movie's success would ride on who was cast as Maria von Trapp. Although Wyler himself would later claim that he was in favour of Julie Andrews, after meeting her on the set of Disney's *Mary Poppins* and seeing some rushes from her performance, Lehman recollected very differently. According to him, Wyler was vehemently opposed to Andrews – who had never been seen on the big screen at that point – and told the writer that he was planning on either using an unknown such as Romy Schneider, or someone like Audrey Hepburn, with whom he had worked before on *Roman Holiday* and *The Children's Hour*. Lehman wasn't opposed to the idea of Hepburn: it didn't matter about her singing voice, or lack of it – they would overdub her with Marni Nixon, later hailed as 'The Ghostest with the Mostest' by *Time* magazine, who had sung for Deborah Kerr in *The King and I*, Natalie Wood in *West Side Story*, and would go on to dub Hepburn on *My Fair Lady*.

Lehman was becoming concerned not only about Wyler's commitment to the movie, but also to the approach which he might take. Wyler originally came from a Jewish family in Alsace – he emigrated from Germany to America after the First World War – and had relatives who had been killed in the Holocaust. Lehman noted that Wyler's desk at Fox was starting to groan under the weight of books discussing the Anschluss, and he felt that Wyler was becoming obsessed with the Nazi invasion side of the story. 'I had a tendency to want to make it, if not an anti-Nazi movie, at least say a few things,' he wrote later. According to Dick Zanuck, Wyler planned to re-envisage the peaceful arrival of the Nazi troops in Salzburg with a blitzkrieg, which would be like the attack on Guernica during the Spanish Civil War. Zanuck was opposed, not seeing the need for such things in a musical. Wyler himself was becoming unhappy, telling his wife that he couldn't face the prospect of making a movie about 'nice Nazis' – although this didn't come to light until many years later.

However, Lehman's primary job was to complete the script on the movie, which he duly did by September 1963. Copies of what Lehman referred to as a 'quick draft' were prepared for Zanuck and Wyler, and the writer was very surprised when the director came to his office to talk about the screenplay. That wasn't the way that the Hollywood hierarchy worked: writers went to directors, not the other way round. Lehman was even more surprised when Wyler, whose reputation also included a penchant for being hard on both his writers and his actors (as Paul Newman would later attest), said that he couldn't find anything to suggest as an improvement on the screenplay. Lehman himself knew that the script was rough around the edges, and needed work; this raised his suspicions even further.

Shortly after this, Wyler invited Lehman to come out to his beach house in Malibu for a Sunday afternoon social event, where Rex Harrison and his wife Rachel Roberts would also be present. Wyler wanted the writer to try to persuade Harrison to sign up for the role of Baron von Trapp, claiming that the actor would be more impressed by an approach from the writer (contrary, it has to be said, once again to the way in which Hollywood usually worked – the writers were never usually deemed that important). Lehman duly went, but noticed that Wyler wasn't really engaged in the social activities – he was spending most of the time deep in discussion with Mike Frankovich, then head of Columbia Pictures. He therefore took himself off for a nose around Wyler's living room, in which there were dozens of scripts, all bar one of which were face up, showing the title page. The only one that was the other way around was for *The Collector*, a Columbia project based on the novel by John Fowles. Lehman knew that the producers on *The Collector* were desperately seeking a director – by chance, during a stopover in London on the trip to Salzburg, he had run into them when they shared their woes on the film – so that night he rang Dick Zanuck and warned him that he thought Wyler was about to abandon ship and sign up for *The Collector*.

Zanuck was therefore forewarned and forearmed for the appearance the next day in his office of Wyler's agent who asked for a delay on production of *The Sound of Music* so his client could make *The Collector* for Columbia. The studio boss was clear: there would be no delay on *The Sound of Music*, for Wyler or anyone else. Wyler duly directed *The Collector*, a dark thriller which was very much the antithesis of the feel-good *Sound of Music*; Lehman claimed it was a 'financial disaster' for Columbia even though it was a critical success, winning prizes for best actor and actress at the Cannes Film Festival.

However, that left *The Sound of Music* once again without a director. Lehman ran into Robert Wise in the Fox cafeteria looking miserable, and Wise explained that a monsoon had hit Taiwan, and consequently shooting on *The Sand Pebbles* had been put on hold. Lehman saw an opportunity, and contacted Wise's agent on the quiet, arranging for a copy of the screenplay to be passed to Wise. According to Lehman, Wise loved the script, slightly to his surprise given the critical negativity about the stage show, and discussed it with his associate producer Saul Chaplin, who had handled the musical aspects of *West Side Story* for Wise. Both men agreed that they would be willing to work on the film together. Lehman's first official notification of Wise's involvement came from a meeting in Dick Zanuck's office when the studio executive told him he might be able to get Wise on board. Zanuck realized that Lehman had been responsible for slipping the script to Wise, but for years, the writer wouldn't admit what he'd done.

Wise's version was that he was approached by the studio to

look at the script, was surprised by its quality, and slightly to his embarrassment, having teased Lehman about working on the film, found himself working on the film. The deal which he came to with the Zanucks probably helped to sweeten the situation: in return for him directing *The Sound of Music*, the studio would back *The Sand Pebbles*, which had run into some financial difficulties, and he would receive 10 per cent of the net profit. That might not normally amount to much, Hollywood accounting practices being what they are, but in the case of *The Sound of Music*, it became an appreciable sum.

Whichever way it came about, in November 1963, Robert Wise signed up to direct *The Sound of Music*. Now all they needed was a cast.

14

SOLVING A PROBLEM

Casting any motion picture or television show is an art. Not only do the actors need the requisite dramatic range to play the part, but their relationships with those around them – particularly when they are meant to be members of the same family – have to be credible, otherwise the audience is quickly pulled out of the story. For *The Sound of Music*, the producers had to find seven children who could quickly be accepted as a family, as well as an actor to play their father who also had that elusive chemistry with the younger woman at the heart of the story.

Although it seems obvious now that Julie Andrews was born to play Maria von Trapp, she was by no means top of everyone's wish list for the part – although screenplay writer Ernest Lehman was adamant from very early on that she was exactly right for the role. When he was involved as director, William Wyler wasn't keen; according to Ernest Lehman, neither was

Richard Rodgers when Lehman had a meeting with the co-writer of the original musical in New York. In fact, Rodgers' comment was an acerbic, 'So what else is new?', which Lehman took to mean that Rodgers was displeased, since Andrews had starred in an earlier Rodgers and Hammerstein production and he didn't feel she was right for Maria – although this wasn't an aspersion on her talent generally.

Various other names were put forward: Rodgers sarcastically suggested Doris Day as a possibility, perhaps because he had been lobbied by Day's third husband and manager, Martin Melcher. Lehman too received the full force of Melcher's attempts to push his wife as the star of the movie, despite the fact that she was over forty at the time, and would be playing a twenty-one-year-old. Director Robert Wise was completely against the idea, and it progressed no further. Out of propriety, since she had originated the role on stage, Mary Martin was considered, but she hadn't made a film in over twenty years, and as Robert Wise later explained, 'the screen is much more demanding, age-wise'. Leslie Caron, Anne Bancroft and Shirley Jones (who would go on to play the part on stage in 1977) were also discussed.

However, as Robert Wise recalled in 1998, it was Julie Andrews whose name kept being mentioned in connection with the part. There were some rumours that she might not be as 'photogenic' as she could be, so Wise decided to cut to the chase, and see how she looked on film. He called the producers of Disney's *Mary Poppins*, and asked if they could see some of the final footage from their rough cut of the film. He, Lehman and Saul Chaplin went over to the Disney lot, and as soon as they saw Andrews as P.L. Travers' magical nanny, they were sold. Wise was convinced that she was going to be a major star, and that they needed to act quickly to snap her up before either Mary Poppins or her other film (*The Americanization of Emily*, which at one stage had been due to be directed by William Wyler) was released. They went straight back to Fox and told them to sign her. Negotiations took a little time: Andrews wasn't sure if she wanted to do another musical so soon after *Mary Poppins*, and she shared Wise's initial reservations about the saccharinity of the material. However, Wise's explanations of his approach (and the promise of a good pay day, according to some sources) convinced her that signing up was the right thing to do.

Born Julia Elizabeth Wells in Walton-on-Thames, in the heart of England's home counties in 1935, Julie Andrews had come to America in 1954 after a strong career as a singing and acting child star in her native Britain (including playing Humpty Dumpty in a pantomime). She played Polly Browne in the Broadway production of Sandy Wilson's *The Boy Friend* aged just nineteen, and the following year auditioned for Rodgers and Hammerstein for their new show, *Pipe Dream*, as well as for the lead in Alan Jay Lerner and Frederick Loewe's adaptation of *Pygmalion*, entitled *My Fair Lady*. Rodgers advised her to take the latter, should that be offered (wise advice, as it turned out: *Pipe Dream* was a rare Rodgers and Hammerstein failure). It was, and Julie Andrews became 'Broadway's most radiant new star' with whom every composer and lyricist wanted to work.

She had her chance to work with Rodgers and Hammerstein on their television special of *Cinderella*, which was broadcast on 31 March 1957, during the run of *My Fair Lady* before Andrews and co-star Rex Harrison brought the show to London. Andrews returned to Broadway in 1960 with *Camelot*, the musical which helped to bring her to the attention of Walt Disney – and to the part of Mary Poppins.

That film was being made at the same time as the screen adaptation of *My Fair Lady*, in which Audrey Hepburn played the part which Andrews had made famous both sides of the Atlantic. Jack Warner of Warner Bros. had decided not to cast Andrews opposite her stage co-star Harrison: as the studio head explained in his 1965 autobiography *My First Hundred Years in Hollywood*, Andrews had charm and ability, but she was a Broadway star, whose name was only known to those who had seen the musical on stage. In 'Clinton, Iowa and Anchorage, Alaska, and thousands of other cities and towns in our fifty states and abroad you can say Audrey Hepburn, and people instantly know you're talking about a beautiful and talented star'. (Andrews had her revenge: when accepting the Golden Globe Award for *Mary Poppins*, which had defeated *My Fair Lady*, she thanked 'a man who made a wonderful movie and who made all this possible in the first place, Mr Jack Warner'.)

Mary Poppins brought all of Andrews' diverse talents to a whole new audience, although small-screen watchers had already seen her demonstrate many of them in a TV special from the Carnegie Hall in New York in 1962 when she and her friend Carol Burnett had made fun of the popular musical, *The Sound of Music*, with the adventures of the 'Swiss Family Pratt' with Andrews as a 'happy nun' singing a 'happy song' about different sorts of food that she sang when she was back home in Switzerland, which may have been rather close in style to 'My Favourite Things'. When negotiations for the film became a reality, she realized that this performance might come back to haunt her, but it was clear that Robert Wise's approach was going to be very different from that taken on stage. Now Julie Andrews needed to learn the words to the real song . . .

Opposite Julie Andrews, Robert Wise cast Canadian actor Christopher Plummer as Baron Georg von Trapp. Again, other names had been considered for the role: some at Fox Studio for a time were very keen on Bing Crosby playing the part, while Yul Brynner, who had starred as the eponymous ruler in *The King and I*, was equally hungry for the role. According to some sources, Wise debated using either Peter Finch or Sean Connery as the Baron, although the latter might have been very young to play the part of the father of a 'sixteen going on seventeen' young lady, and it is claimed that Curt Jurgens (star of *The Enemy Below* and later the Bond villain Karl Stromberg in *The Spy Who Loved Me*) screen-tested for the part.

It was Wise's wife who suggested Plummer, and the idea of appearing in a musical apparently fitted with the Canadian's own career plans. In his autobiography, he claims that he accepted the role because he had a 'secret plan to one day turn Cyrano de Bergerac into a Broadway musical'. Working on *The Sound of Music* would give him some valuable experience. (Plummer did end up playing Cyrano in a musical adaptation written by Anthony Burgess and Michael J. Lewis in 1973.) He wasn't necessarily drawn by the character as written in the draft screenplay, but that was something that could be dealt with.

Christopher Plummer in fact was only thirty-four when he was cast as the Baron. Born in Toronto in 1929, he studied to be a concert pianist when younger, but found a taste for acting. He learned his trade as part of the Canadian Repertory Company and the Bermuda Repertory Theatre, before making his Broadway debut in *The Starcross Story* – for its one and only performance in January 1953. He made his mark on the stage for many roles including in Archibald MacLeish's *J.B.* on Broadway, and as part of the Stratford Shakespeare Festival and the Royal Shakespeare Company in Canada and England.

However, for a time it seemed as if Plummer would not stay on the movie for long. Before shooting began in Austria, the studio wanted to lay down a guide track of the songs, with Plummer and Julie Andrews, and there was a possibility that some of it might end up in the final cut of the film. Plummer, who was well aware that he wasn't the best singer in the world and was taking lessons to ensure that he didn't embarrass himself when it finally came to record the soundtrack, baulked at the prospect. The studio was insistent; Plummer was equally firm – he wasn't prepared to do it and threatened to walk off the film. Luckily, his agent Kurt Frings, was able to calm both sides down, and agreed with Fox that Plummer could 'mumble the guide track' and then record it properly later. The star was formally welcomed back to *The Sound of Music* by Dick Zanuck in front of the entire cast and crew. However, it wasn't the last time that his musical contribution to the movie would cause friction.

The producers didn't just have to think of the other von Trapp family members. There were other key adult roles to be filled. The Mother Abbess, who sends Maria off to be governess to the von Trapp children, was played by Peggy Wood, although she wasn't the first one considered. Irene Dunne, the star of the screen version of Jerome Kern and Oscar Hammerstein's *Show Boat*, was high on the list, even though she hadn't actually appeared on screen for over a decade. Jeanette MacDonald – who had starred in Richard Rodgers and Lorenz Hart's *I Married An Angel* on the big screen – was actually signed up for the role, according to some biographies, but had to have heart surgery to deal with a long-standing condition in late 1963, so was ruled out of contention. Peggy Wood, a veteran of stage and screen, was cast, although she was aware that she would not be able to reach the high notes for 'Climb Ev'ry Mountain'; her singing was dubbed by Margery McKay.

The junior key members of Nonnberg Abbey were equally talented stage and screen actresses: Sister Berthe was played by composer and cabaret artiste Portia Nelson, with Anna Lee, the former wife of Julie Andrews' director on *Mary Poppins* Robert Stevenson, as Sister Margaretta. These two would form a brief comedy double act at the end of the movie, sabotaging the Nazis' car. Sister Sophia allowed Marni Nixon to make her stage debut, and she and Andrews became firm friends on the set.

For Max Detweiler, the slightly down-at-heel would-be impresario, Robert Wise initially considered using either Victor Borge, the Danish musical comedian (who was interested in a film debut if the part was strengthened), or Noël Coward. The role went to British actor Richard Haydn, who had voiced the Caterpillar for Disney's animated version of *Alice in Wonderland* and appeared as Baron Popoff in the 1952 movie of *The Merry Widow*.

Baroness Elsa Schraeder, his counterpart in the stage show – although not so much in the revised version of the script – was chosen from a list of glamorous ladies including Cyd Charisse, Eva Gabor and Grace Kelly. Eleanor Parker, who had been nominated three times for Academy Awards in the 1950s, took the part, which, like Max, now did not require the actor to sing.

British actress Norma Varden, who had worked with Wise on *Madame Fifi*, one of his first films for RKO in 1945, lobbied the director to play the Mother Abbess, but Wise knew they were looking for someone who could sing. He did however cast her as the housekeeper, Frau Schmidt. In the end, since Peggy Wood's singing was dubbed, it might not have been so big an issue, although Wood, of course, had a bigger reputation.

For the Nazis, Wise cast Ben Wright as Herr Zeller, the Third Reich supporter who ends up becoming the Gauleiter for the Salzburg area, and the von Trapps' implacable foe. The British actor had played many roles as French and German natives during a long career on TV and film, and had the chilling air that Wise required for the role.

The character of Rolfe changed quite considerably between the stage and screen, and Wise needed an actor who could play the young lover who finally puts his new masters first. Daniel Truhitte was born in Sacramento in 1943, and was singing and dancing from the age of six. He had auditioned for the stage version, but claimed he didn't get called back because they were looking for a natural blond (Truhitte is dark-haired). For the film, the producers had a considerable problem finding the right actor – Truhitte recalls that Jon Voight, who had appeared on the show on Broadway as Rolf, didn't pass muster – and he was one of the last actors cast . . . not long after the girl with whom he would be matched, Charmian Carr.

* * *

Robert Wise didn't want the von Trapp children to be a homo-
geneous bunch. Many of the stage productions had gone for
the stereotypical Aryan look – blond-haired and blue-eyed –
but he knew that they needed some variety. That was as well
as being able to sing, dance, act and be of the requisite height
for numbers in the movie that relied on them being of differing stature. This ruled out potential siblings such as members
of the Osmond family (the older brothers Alan, Jay, Merrill
and Wayne apparently auditioned). Kurt Russell, Richard
Dreyfuss and Sharon Tate were among the other later-famous
names who tried for roles in the film unsuccessfully.

Wise and his team of casting agents scoured London, New
York and Los Angeles for potential members of the family,
before arranging to audition two hundred of them in various
groups. The only absolute proviso that Wise made was that
none of the children should have appeared on stage in *The
Sound of Music* – the performance he would be looking for was
completely different. In the end six of the seven children were
cast in Hollywood – the exception was Nicholas Hammond,
who played Friedrich, whose screen test was in New York.

Hammond, the son of an American army officer and a
British actress, was born in 1950 and spent part of his child-
hood in France. On the way back to America, the family
stopped off in London, where the young Nicholas saw Julie
Andrews give her final performance as Eliza Doolittle in *My
Fair Lady*. This, combined with viewing films in the ship's
cinema on the voyage home, encouraged him to want to act,
and once settled in their new home in Washington D.C., his
parents spotted an advert for auditions for Peter Brook's movie
version of William Golding's *Lord of the Flies*. This marked
his screen debut, and soon after returning from location in
Puerto Rico, Hammond was cast by legendary theatrical producer Irene Selznick in *The Complaisant Lover*. By the time
he auditioned for *The Sound of Music*, he had amassed a size-
able list of roles.

The actor recalled many years later entering the audition hall and seeing hundreds of children all singing away. He had fifteen minutes to learn a scene, but impressed the casting director, who invited him back to meet Robert Wise and Saul Chaplin the next day. They questioned him closely about his experience before carrying out another screen test, with Hammond performing his lines with a British accent (not something which was hard for him, given his background and his role in *Lord of the Flies*). The screen tests were shown to the studio executives in California, and Hammond was cast.

Heather Menzies remembers not really taking on board what she was auditioning for when she went for the part for Louisa – something to do with 'Julie Harris', musical instruments and Australia was all she could remember when she was talking with school friends later. It's perhaps not too surprising: the audition process was all still quite new to her. Born in December 1949 in Canada to Scottish parents – her father had been a prisoner of war for the majority of the Second World War and emigrated for a fresh start – she moved with them and her older brother Neil to Florida. When she was eight the family moved to California, where she enrolled at the Falcon Studios and learned acting, singing, tap dancing and fencing. Acquiring an agent via the mother of one of her friends, she debuted on the TV series *My Three Sons*, and her second audition was for *The Sound of Music*. She knew nothing about the stage version and was happy to chat with Robert Wise and Saul Chaplin about the lucky St Christopher medal she always wore to auditions. After various call backs she screen-tested one Friday, and the following Monday she heard that she had got the part – in passing, as her mother was more concerned with getting her younger sister out of the door for a commercial audition!

Duane Chase was thirteen when he went for the audition as Kurt, and by that point was an old hand at filming commercials. The native Los Angeleno, born there in December 1950, was the youngest of three children by some considerable margin, with his older siblings acting when they were younger. He wasn't necessarily set on an acting career – filming commercials for Mattel toys or the International House of Pancakes (IHOP) was fun, and a way to fill his college fund so he could fulfil his real dream of becoming a scientist. He loved to build things in his garage and took extra maths and science classes, as well as singing lessons. He hadn't done any film work prior to *The Sound of Music*, but Wise had seen him in the IHOP commercial, and invited him for an interview. That seemed to go well, and he waited to hear if he'd been granted a screen test – but was delighted when he was called back to learn that he had been chosen.

Angela Cartwright, who played Brigitta, was the first to be confirmed in her role, although she also screen-tested for Louisa. Born in Altrincham, Cheshire, Cartwright emigrated with her family firstly to Canada, but, aged three, she accompanied them to Los Angeles, where her father worked for the Apollo space programme as an illustrator, and then as an art director, starting with *Tora! Tora! Tora!*. Angela and her sister Veronica (later seen as Lambert in Ridley Scott's *Alien*) became child stars, appearing in multiple commercials. Her first film role was in *Somebody Up There Likes Me*, playing Paul Newman's daughter; the director was Robert Wise. She then got a recurring role in the sitcom *Make Room For Daddy*, which was just coming to the end of its eleven-season run when the auditions came up for *The Sound of Music*. Her parents were happy with her trying out for something different, and she filmed two auditions, wearing a blonde wig to cover her naturally dark hair for Louisa. She later noted that her casting as Brigitta may have allowed them to diversify the looks of the children even further.

Debbie Turner wasn't the only member of her family to audition for the film: her sister Michele tried out for the role of Brigitta when she successfully tried for Marta. All three Turner girls were child actors – her older sister Patricia was in *The Ten Commandments*. Her parents were Canadians who had emigrated from Manitoba to escape the terrible winters there – the temperature often remains twenty degrees below freezing for weeks on end – and they encouraged the girls' acting ambitions. Her mother was contacted by the girls' agent, Mary Grady, about the auditions and both girls went in to sing for casting director Michael McLean. However, it was Debbie who was invited to meet Wise and Chaplin, and sing once more for them. Turner recalls that there was a three-month gap before she went for the screen test just before Christmas 1963, opposite Shelley Fabares as Liesl, and then a few more weeks before she received the news that she had the part; a contemporary newspaper report, however, notes that she auditioned in November, and screen-tested in January.

Five-year-old Kym Karath impressed Robert Wise at her audition with her calm demeanour – and by the fact that she confidently sang 'Sixteen Going on Seventeen' as her piece, after admitting that she knew all the songs from *The Sound of Music*. The daughter of two Greek immigrants, Karath was born in August 1958 in Los Angeles, with her older siblings also involved in the entertainment world. She was cast as Henry Fonda and Maureen O'Hara's daughter in the movie *Spencer's Mountain* when she was just three years old, after producers spotted her in her father's restaurant, which was just across Melrose Avenue from the Desilu studios (where *I Love Lucy* and later *Star Trek* were filmed).

The six screen siblings were already in rehearsals before their older 'sister' was cast: Nicholas Hammond recalled that practice for the routine for 'My Favourite Things' featured a different person playing Liesl every day. Wise auditioned numerous future stars, including Kim Darby, Patty Duke, Mia Farrow, Teri Garr, Victoria Tennant and Lesley Ann Warren, but none of them had the qualities that he was after. Hollywood agent Marian Garner suggested that her friend Rita Farnon's daughter Charmian might be suitable. Charmian was actually twenty-one years old, born in December 1942, but she could pass for sixteen. The family had moved from

Chicago to San Fernando in 1956, and she was crowned Miss San Fernando in 1960, receiving the crown from her sister, the previous year's recipient. Charmian drove herself to the Fox lot for her audition (during which she pronounced her character's name Lysol, like the disinfectant spray, rather than Lee-sall) and read for the casting director. Two further auditions followed, but Robert Wise had concerns about her eyes being too blue, so she had the role provisionally until a screen test could be arranged. Once that was sorted, she joined the rest of the children in rehearsal.

Robert Wise didn't just need talented people in front of the camera; he required some of the best industry professionals to ensure that everything looked exactly as it should on screen. Christopher Plummer gives a lot of credit for the film's lack of fairy-tale sentimentality to the work of the director of photography, Ted McCord, a veteran of Hollywood for nearly fifty years at that point. Plummer noted that McCord had invented a lens which 'gave back to the countryside all its natural beauty, just as one views it with the naked eye'. He had begun work as a camera assistant at the Hobart Bosworth Production Company in 1917, with his first film as cinematographer coming four years later. He made hundreds of films, many of them Westerns, between the wars, and had served as a captain in the US Army Photographic Unit when the Allies entered Berlin. Returning to civilian life, he lensed John Huston's *The Treasure of the Sierra Madre*, and Elia Kazan's *East of Eden*. He and Robert Wise had recently worked together on *Two for the Seesaw*, released in 1962, a very different stage adaptation from *The Sound of Music*.

The production designer was Boris Leven, who had won an Academy Award for his work with Wise on *West Side Story*, and had also designed *Two for the Seesaw*. The mix of interior and exterior designs seen in the earlier musical would need to be replicated here. Costume designer Dorothy Jeakins brought a wealth of experience to the picture: not only had she worked on film musicals such as Rodgers and Hammerstein's *South Pacific*, but she was the designer for the Los Angeles Civic Light Opera Company. Her motto of 'make beauty' can be seen to have inspired the costumes throughout the movie.

Wise's own career had also been varied. He was nominated for an Academy Award for his film editing on Orson Welles' *Citizen Kane* in 1941, during which he gained insight into the world of special optical effects – he used these to great effect in his science fiction parable *The Day the Earth Stood Still* in 1951, as well as in *West Side Story*. His directorial career began with the horror movie *The Curse of the Cat People* for Val Lewton in 1944, and he directed legends Boris Karloff and Bela Lugosi together in *The Body Snatcher* the following year. He tackled many different types of movies – from the James Cagney Western *Tribute to a Bad Man* to the biopic of a convicted killer in *I Want to Live!* – and immediately before embarking on the von Trapp family story, he directed the psychological horror movie *The Haunting*. *The Sound of Music* would be another change in direction, but, as Wise himself pointed out to a group of American Film Institute students in 1980, what he was looking for in projects throughout his career was 'good, exciting, gripping, original material'. Certainly, *The Sound of Music* would have looked and sounded very different with someone else at the helm.

15

REWRITING THE STORY

Towards the end of his long career, Ernest Lehman noted that one of the secrets of being a successful screenwriter was to know what to keep and what to ditch from the source material. What works on stage or on the printed page might not translate to the cinema screen, and in the case of a musical there is always the problem (highlighted by William Wyler when he was contemplating working on *The Sound of Music*) of finding a natural way of getting from dialogue into the song. 'You want the audience to be already enjoying the song and the musical moment before they realize what is happening,' Lehman explained.

Lehman's version of *The Sound of Music* takes Howard Lindsay and Russel Crouse's original book, as well as the lyrics and music by Rodgers and Hammerstein, and gives them a major reworking. Unlike the original musical, which was by its very nature confined to a stage, Lehman had the opportunity to expand the canvas, and the trip he took along with William Wyler to Salzburg showed him the marvellous opportunities which were available there. The city itself, with the castle and abbey high on a hill looking down on both old and new towns, as well as the proximity of the Alps, gave the writer inspiration and enabled him to achieve certain story-telling aims, such as convincing the audience that Maria has had ample time in Captain von Trapp's absence to teach the children to sing.

The screenplay is based on the stage show, rather than on the memoirs of Maria von Trapp or the two German films which followed. According to Lehman, he never saw *Die Trapp-Familie*; all he ever viewed was the sequel, *Die Trapp-Familie in Amerika*, which, as he pointed out, had nothing to do with *The Sound of Music*. However, he did meet up with Maria von Trapp herself; William Wyler said that he had a meeting with Maria in New York prior to the Salzburg trip (although since he also said he signed Julie Andrews on the set of *Mary Poppins*, he clearly wasn't averse to indulging in some revisionist history when it suited him). Lehman remembered that Maria was 'all over the place' and 'very visible and full of advice': he had seen her attend a performance of the stage show when she took a bow since it was based on her story. He could only recollect one meeting, over lunch at the St Regis Hotel, in which she said, 'When the Lord closes a door, somewhere he opens a window'. Lehman used this line in the movie, not realizing how it had also been used for dramatic effect at the end of *Die Trapp-Familie* (and it does appear in the stage show). Otherwise, the writer said, although he was grateful for the meeting, he wasn't able to use anything else from the matriarch of the von Trapp family.

It's worth noting that Maria herself doesn't mention having this meeting with Lehman. In her 1972 autobiography, she says that she and the family heard rumours about the proposed 20th Century Fox movie, and decided it was a chance to get the character of the Baron changed from the rather strict portrayal in the stage show. It took her some time to track down 'the producer' (whom she doesn't name), and get him on a person-to-person call from the Lodge in Vermont. When she explained her concerns, she was told that they were not concerned about 'persons and facts', they hadn't read the book, and they were going to make their own version of her story. This wasn't going to be a documentary, but a musical. From there on, she said, they had no input into the movie, save by a chance meeting with Julie Andrews in Salzburg during filming. (Members of the cast had a different take on that encounter too, as discussed in the next chapter.)

One person who definitely did have an impact on Lehman's screenplay was Christopher Plummer, who also expressed his concerns about the characterization of the Captain. In the first draft screenplay, Plummer thought he was 'still very much a cardboard figure, humourless and one-dimensional'. Robert Wise understood Plummer's feelings, and brought Plummer and Lehman together on a cabana on the Fox lot for the pair to discuss the situation. Plummer recalled that Lehman 'made me feel that all his invaluable ideas were mine alone' and although it was 'impossible to turn von Trapp into Hamlet', the result was a captain with 'some edge to him'.

Plummer had been cast while Lehman was taking a vacation after Robert Wise signed on to the movie – this was to allow Wise and Saul Chaplin to visit the Salzburg locations to get up to speed – and Lehman respected the actor's input into the character. For five intense days, Lehman and Plummer went through every single line of dialogue and movement in the movie, rewriting it from top to bottom, to make the Captain much more of a 'real, living human being'.

This had a knock-on effect on other characters in the movie. The role of the Baroness was significantly altered between the stage play and the film – bringing the underlying emotions, if not the events, back much closer to the real relationship between Georg von Trapp, Princess Yvonne and Maria – which made the Baroness a much more credible character than the almost laissez-faire person in the original stage musical.

*   *   *

Lehman's screenplay opens with the camera flying through the clouds over the Alps, and descending past sheer rock faces towards the valley below, eventually reaching an Alpine meadow where we find the grey-smocked Maria singing 'The Sound of Music'.

This immediately indicated to those who had seen the stage show that this movie would be a different take on the material. The pan down to Maria was a trick that Wise and Lehman had used for the start of *West Side Story* (Lehman would later lament that he couldn't repeat it for the start of his version of *Hello Dolly!*, given the time period in which it was set). The song itself lost its opening verse for the movie version, as if the audience has come across Maria in the middle of her hymn to nature.

As she finishes her song, Maria hears church bells and realizes the time. Grabbing her wimple from where it lies on the grass, she heads back to the convent. As the main titles roll, we learn it's Salzburg in the 'last golden days of the Thirties'.

To accompany the credits, an overture plays, consisting of themes from 'The Sound of Music', 'Do-Re-Mi', 'My Favourite Things', 'Something Good' and 'Climb Ev'ry Mountain' scored by Irwin Kostal, providing the audience with their first exposure to one of the new songs for the movie. Richard Rodgers had not needed to write an overture for the stage show, since it opened in the abbey with the religious chanting.

In Nonnberg Abbey, the nuns are complaining about a lack of 'Maria' and noting that she's not an asset to the abbey. As they sing, Maria arrives, realizing she's in trouble. She's summoned to see the Mother Abbess, and, even though the Abbess doesn't seem to worry, has to beg forgiveness for going out onto the Untersberg. She wasn't worried about getting lost – that is her mountain. The Mother Abbess asks her what she's learned, and Maria says it's to find out the Will of God and do it wholeheartedly. At this, the Mother Abbess explains, to

Maria's horror, that she will have to leave them, which will give her a chance to see if she really feels she's ready for the convent life. She's to become the governess to Captain von Trapp's seven children.

The stage show included the song 'My Favourite Things' sung by Maria and the Mother Abbess during this scene; it was moved to a more appropriate place during the thunderstorm. The reprise of that number was replaced with a completely new song:

Maria leaves the abbey and heads down into Salzburg, catching a bus out to Aigen, singing 'I Have Confidence' until she arrives at the gates of the villa von Trapp – when all her confidence once again deserts her.

This was the first of two new songs in the film, credited to Richard Rodgers for both music and lyrics. Ernest Lehman and Saul Chaplin came up with some suggested lyrics for the scene, which Rodgers took away and added to himself, as well as composing the tune. Unfortunately, his version didn't accomplish everything that Lehman needed from the song, so various verses were added by the writer and producer, although they kept this quiet even from Julie Andrews. Lehman didn't think that Rodgers was that concerned about it.

Maria is greeted at the front door by Franz, who asks her to wait for the Captain. Ever inquisitive, Maria opens the door of one of the rooms, to reveal a dusty ballroom. She's pretending to dance when the Captain arrives and he brusquely tells her there are rooms not to be disturbed in the house. She's the latest in a long line of governesses to the children, and although he's not impressed with what he sees, he instructs her in her duties – which don't include time for the children to play.

Lehman removed a scene showing the Captain treating all of the staff in this way; he also doesn't give Maria a surname – she's simply 'Fräulein Maria'.

The Captain then uses his bosun's whistle to summon the children, who arrive in military formation – bar Brigitta who eventually wanders in, her nose in a book. Each has their own distinctive whistle, which the Captain demonstrates, and expects Maria to copy. She says she won't use the whistle, nor will she respond to one herself. As he leaves, Maria blows the whistle, bringing the Captain up short, but she explains that she doesn't know his signal. She can call him 'Captain', he explains curtly, and leaves. Maria tells the children that she's never been a governess before and they start to give her deliberately bad advice.

In the original stage musical, after Maria introduces herself to the children she gets them singing 'Do-Re-Mi', and then we jump to the first scene between Liesl and Rolf. Again, Lehman moved the song to later in the story.

Maria is taken to her room by Frau Schmidt, and finds a frog in her pocket. She's therefore not surprised to find another practical joke waiting for her over dinner and she simply says she's happy to have been made to feel accepted. This provokes the children to tears, to their father's surprise.

This was the only scene in the entire film which Ernest Lehman wasn't happy with the way it appeared on screen and wished could be reshot. It was designed to show the start of the children's friendly relationship with Maria – the script indicates that they are surprised and pleased that they're not in trouble for their practical joke – and that they are feeling guilty about putting a frog in her pocket, and then a pine cone on her seat. However, Lehman felt it was 'over-directed', and that the children cried rather too easily.

The Captain tells the children he's going to Vienna but will be bringing Baroness Schraeder back to visit them all. A telegram arrives, delivered by Rolfe, and Liesl asks to be excused so she can go to see him. Outside the young lovers talk about creating telegrams to give Rolfe an excuse to visit the house; Rolfe inadvertently mentions that a German colonel is staying nearby but tells Liesl to forget that and not to tell her father, who's 'so Austrian'. Rolfe is concerned about Liesl's attitude to life, and they sing 'Sixteen Going on Seventeen' dancing around the gazebo. A storm has begun and Liesl runs off into the night.

In Maria's room, Frau Schmidt tells the new governess about the way the house has changed and that new curtains are coming.

Lehman removes the discussion about there being no music allowed in the house from the stage version (which made no sense anyway, since in the stage version Maria had already been singing with the children).

After Frau Schmidt has gone, Liesl comes in, soaked from the storm, through the window. Maria tells her to change and she'll keep her secret. The children start to come in – first Gretl, then the other girls, then the boys. To stop them being frightened of the thunder and lightning, Maria tells them she thinks of 'My Favourite Things'.

Julie Andrews described Lehman's decision to move this song from the start of the story to here as 'inspired'; it showed Maria's ability to cheer the children up by reminding them of everything cosy and comfy. Rather than jump into the song cold, Andrews speaks the first lines of the lyrics.

The singing is interrupted by the Captain, who's unhappy at the lack of discipline. Maria covers for Liesl, then, once the children have left, she and von Trapp briefly clash. They may be children – but he is their father.

Sometime later, Maria has made clothes for the children from the old curtains and takes them out through Salzburg, ending up having a picnic in a meadow. She says they should learn a song to sing for the Baroness when she arrives, and when they say they don't know how to sing, she teaches them 'Do-Re-Mi', which they joyously sing all around the area over the coming days.

One of the big set pieces of the movie, 'Do-Re-Mi' was used both to indicate the growing affection between the children and Maria, but also the passage of time while the Captain is in Vienna. Lehman was particularly pleased with the sequence because it achieved everything he wanted in story terms – notably that Maria really was teaching the children to sing, so their honed ability in the next few scenes was credible.

On his way back from Vienna with Baroness Elsa and their friend, self-styled 'sponge' Max Detweiler, the Captain spots what he thinks are local urchins in the trees. Arriving at the villa, the Captain and the Baroness chat: he's far more at home in the mountains than in the unnatural world of Vienna, and he tells her she's been his saviour. She's also searching for something, she tells him. He goes to find the children, as Max and Elsa talk; she thinks she's there on approval. Max just wants her and Georg to marry to keep Elsa's inheritance in their circle.

Max has been making calls in his hunt for a choir for the Salzburg Festival, and receives a telegram delivered by Rolfe (who gives a Nazi salute). The Captain gets angry at Max's attitude towards the Nazis – what will happen will happen; don't get caught in the crossfire – and Georg admits to Elsa he's in a world that's disappearing.

The song 'How Can Love Survive?' was removed from the film; the character of the Baroness is altered: she's not in charge of a corporation any more, but the provider of parties in Vienna. Her cynicism is nowhere near as obvious, and she rebukes Max for teasing her about her feelings for the Captain.

The children and Maria come into view – in a boat on the lake, which capsizes when they stand to wave at their father. The soaked family come on shore and are introduced to the Baroness before being sent inside to change. Elsa and Max diplomatically withdraw when the Captain starts to berate Maria. She tells him he doesn't know his children and their argument reaches a peak with him telling her to return to the abbey, when they hear music from inside the house. It's the children singing 'The Sound of Music'. He goes in to listen, and ends up joining in. Maria looks in, then heads upstairs, but the Captain stops her and asks her to stay.

Some time later, the Baroness, Max and the Captain are watching a puppet theatre presentation of 'The Lonely Goatherd'. Everyone, especially the Captain, is impressed, and there's a long gaze between Maria and him at the end – which the Baroness spots.

'The Lonely Goatherd' was originally the song Maria cheered the children up with during the thunderstorm; the new placing in the story was inspired by the famous Salzburg Marionettes, founded in 1913, whom associate producer Roger Edens saw during the first location trip with William Wyler. In the end, the troupe was not willing to take part and American puppeteers Bil and Cora Baird created the scene. In what one Salzburg travel guide describes as 'the consumerist fall' of the Salzburg Marionettes, they did create their own version of the whole of *The Sound of Music* in 2007, which plays to packed houses. Lehman felt that the movie needed some spectacle at this point; coincidentally, *Die Trapp-Familie* also shows the children and Maria presenting a play at this juncture, and uses it to display the growing affection between Maria and Georg.

Max says he's found his new act – the Trapp family. The Captain thinks he's joking, and when he realizes he isn't, says bluntly it won't be happening. The children ask their father if he will sing for them and he sings 'Edelweiss'. The Baroness again spots his interaction with Maria, and then suggests that the Captain should throw a party for her before she returns to Vienna.

In the stage show, 'Edelweiss' only appears at the end of the story; Lehman adds it in here to show the increasing warmth between the children and their father, as well as between him and Maria – and contrasts that with the elegant, sophisticated Baroness and Max, giving Elsa a line about wishing she'd brought her harmonica. She's more at home in the stately world of a dance than the domestic bliss of the Captain with the children, hence the suggestion of a grand party. The incident that we see in the film happened off stage in the original – Brigitta talks about her father stopping singing when they're all together because he was looking at Maria.

At the party, Herr Zeller shows his dislike of the Austrian flag being so obviously on display, as the children watch the adults' grown-up antics. Liesl and Friedrich dance together before the Laendler begins, and Kurt begs Maria to show him how it's done. She starts, but to everyone's surprise, the Captain cuts in and the two dance perfectly – Maria becoming rather flushed. The Baroness is clearly jealous and makes some pointed remarks to Georg as Maria gets the children ready to say goodnight.

The stage version of the party emphasizes the growing worries about the impending Anschluss far more than its screen equivalent at this stage (that discussion comes after the children have gone to bed); Lehman downplays that element in favour of the growing romance between Maria and the Captain and the jealousy of the Baroness. In the stage show, she doesn't witness the Laendler, only the effects of it on Maria; and prior to the children singing their goodnight song, Brigitta tells Maria that her father is in love with her; although Brigitta's ability to notice things is retained in Maria's diatribe against the Captain about his children, it's not built on as much in the film as it is in the original stage version.

The children sing 'So Long, Farewell' as they head up to bed. Max is certain they'll be a success at the festival and tells Maria that she must join them for dinner, despite the Baroness's clear dislike of the idea. He wants to use her to persuade the Captain to let them sing.

In the original stage musical, it's the Captain who wants Maria to join them, and Max who's against the idea of the governess being at the table; rather than Maria, it's Elsa whom Max targets to try to get the von Trapp family singing.

The Baroness goes to help Maria change and tells her the Captain is in love with her – although he'll get over it. Horrified, Maria says she must leave, and the Baroness does nothing to stop her. In fact, when she returns to the party, she grabs champagne and tells Max she's celebrating – and tells him that if he wants to influence Georg, it's her, not Maria, he needs to talk to.

Sadly, back in the clothes she arrived in, Maria leaves the villa, leaving a letter as she goes. [Fade to the intermission.]

The stage show doesn't feature any such confrontation between the Baroness and Maria; again this is much closer to the reality of the discussion between Princess Yvonne and Maria, although the young governess didn't actually follow through on her threat of leaving. In *Die Trapp-Familie*, this was when Georg declared his love too.

Lindsay and Crouse's original version of the book for the stage show ended Act 1 with Maria's exit from the villa, but Rodgers and Hammerstein wanted to finish the first half with a resounding anthem – 'Climb Ev'ry Mountain'. Lehman returned to the initial idea, sending the audience out into the intermission on a low note.

During the intermission, an entr'acte played, scored by Irwin Kostal. This included themes from 'I Have Confidence', 'So Long, Farewell', 'Do-Re-Mi', 'Something Good' and 'The Sound of Music'. Rodgers' original scoring for this featured 'The Sound of Music', 'Sixteen Going on Seventeen', 'Do-Re-Mi' and 'The Lonely Goatherd', which led into the children singing at the start of the second act.

The second part starts with the children listlessly playing ball with the Baroness, who admits to Max she plans to send them off to boarding school. Max tries to encourage the children to sing, but they're not interested without Maria. Their father tells them that Maria missed her life at the abbey and that's why she left. They won't have a new governess – they'll have a new mother, it was agreed the previous evening. They are not impressed but dutifully kiss the Baroness.

That afternoon, the children go to the abbey to try to see Maria but they're told she's in seclusion. Hearing of their visit, and that Maria still isn't talking, the Mother Abbess calls for Maria to be sent to her. Maria explains she left the von Trapps because she was frightened and the Abbess explains she can't just hide there; she must face her problems and 'Climb Ev'ry Mountain'.

Transposed from the end of Act 1, this latter scene is pretty much the same as Lindsay and Crouse's original, although since the von Trapp children haven't visited, it's Maria who chooses to speak to the Abbess, rather than being summoned.

The children are being asked by their father where they've been, and the story they concoct ends up with him not letting them have any tea. They're miserable, and try to cheer themselves up with 'My Favourite Things', and as they sing, Maria arrives.

Lehman split the stage show Act 2 opening into two scenes, which served to show the growth in the relationship between the Captain and his children, and the way in which the Baroness really isn't fitting in – the Captain is almost teasing in his interactions.

The children are delighted to see Maria, and tell her their father is marrying. The Baroness is equally delighted when Maria gives her and Georg her congratulations and says she's only back till a replacement can be found. That night, Georg and Elsa talk on the veranda after Maria has walked down by the lake. Georg starts to tell her that he doesn't think it's going to work, but she pre-empts him, and says he's too independent for her, so she's going to leave. Somewhere out there is a young lady who will never be a nun.

And here is where stage show and film musical diverge dramatically. In the original, it's the Baroness's willingness to kowtow to Austria's potential new rulers that drives the wedge between her and Georg (the song 'No Way to Stop It'), and it's only when Maria arrives to congratulate her on the engagement that she breaks it off.

The Captain goes to find Maria, and tells her the engagement is off; they declare their love, singing 'Something Good', and go to ask the children for permission to marry.

'Something Good' was the second song that Richard Rodgers wrote on his own for the movie, replacing 'Ordinary People' from the stage show, a song that he and Oscar Hammerstein had always intended to rework. Lehman admitted he was fond of the song, and held on to it in his draft screenplays for longer than he should have done – even though he later called it the 'weakest song in the play' – but eventually agreed with Robert Wise and Saul Chaplin that it needed to go. Rodgers was more than happy to produce something fresh – he had been composing both lyrics and music for projects since Hammerstein's death in 1960 – and enjoyed the chance to write once more for Julie Andrews. (The much-vaunted 'live' production of the musical on NBC in 2013 also used 'Something Good', although it stuck with the stage show for everything else.)

Cut to the abbey where Maria is being prepared for her wedding. Liesl is chief bridesmaid and Max is the Captain's best man as Maria walks down the aisle, watched by the nuns. Their wedding is blessed as the nuns sing 'Maria', and a bell peals out . . .

Quite sensibly, Lehman eliminated all the dialogue from this scene, and created one of the most dramatic jump cuts . . .

. . . and we realize it's a few weeks later. The Anschluss has happened, and the Nazis are in Salzburg, their cars and troops in the cobblestoned square of the Residenzplatz. Herr Zeller, now the Gauleiter of the Third Reich, comes to the Salzburg Festival Hall Amphitheatre, where the von Trapp children are rehearsing. He's been trying to find the Captain, and the housekeeper has sent him to see Max; Zeller also wants to know why there was no Nazi flag flying. The Third Reich needs the Captain's services – as is proved by a telegram that Rolfe brings to the amphitheatre and brusquely hands to Liesl, all romantic feelings apparently gone. He has more important things to be concerned over – as should Liesl's father.

Another scene which is opened up from the stage show, and explains in part why the fictional Kaltzberg Festival of the original becomes the genuine Salzburg Festival for the film: the location allows the magnitude of what the children are undertaking to hit home. In the original, Rolf delivers the telegram to the house, and Maria thinks that he may be trying to warn the family of the dangers; in the movie, Rolfe has

embraced the Nazi creed fully by now, and all trace of friendship towards the family has disappeared.

*Max takes the children home where they find Maria and
the Captain, who furiously tears down the Nazi swastika. The
children excitedly talk about singing in the festival, and the
Captain is not happy with Max, who explains that it's for the
good of Austria – although the Captain doesn't think there is
an Austria any more, even if the Anschluss took place peacefully. Max asks Maria to try to persuade him; Liesl is upset by
Rolfe's behaviour, but she and Maria reprise 'Sixteen Going
on Seventeen', giving her a new perspective.*

Lehman's reordering of events makes more sense of the
reprise of the song: in the stage show, it comes before Rolf
arrives with the telegram.

*Georg has read the telegram: he has to report to Bremerhaven
the next day to serve in the navy. To refuse would be fatal;
to accept, unthinkable. They know they will have to leave
Austria – that night.*

*The boys, Max and the Captain push the car out into the
road, so that Franz and Frau Schmidt won't hear the engine
start. They're about to get in when the Nazis show their hand:
Zeller is waiting for them, with orders to take von Trapp to
Bremerhaven. The Captain says they can't go as they're
performing in the festival; that's where they were heading.
Although Zeller doesn't believe that the Captain is part of the
singing family, he escorts them to the amphitheatre.*

In the stage play, Admiral von Schreiber himself comes to
visit Captain von Trapp since he's held in such high regard.
Over Zeller's objections, the admiral permits the von Trapps
to sing – although the Captain has to demonstrate he knows
the music. It's Maria here who comes up with the excuse of
the festival to buy them time, rather than the Captain, as in
the film.

*At the Festival, the family sing 'Do-Re-Mi', then the
Captain gives a heartfelt rendition of 'Edelweiss', with which
the entire audience joins in. Max as compère says this is the last*

time the family will be heard together, as the Captain is going off to do his duty, and they sing 'So Long, Farewell'.

It was Robert Wise's idea to make 'Edelweiss' something of a patriotic call to arms by the Captain, in a scene that is reminiscent of the singing of the Marseillaise in *Casablanca*.

Max plays for time as much as he can, announcing the winners in reverse order. But when the family von Trapp are declared victors, they're nowhere to be found. At Nonnberg, the Abbess shows them a hiding place as the sisters very gently and peacefully allow the SS to enter. In the graveyard, the von Trapps have to rethink: they were going to drive in the abbey caretaker's car to the border, but the Abbess tells them it has been closed. They will need to drive to the mountains and then cross by foot.

As the soldiers search the graveyard, the family hides, and it looks as if the coast is clear – until Rolfe comes in. He hears Liesl gasp but doesn't react; he fakes leaving then shines his flashlight on them all as they emerge from hiding. The Captain sends Maria and the children away, as Rolfe says it's only the Captain they want. Risking being shot, the Captain takes the gun from Rolfe, but when he tells the lad that he'll never be a Nazi, it's too much, and Rolfe calls for his lieutenant. The Captain races after his family as the Nazis run for their cars. The von Trapps speed past the Nazis, but their cars won't start because two of the nuns, Sister Margaretta and Sister Berthe, have 'sinned', and removed the distributor caps from the engines.

Lehman reworked the ending considerably. In the play, Rolf spots the family but doesn't betray them after Liesl looks pleadingly at him. Not finding any sign of them, the Nazis depart, leaving a guard at the gate; the von Trapps therefore have to walk from there 'over that mountain' to Switzerland.

The writer felt that the change in Rolfe was needed to make him more human, and that his betrayal contrasted nicely with the trick with the distributor caps by the nuns – a small piece of humour in an otherwise grim sequence as the movie draws to its close.

The movie ends with the von Trapps making their way laboriously up the mountain, away from the Nazis to freedom.

'Don't they know geography in Hollywood?' Maria von Trapp complained in 1967 about this scene. 'Salzburg does not border on Switzerland.' To be fair to Lehman, he doesn't actually say in the screenplay that they are heading for Switzerland – unlike the original Lindsay and Crouse book – and he wasn't responsible for the choice of Obersalzberg as the location of the shot.

As Ernest Lehman was forced eventually to admit to Dick Zanuck, *The Sound of Music* was a great movie and his opening out of the story played a key part in achieving that greatness.

16

FILMING *THE SOUND OF MUSIC*

As far too many Hollywood producers – let alone audiences – have learned to their cost, you can have the most literate and perfect script ever devised; you can have a talented cast at the top of their game; and a director who has a complete command of the material – and you'll still create a turkey. There is no sure-fire way of ensuring that any movie will not only work on its own terms but also provide the general audience with sufficient material to interest them not just in coming to see it once, but to return repeatedly – and nowadays, to purchase it in download or disc form.

In later years, director Robert Wise would start to feel niggled when people tried to work out what it was that made *The Sound of Music* work. 'People just feel good when they see it,' he said. 'There's a sense of warmth, of well-being, of happiness and joy.' With a common determination amongst cast and crew not to let the film become the sugar-fest which critics had accused the musical of, they embarked on over six months of rehearsal and filming.

The movie relied on the children being believable, and before the cameras started rolling at the end of March, they were rehearsed meticulously in the many routines they would be carrying out. Choreographers Marc Breaux and Dee Dee Wood, who had worked with Julie Andrews on *Mary Poppins*, were responsible for the routines, which took maximum advantage of the space afforded them by the movie camera rather than the restrictions of the proscenium arch. 'My Favourite Things' was going to be the first number filmed, and it was carefully monitored by everyone involved in the production – Ernest Lehman wanted to ensure that the film avoided the 'set piece' mentality that many filmed musicals fell into, and after seeing a run-through of the number, asked Breaux and Wood to make the whole pillow fight seem more spontaneous.

The children fell into a routine during this time, attending school in the classroom on the Fox lot for three hours in the morning (barring Charmian Carr, who was well past school age, and Kym Karath, who was too young), and rehearsing for the rest of the time. Some of this would be musical, working with vocal supervisor Bobby Tucker and then music supervisor Irwin Kostal and Saul Chaplin to learn the harmonies for all the songs; other times, they'd be practising with dialect coach Pamela Danova to ensure their accents were the mid-Atlantic 'not quite British' sound the producers wanted. The children also had to brush up their bicycling skills: the moment in 'Do-Re-Mi' where they cycle around Salzburg was heavily rehearsed in Los Angeles to ensure that they could achieve the intricate two-wheeled choreography. (Debbie Turner later claimed that she deliberately hit Duane Chase's wheel during filming.)

The music had to be laid down before filming began too, and recording of the tracks, along with full orchestra, began during March, with Kostal in charge. This was what

Christopher Plummer had been worried about – and in the end, had to agree that some of his vocal part would need to be dubbed. Four extra children's voices were drafted in to help enrich the sound of the Trapp Family Singers, which included Darleen Carr, Charmian's eight-year younger sister, who dubbed some of Duane Chambers' higher notes. (This didn't mean that the actors didn't need to sing on location – it's very obvious when people are miming, so they would sing along to the pre-recorded songs.)

One painful practical matter had to be dealt with: Nicholas Hammond's hair, which was meant to match Heather Menzies' blonde tresses. Rather than a gradual bleaching to turn his chestnut brown into the blond, it was done in one session, resulting in Hammond getting blisters on his scalp.

On Thursday 26 March 1964, filming officially began on *The Sound of Music*. Stage 15 of the Fox lot in Los Angeles was the home for five days' shooting of the scene in Maria's bedroom leading up to the singing of 'My Favourite Things'. This was an appropriate starting point, as it marks the first time in the story that the children and Maria really start to bond. According to all accounts, that bonding was happening in real life too as the seven young actors and Julie Andrews started to become closer – Debbie Turner and Kym Karath in particular had fond memories of the scene, while the older ones were conscious of the amount that they had to get right. Charmian Carr, who was the least experienced of the actors on set, had problems with her entrance through the window, and was forever grateful to Robert Wise for the care he took in ensuring that she didn't feel too pressured, asking Andrews to give the cue line louder to make sure Carr heard it. Andrews herself did her best to put the children at ease, teaching them to sing her song from the then-unreleased *Mary Poppins*, 'Supercalifragilistic' – not just the ordinary way round, but backwards too.

The abbey cloister was prepared on Stage 16 next door for scenes to be filmed there for four days, starting on 2 April, with the graveyard escape following in the last days of the first batch of studio filming. The set for the latter was built on Stage 5 and based on St Peter's Cemetery and Catacombs in Salzburg: although these are well worth a visit (and the von Trapp family's real musical director, Father Wasner, is buried there), it wasn't where the scene was filmed – as visitors quickly realize, the geography of the cemetery doesn't correlate to what was required in the movie. (That didn't stop tour guides for some years stating the opposite!) Nicholas Hammond recalled that their on-set teacher, Frances Klamt, ensured he didn't spend too long with the young actors playing the Nazis, in case their language was inappropriate for his ears. It was baking hot that April (one day reached 105 degrees Fahrenheit), and despite the air-conditioned set, the cast felt very uncomfortable in their 'performing costumes'.

Maria's first dinner with the von Trapps was also in this opening group of scenes, and, to their initial delight before each take, fresh pieces of chocolate cake were produced for the children to eat.

With the rest of the studio material kept for the return from Austria, cast and crew prepared for the trip to Salzburg, for what was expected to be a six-week location shoot. It ended up being considerably more. As Eliza Doolittle, Julie Andrews may have sung about the rain in Spain falling mainly on the plain; in Salzburg, it fell mainly on the sixty-strong *Sound of Music* production. (In the week of 18 May, the movie lost one day to a public holiday, and two others completely to rain; a shot by the horse fountain was all that was achieved on one of the other days.) There never was any question about using Salzburg as much as possible: as Robert Wise explained in the production notes given out at the advance screenings of the film, 'Salzburg was more than just the city where this story took place. It was an atmosphere, and this is what we wanted to capture on film in order to make audiences feel the aura that surrounded the people with whom we were involved.' Despite Wise and his team using their best logistical endeavours, and creating a makeshift interior to film as many other scenes as they could, some of the team were still out in Austria eleven weeks later, with one of the iconic images of the whole movie – Maria in the meadow at the start of the film – the last thing to be completed at the start of July.

Once what the children regarded as the boring part of the preparations were complete – such as the necessary inoculations – they and the adult cast embarked on their Pan Am flight from Los Angeles to Salzburg. They were treated like royalty, eating Chateaubriand in first class, with Debbie Turner and Angela Cartwright's sister Veronica's birthdays given a special celebration. Many of the crew had gone ahead, but the cast were brought over at the last moment, and thrown straight into work as soon as possible.

They were divided into different hotels: Robert Wise, Julie Andrews and her eighteen-month-old daughter stayed at the Österreichischer Hof (now the Hotel Sacher) on the west bank of the river; the children were at the Hotel Mirabell, along with their parents who were accompanying them as chaperones, as well as some of their siblings who were along for the trip; and the other adult cast members went to the Hotel Bristol. Charmian Carr was originally billeted with the other 'children', but it soon became clear that this wasn't appropriate – she might have been playing a sixteen-year-old, but she was an adult, and deserved to be treated as such. She was therefore moved to the Bristol.

Christopher Plummer had also initially been listed for the Österreichischer Hof, but ended up at the Bristol, where, by his own admission, he spent rather too long in the bar, which led to a few problems on set. Carr, though, like many others, was delighted by Plummer's attempts to 'vent my spleen on the poor innocent baby grand [piano] in the Bristol bar night after night'. (In his autobiography, Plummer noted that he seemed determined to 'present myself as a victim of circumstance' and that he was almost being forced into making the movie; 'I was also a pampered, arrogant young bastard', he wrote with the benefit of forty-five years' hindsight.) When he was granted some time off from filming, he travelled around the neighbouring countryside, and indulged in the local cuisine – to the extent that Robert Wise advised him to quickly lose some weight when he returned to the set. (Plummer says this was straight after the filming of the wedding scene at Mondsee, although this doesn't fit with the accepted chronology of filming.)

The younger children behaved exactly as you might expect a group of children thousands of miles from home to behave: they played pranks on each other and the other hotel guests, switching breakfast menus and shoes around outside the doors, and running around the corridors. They still had to attend school, although their American tutor Frances Klamt didn't accompany them; Jean Seaman was hired as the location teacher, and used her initiative to give the children a good grounding in the culture and geography of the area in which they were staying – the field trips to the Alps, the salt mines and the ice caves all formed part of their education, as did visits to the waterpark at Hellbrunn Palace, the Salzburg Marionette Theatre, and Hitler's Berchtesgaden (although no one pointed out that this was where their fictional characters' trip would have ended up if they'd followed the route!).

One of the first scenes to be filmed was the wedding, which was actually not shot in Salzburg itself, but at Mondsee Cathedral, about half an hour's drive north-east of the city. The small town is at the top of Lake Mondsee and around six hundred extras were hired to fill the cathedral, which was doubling for Nonnberg Abbey (whose church is considerably smaller and much less photogenic). Ted McCord and Wise tracked the camera up the north aisle of the cathedral, following Maria, as she walked up the majestic steps to the altar.

The next location was the Felsenreitschule, the Rock Riding School, where the Salzburg Festival takes place. Built in 1693 by a local archbishop who turned a local quarry into a riding school, it had become a concert venue in 1926. The building was remodelled five years after filming took place, so although the exterior still remains the same, the interior of the location is now very different from how it looked both when the von Trapps lived in Salzburg, and when the movie was later shot there.

Access could only be gained at night, so makeshift cots were built for the children to sleep in between takes, and a real audience of extras was brought in to attend the movie's re-creation of the festival – which gave many of the cast a buzz that helped them through the difficult shoot.

Rodgers and Hammerstein's final song together, 'Edelweiss', was the centrepiece of this part of the filming, and it seems that Robert Wise for some reason believed that it was the real Austrian national anthem from before the Second World War that the composers had incorporated into the show. Of course that wasn't the case, so the hundreds of extras had to be taught this (luckily very simple) song before the highly effective finale could be shot.

After that came the few scenes that could be shot at the real Nonnberg Abbey, high above the town. The Mother Abbess had refused permission for any scenes to be shot inside the building itself, but did allow the crew to shoot in the court-yard and through the exterior gate that leads to the church entrance for the scene in which the von Trapp children come to find Maria. Since this wasn't the main entrance to the con-vent (which is slightly further around the corner), there wasn't any form of bell by the gate; the set designers therefore added one, which remained in position for many years, although it has now gone. The distance from there to Untersberg moun-tain – where Maria apparently is singing at the start of the film when she hears the abbey bells pealing – is quite con-siderable (around twenty kilometres using the recommended walking route), suggesting that Maria was quite remarkably gifted to be able to get back so quickly!

From there the crew began to film all around Salzburg for the montage sequences which formed both 'I Have

Confidence' and 'Do-Re-Mi'. Both had been worked out and rehearsed in the minutest detail before leaving the United States: Saul Chaplin and choreographer Marc Breaux had made a specific trip to Salzburg, prior to the start of shooting, to work out exactly what scenes would be shot where. Armed with a recording of 'Do-Re-Mi', the pair timed exactly how long it took to travel from street to street, and along each thoroughfare, receiving some considerable interest from the locals. As the publicity notes explained, 'From time to time, the strange Americans would halt in front of a Salzburg landmark and go through what appeared to be some sort of tribal dance'. Neither Chaplin nor Breaux spoke sufficient German to explain themselves, but the local police seemed content with the explanation that they were American! These ideas were transferred to storyboards created by Maurice Zuberano, which then formed the basis of the routine – some elements, such as a dance in and out of topiary, were removed. The sequence concludes in the Mirabell garden – whose flowers had unfortunately been cut shortly before filming took place, much to Robert Wise's chagrin.

One of the few scenes cut by Robert Wise from the final version of the movie was filmed at this point, which would have come partway through 'Do-Re-Mi' (not 'My Favourite Things', as some sources suggest). Liesl and Maria are by the horse statues, when Rolfe cycles by. He stares at Liesl's costume – having never seen her wear anything other than the formal wear her father demanded – as she invites him to join them for a picnic; he says picnics, and indeed her outfit, are for children. Liesl introduces him to Maria, but Rolfe hastily disappears. Wise and Chaplin felt that this was an unnecessary intrusion into the flow of the song.

On 14 May, the day before they shot the sequences in the Mirabell Gardens, the cast and crew were filming in the Residenzplatz, and received a visitor: the real Maria von Trapp. According to her account, this was 'by mere chance': she coincidentally came into Salzburg from Italy with her daughter

Rosmarie and granddaughter Barbara, and heard that filming was taking place. That allowed her a fleeting opportunity to meet Julie Andrews and the rest of the cast. Certainly her arrival on set was unexpected, but Robert Wise (and no doubt the movie's on-set publicist) recognized the benefits of Maria being seen to be giving the movie her tacit approval, and held up shooting to allow her to chat with Andrews and Wise's wife Pat. Maria was very taken with Christopher Plummer, giving him a kiss on the lips and telling him that she wished her husband had looked as good as him. Maria appeared in the background of the scene, but hadn't anticipated the rigorous needs of a film production – after around twenty takes, she admitted that this had slaked her thirst for Hollywood fame and fortune.

Another scene in the Residenzplatz had inherent difficulties: even though Robert Wise didn't intend portraying the Nazi Anschluss in as graphic terms as William Wyler had, he still needed shots of Nazis on the streets of the city. While Wyler had been greeted with a certain lack of concern when he talked to the mayor about the possibility the previous year, Wise received a less benign reaction, with the town fathers telling him that they did not want such scenes since they would stir up old memories. Wise countered this by suggesting that he could simply cut to newsreel footage of the real Anschluss; perhaps not too surprisingly, a compromise was quickly reached for the scene which forms the dramatic jump cut from the wedding.

They had problems of a different sort on another day during this part of the filming: Christopher Plummer took offence at not being given a call sheet – the schedule for the following day's filming – and turned up during the filming, ranting and raving at the director, crew and anyone who would listen about their lack of manners. He was gently told by assistant director Reggie Callow that he actually had a day off – that was why he didn't get the sheet.

By the end of May – which is when the unit should have

been packing up, ready to return to Los Angeles, according to the original schedule – there were still plenty of scenes left to film. The real von Trapp Villa in Aigen wasn't suitable for filming: the alterations made when it was used as Himmler's headquarters during the Second World War created a less photogenic atmosphere than the two locations found by the film-makers: the seventeenth-century Frohnburg Castle, and Leopoldskron Castle, a short distance away, had the terrace, and, more importantly, the lake for the critical scene where Maria and the children greet the Captain and Elsa on their return from Vienna.

This was shot at the end of May and the start of June, and nearly ended in disaster on 28 May, when Kym Karath fell in the water. The little girl was originally going to be doubled for the scene, since she couldn't swim, but when it was rehearsed with Karath's double, Wise was unhappy with the way it looked. He therefore approached Karath's mother and told her that they really needed the girl to be in the shot. There was no need for concern – there would be someone on standby, but Julie Andrews herself would be catching her. Perhaps encouraged by Wise's talk about teamwork, Karath herself pestered to be allowed to do it.

The first take went perfectly, with Karath falling in the water, and Julie Andrews catching her right away. Unfortunately, Wise decided he needed another take (which meant that the children had to dry off and get changed), and this time things weren't as smooth. Wise had hoped to get a shot of the boat capsizing, and then the children and Maria wading to shore. That wasn't how it played out: Karath and Andrews fell in opposite directions, the young girl sinking in the murky water like a stone towards the bottom of the lake, where leeches awaited. Assistant director Reggie Callow's son Alan jumped in and saved her as Karath's mother had to be held back. Karath was given to Heather Menzies to bring to shore, and she promptly puked up all over her friend. (Kym Karath's sister Francie later married Alan Callow.) The rest of the scene was shot on the following Monday, 1 June, and required the children to be covered in water from the lake using watering cans so they would look wet.

Water became a recurrent feature for the next month. Salzburg is renowned for its rainy days – holiday websites nowadays advise people travelling there to plan on having at least a few wet days during any vacation, and June, especially, is a rainy month. This put *The Sound of Music* further and further behind schedule: scenes at the two castles were shot whenever the rain clouds cleared for a few minutes, and Ted McCord rigged up tarpaulins, which would allow some scenes to be shot despite the precipitation. Cameras may not 'notice' the rain to the same extent that the human eye does, but of course they do notice its effects on the people standing in it!

However, by the end of June, the scenes were completed, and the production could move up into the Alps for the picnic sequences, and the escape from Austria. By this point, and particularly given all the waiting around because of the rain, the children were beginning to lose focus, and they were brought up short when Robert Wise gathered them all in a barn, and read the riot act, reminding them that they were not there on holiday, but to do a job of work for which they were being paid. Wise was well aware that there was still a lot to do even once they had finished filming in Austria, and it seems that his words – and the fact that he had not needed to chide the children in this way before – had a positive effect.

The filming was still beset with weather problems. The equipment had to be taken up the mountain in an ox-drawn cart, and star Julie Andrews hitched a lift, keeping the important equipment dry with her umbrella. Ted McCord would keep a close eye on the clouds and give as much warning as he could to the cast so they could get ready to shoot in the few precious minutes of sunshine. (Andrews would later note that the inclement conditions added to the lack of fairy-tale feel to the film: it wasn't all sunny blue skies all the time.) Nicholas

Hammond recalls that it was on the third day waiting on the mountaintop in Werfen that they were finally able to put into practice everything they had learned in the rehearsals for 'Do-Re-Mi' months earlier. A few days later, they shot the escape – for once, scenes which didn't require a lot of dialogue to be learned or shot.

Shooting at Werfen concluded on Saturday 27 June, and after a day off, the children filmed their final scenes on the steam railway on a foggy Monday. They departed the next morning for Los Angeles, changing planes in New York, where they missed their flight, and had to wait a further six hours. It was 1.40 a.m. before a very tired group of children and parents arrived back on the west coast.

Charmian Carr and Julie Andrews weren't with them. Carr was needed for some promotional filming on a tourist documentary called *Salzburg: Sights and Sounds*, while Andrews still had to get her first scene in the can. Robert Wise and Saul Chaplin were coming under intense pressure from Dick Zanuck to wrap location filming and return, but Wise was adamant that he needed that shot. He begged for one more day, otherwise he would come back and try to find a way of re-creating the scene in California. Zanuck granted his request, and on Thursday 2 July, the crew were able to get the shot.

Not, it has to be said, without some problems. As Julie Andrews has made clear, it was not her favourite scene in the movie. Filmed at Mehlweg, a village about a dozen miles south of Salzburg, it required Andrews to start at one end of a field, while a helicopter, with a cameraman leaning out from the side, would approach from the other end, swooping down through the trees towards her as she would turn, just before bursting into song. The problem was that when the shot was complete, the helicopter had to go around for another take – and the downdraught would leave Andrews flattened into the ground.

Andrews, Wise and the rest of the crew returned to Los Angeles on 3 July, with interior scenes starting to be filmed at the beginning of the following week. The film was now way over budget – around 10 per cent – and the pressure was on to get it completed as quickly as possible. That didn't mean that there weren't further mishaps on Stages 8 and 15 where the interiors of the villa and the pavilion were re-created. The latter was rather bigger in the studio shots than it was on location (as is clear if you join the thousands who visit the gazebo in Salzburg at its new home at the Hellbrun Gardens).

In fact, the pavilion set almost seemed cursed. Charmian Carr and Daniel Truhitte had to film 'Sixteen Going on Seventeen' there, and once rehearsals were complete, Carr was given a new pair of shoes to wear for the take – but they had failed to put rubber skids on the soles, which meant that when Carr jumped up on to one of the benches, she didn't stop, and smashed through the plate-glass window. Since she had sprained her right ankle very badly, the studio doctor was called to give her an injection – Carr was told it was vitamin B12, but she always suspected it was a cortisone painkiller – and she was able to complete the scene with her ankle bandaged. The make-up department tried to hide it, but it can still be seen on original copies of the film; it has been digitally removed for the recent DVD and Blu-ray versions.

The other scene set there is the duet between Maria and the Captain, 'Something Good'. Julie Andrews and Christopher Plummer had, on the whole, been consummate professionals throughout the filming, but on the day this scene was due to be filmed, something gave. Lighting a glass structure is not easy, and Ted McCord had to use some old-fashioned Klieg lights, which made an unfortunate farting sound whenever they were fired up. Plummer and Andrews didn't exactly look like a respectable Austrian war hero and a former postulant as they both cracked up when they heard the sound. It wasn't helped when Plummer found the idea of singing nose to nose with his co-star less than serious and got a fit of the giggles. Robert Wise ordered an extended two-hour lunch for his stars to pull themselves together and stop their 'unprofessional idiotic laughter'. They couldn't, and in the end Wise had to shoot the scene in silhouette.

Those two scenes were filmed in reverse order at the very end of production; before then, the party had to be put on film, with the Laendler and then 'So Long, Farewell'. These passed without too much incident, although Nicholas Hammond, at least, wasn't happy about the amount of dancing he had to do. He enjoyed the next sequence far more: the puppet show with Bil and Cora Baird for 'The Lonely Goatherd', for which the children and Julie Andrews had to learn how to manipulate the marionettes themselves for a number of scenes.

After the moment when Captain von Trapp sings 'Edelweiss' with his children, the final scene for the whole cast together was the reprise of 'The Sound of Music', sung by the children for the Baroness. This moment – the one that had nearly provoked the cynical William Wyler to tears when he saw it on stage – was highly emotive for all involved, as they realized that after nearly a year, from first auditions to wrap, *The Sound of Music* would no longer feature in their daily lives.

17

THE BIRTH OF A PHENOMENON

The Sound of Music was still over budget and running late when Robert Wise finally declared it was a wrap at the end of August 1964. Over the next few months, he worked with editor William Reynolds to create the final version of the story – in addition to the meeting between Rolfe, Liesl and Maria in Salzburg, another scene, showing the Captain looking up at Maria's window, was also removed after they saw the full movie. Reynolds admitted at the Oscars ceremony that his technique for the film was simple: 'When in doubt, cut to Julie Andrews.' Irwin Kostal wrote the score using Richard Rodgers' melodies as his base, and a rough cut was prepared for preview.

The first audiences for *The Sound of Music* were in Minneapolis, Minnesota and Tulsa, Oklahoma, not places where people would necessarily have been familiar with the stage musical or, more generally, the von Trapp story. The previews took place in mid-January 1965, with the audiences, as always, asked to score the film. No one at all thought it was 'fair'; only five people thought it was 'good'. But to the relief of Robert Wise and everyone else involved, no fewer than 460 people deemed it 'excellent'.

There was someone else whose opinion would be valuable, if only as a marketing tool: Maria von Trapp herself. She was invited to a preview screening, and told Julie Andrews that she was delighted that she was playing her as a tomboy. In years to come, her stock answer about the movie was that she really liked it very much, particularly the opening shot, which matched what she had been able to see at breakfast every day. However, much as 20th Century Fox were happy to have her seal of approval – and they quoted her in the press notes – that didn't extend to arranging for her to attend the premiere, either in New York or Hollywood. Maria said that she took it for granted she would be invited, and when she queried the situation, she was told that they were sorry, but there were no seats available.

The film premiered in New York on 2 March, and the East Coast press were not kind. *The New York Times* particularly criticized Christopher Plummer for 'Looking as handsome and phony as a store-window Alpine guide', and suggested it was the story's 'cheerful abundance of kirche-küche-kinder sentiment and the generally melodic felicity of the Richard Rodgers–Oscar Hammerstein 2d musical score' that made it work. Pauline Kael called it a 'mechanically engineered' piece, which would offend those who 'loathe being manipulated' emotionally. Judith Crist in the *Herald Tribune* dubbed it 'The Sound of Marshmallows'.

Luckily the West Coast critics didn't agree. The film was given a gala premiere in Hollywood on 10 March, with *Variety*'s Whitney Williams calling it 'a warmly pulsating, captivating drama set to the most imaginative use of the lilting R-H tunes, magnificently mounted and with a brilliant cast headed by Julie Andrews and Christopher Plummer which must strike a respondent chord at the box office'. The *Hollywood Reporter* noted that the film had restored faith in the motion picture industry. The *Los Angeles Times* hailed it as 'three hours of visual and vocal brilliance, all in the universal terms of cinema'. *Life* magazine put Julie Andrews on its cover, noting that her 'radiance floods the screen', and presciently noted that *The Sound of Music* was 'destined to be one of the biggest hits ever'.

And the audience – which included a roll call of the great and the good of Hollywood in the mid-1960s – loved it. There were huge rounds of applause throughout the film and at the end; Nicholas Hammond recalls that you couldn't hear what happened after 'Do-Re-Mi' for three or four minutes because people wouldn't stop. The children lapped it up, and were then caught up in the publicity whirl, shooting picture spreads for the *Ladies Home Journal*, and being interviewed on the *Ed Sullivan Show* (as well as the long-running children's TV programme, *Sonny Fox's Wonderama Show*) on 18 April.

Charmian Carr was still under contract to Fox, and travelled the world for two years promoting the film, which was released on what was called a 'road show' roll-out around America, which meant that it was more like going to the theatre than the cinema with souvenir programmes and tickets sold in advance. Promoted with the tagline 'The Happiest Sound in All the World', the film topped the box-office charts for six consecutive months. It made back its costs of $8.2 million and then some – by the end of 1965 its net profit was over twice the budget, and the film became the most successful picture of all time in 1966. It was overtaken by *The Godfather* in 1972 and now sits at 233rd for domestic takings; however, when ticket-price inflation is taken into account, it is the third highest in history, behind *Gone with the Wind* and the original *Star Wars* (aka *Episode IV: A New Hope*).

It was similarly successful around the world. Whether known as *Sonrisas y Lágrimas* ('Smiles and Tears') in Spain, *La Novicia Rebelde* ('The Rebellious Novice') in South

America, or *Charms of the Heavenly Sound* in Thailand, it brought money back into Fox's coffers, with the studio heading towards making a $20 million pre-tax profit for 1966.

The Sound of Music was nominated for ten Academy Awards – although Ernest Lehman, whose reimagining of the original musical was central to the film's success, was not among those honoured (Wise's reaction when he heard this was 'You woz robbed'). It won Best Picture, Best Director, Best Sound (James Corcoran and Fred Hynes), Best Musical Adaptation (Irwin Kostal) and Best Editing. Julie Andrews, who had triumphed the previous year for *Mary Poppins*, lost to Julie Christie. She did however win a Golden Globe, and the film won Best Musical or Comedy. Lehman was recognized by his peers: the Writers Guild of America awarded him the Best Written American Musical. Julie Andrews' growing success was acknowledged when she was asked to write her name and place her feet and hands in the wet cement outside Grauman's Chinese Theatre on Hollywood Boulevard.

The film's appeal has seen it appear in multiple 'Top 100' lists compiled by the American Film Institute: it came fourth in the Greatest Movie Musicals lists (Wise's *West Side Story* was second); the title song was tenth in the 100 Songs list, with 'My Favourite Things' and 'Do-Re-Mi' also making the cut; and it was fortieth in the 2007 list of 100 Best Movies (after coming fifty-fifth in the initial list compiled in 1998).

The only place that *The Sound of Music* – or *Meine Lieder, Meine Träume* ('My Song, My Dream') – wasn't a hit was in the places whose history it drew upon: Germany and Austria. The branch manager at Fox's Munich office felt that the film's depictions of the Nazis were not the right way to end the story, so he prepared copies of the movie that brought the film to an end after the wedding, removing the portion relating to the Anschluss and the escape from Austria entirely. Robert Wise was furious when he heard about this, and Fox ensured that a correct version was released. It bombed, however: the full film played a mere three weeks in Salzburg. Less controversial edits were made to the French print: the original renditions of both 'Maria' and 'Climb Ev'ry Mountain' were removed as it was felt that nuns shouldn't be singing non-religious songs.

The cast and crew went their separate ways after the film's release, with the nine von Trapps – the children plus Andrews and Plummer – only reuniting for the *Oprah Winfrey* show in 2010.

Andrews had a successful screen career, appearing in *Hawaii* and *Thoroughly Modern Millie* straight after *The Sound of Music*, before making a move to television following the less than rapturous response afforded to her next collaboration with Robert Wise, *Star!*, a biopic of Gertrude Lawrence. On one of her TV shows in 1973, she reunited with Maria von Trapp. Following surgery on her throat in 1997, her singing voice was never the same, but she has attracted a new wave of fans for her other acting roles, including in the *Shrek* series of films, and as a writer both of fiction, with her daughter, and autobiography.

Christopher Plummer has also had a distinguished career. He won a Tony Award for his role as *Cyrano* – rather ironic, given that his singing voice was dubbed by Bill Lee for portions of *The Sound of Music* – and played Sherlock Holmes in the Jack the Ripper story *Murder by Decree*. He gained a different set of cult fans for his role as General Chang in *Star Trek VI: The Undiscovered Country*, and great critical acclaim as Mike Wallace in the movie *The Insider* in 1999. He won an Academy Award and Golden Globe for the character of Hal in the 2010 movie *Beginners*. Although he spent many years being critical of *The Sound of Music*, his 2008 autobiography contains his admission that, after many years, he could finally see what others found.

Charmian Carr gave up acting when she started a family, and now runs her own interior design company. She wrote two books with Jean Strauss about her time as Liesl: *Forever Liesl*, and *Letters from Liesl*, and during the publicity tour for the first one she had the chance to spend time with the character she played in the film – Agathe von Trapp. She is often involved with the *Sing-A-Long-A Sound of Music* events (discussed in chapter 20).

Nicholas Hammond stayed in show business, although he followed advice given during the making of *The Sound of Music*, and gained his degree from Princeton. He was regularly cast in 1970s American TV shows, and took the lead role in the small-screen version of *The Amazing Spider-Man* in 1977. He emigrated to Australia in the mid-1980s, where he now combines acting and writing, winning first prize at the New International Film and Television Festival on two occasions.

Heather Menzies also remained an actor, appearing in *Hawaii* as Julie Andrews' younger sister. She became the female lead of the TV spin-off of the 1976 science fiction film *Logan's Run* (for which Nicholas Hammond screen-tested as Logan). Like Carr, she stopped to raise her family from her marriage to actor Robert Urich. Following his death from cancer in 2002, she spends her time helping to run the Robert Urich Foundation for Cancer Research and Patient Care.

Duane Chase retired from acting when he hit his late teens, and studied geology, before entering the computer field. He now designs computer software for geologists and geophysicists.

Angela Cartwright's acting career continued with her casting in the CBS science fiction show *Lost in Space*, which ran for three years. She too stopped acting when she was raising her family, running an eclectic gift shop called Rubber Boots in Toluca Lake, California, and enjoys photography and art.

Debbie Turner changed agents after *The Sound of Music* came out in a bid to escape typecasting, but when that didn't work out, she retired from the profession, returning to school, skiing competitively and studying psychology and art. She eventually started her own business designing and creating permanent floral arrangements.

Kym Karath stayed acting throughout her teens and early

twenties, but gave it up after her son Eric suffered seizures and a stroke shortly after he was born and was left with brain damage. Together with other parents from her son's school she helped to start the Aurelia Foundation, which recognizes the need for increased discovery and development of special needs children as they leave the school environment. She continues to write and act, alongside promoting this work.

Robert Wise continued directing for cinema until 1989, and won a Daytime Emmy for his last directing job, Showtime's *A Storm in Summer*. After success with *The Sand Pebbles*, he reunited with Julie Andrews for *Star!*, which wasn't critically well received, and alongside his directing, he also became involved with various film-industry bodies, including the Directors Guild and the American Film Institute. One of his last projects before his death on 14 September 2005 was a director's cut of *Star Trek: The Motion Picture*.

To the end, Robert Wise stayed in touch with his *Sound of Music* family, and when he met up with Charmian Carr when he was 85, he admitted that he found one thing puzzling – out of all the many films that he had made, the only one people ever asked him about was *The Sound of Music*. Perhaps that might be for the reason that he himself suggested at an AFI seminar in May 1975: 'The Sound of Music just happened to come out when the world was hungry for this kind of warm, emotional family entertainment.'

PART FOUR: THE TRAPP FAMILY GET ANIMATED

18

LONELY ANGELIC CRY-BABIES

Most fans of the 1965 film of *The Sound of Music* are aware that the movie was based on a stage musical; many probably know that it is (albeit sometimes loosely) based on a true story, even if they don't know the ins and outs of that tale. However, there are probably only a few dozen people in the Western world who realize that the story of Maria Kutschera and her time with the von Trapp children has been retold subsequently – and at great length.

Released in 1991, *Trapp Ikka Monogatari* ('The Story of the Trapp Family') was part of the World Masterpiece Theatre series, which was created by Nippon Animation in 1975 to cash in on the success of Isao Takahata and Hayao Miyazaki's 1974 adaptation of Johanna Spyri's 1881 children's book *Heidi*. The idea of *Heidi, Girl of the Alps* – and the series that followed – was to create an animated series which artistically stood head and shoulders over the normal television anime. *Heidi* boasted over eight thousand cells in each twenty-five-minute episode, which allowed it a fluidity of movement and attention to detail that showed its superiority. (For comparison, an ordinary twenty-five-minute live action film would have around 15,000 frames.) The animators may not have been pleased that this level of quality would be expected from them all the time, but they rose to the challenge, producing material which appealed to adults and children.

Over the next two decades, the series adapted many Western children's classics into the anime form, including *Anne of Green Gables*, *The Adventures of Tom Sawyer*, *The Swiss Family Robinson*, *Pollyanna*, *Little Women*, *Little Lord Fauntleroy* and *Peter Pan and Wendy*. It wasn't only English-language stories that were adapted: the Finnish novel *Paimen, piika ja emäntä* by Auni Nuolivaara appeared in 1984, Lisa Tetzner's *Die Schwarzen Brüder* in 1995, and Hector Malot's *Sans Famille* a year later.

Maria von Trapp's memoirs were mined for *Trapp Ikka Monogatari*, perhaps in an attempt to revitalize the series, which was beginning to show its age. Its setting in the Alps was also reminiscent of *Heidi*, and of another World Masterpiece Theatre success, *Treasures of the Snow* aka *My Annette: Story of the Alps*, which managed to glean forty-eight episodes from a 1950 children's book by Patricia M. St John (as with many of the stories, including the *Little Women* adaptation, the writers had no qualms about adding incidents to pad out the plot to the required length).

Forty twenty-five-minute episodes were created by screenwriter Ayo Shiroya. Directed by Kôzô Kusuha, Jiro Saito, Fujino Sadohara and Nobuaki Nakanishi, they were first broadcast between 13 January and 28 December 1991. (The sixteen hours were later condensed down to an eighty-five-minute feature-length TV movie.) Each episode began with Maria – a young blonde girl – standing in postulant's robes raising her hands to heaven, and we pull back to see she is standing on a rock looking out at the countryside. Through the magic of animation, she is suddenly in full Austrian dress, and bursts into song. This was a Japanese version of 'Do-Re-Mi' on the original TV broadcast, to emphasize the links between this and *The Sound of Music*; an original song, 'Hohoemi no Mahou'/'Smile Magic', was written for the subsequent releases in other media – which includes a lyric wonderfully translated by multiple different sources as 'We're all lonely angelic cry-babies inside flying up the stairs of our dreams, two at a time.'

Maria spins round in a meadow, filled with edelweiss, and then walks through the countryside, with the Alps behind her, seeing churches and animals. She jumps with the setting sun behind her, and then perches above a particularly dim-witted-looking cow. After relaxing against a tree (shades of the original stage direction for the discovery of Maria at the start of the musical), she looks up to see a rainbow, which arcs from behind the Alps, and then she dances off with the cow following . . .

Episode 1: 'My Aspiration to be a Catholic Nun'

The story opens with some well-created establishing pictures of Salzburg. Maria arrives at the station, from where she is directed to Nonnberg Abbey (which is extremely accurately depicted). The nuns originally think she just wants charity soup. Addressing the Mother Abbess as 'boss', and dressed in her hiking gear, she asks to be admitted as a postulant, and the Abbess agrees. Dressing in her robes, she tries to help her new sisters by abseiling out of a window to go to collect some clothing before it rains – much to the consternation of some of the nuns – but only manages to get wet. At dinner she meets Rafaela, another novice, who becomes her friend, and starts to learn the rules of behaviour. Her roommates aren't particularly friendly because they're preparing for their exams.

Maria decides to climb the abbey tower to see the Alps and tells Rafaela that she decided to become a nun while standing looking at the hills. Unfortunately they're caught, but this is just the start of Maria's regular breaking of the rules

– whistling, helping others. When she's caught out on the roof, the Mistress of Novices tells her that she's not suitable for the abbey, and seems not to care that she has nowhere else to go. The Mistress of Novices and the Mother Abbess pray about her future, as, once again in her own clothes, Maria heads back towards Salzburg.

Episode 2: 'My Future as a Sister'

Rafaela finds Maria and stops her from leaving; the Mother Abbess is looking for her. Maria promises to try to obey the rules, but even when she tries, she can't help things going wrong. She's sent to help Rafaela teach, but even at the school, she's regarded as a problem child.

She and Sister Laura are teaching Bible study when young Thomas tries to sneak in late; Sister Laura punishes him, but Maria is concerned when she learns he's late because he was helping with the housework. She's advised not to interfere. When Sister Laura is called away, Maria gets the children to move the desks against the wall, and gets out her guitar, leading them in a folky song, but before she can start singing a hymn, she's interrupted by Sister Laura's return. She's told that she may have studied at a prestigious college in Vienna, but there they do things by the book. There's an inspector coming from the diocese next week, and Maria is cause for concern. Worrying she'll be struck by lightning from the bishop's staff, Maria wonders what to do. Warned that the bishop thinks everything derives from the sun, she primes the children with appropriate answers, and is highly praised.

Later, she's marking books when she's called to see Mother Abbess. Baron von Trapp needs someone as a governess, to look after his daughter as she recovers from an illness; they are going to send Maria for nine months. Maria is concerned about the Baron (imagining him as a piratical figure), but more concerned for his children. In the old clothes she's given, she leaves in tears for Aigen and sits in the square waiting for the bus . . .

Episode 3: 'The Captain and his 7 Children'
The bus takes Maria to Aigen where a local tells her she's the twenty-sixth teacher. She walks to the house where Hans lets her in. She admires the chandelier and the Austrian flag as she waits for the Baron. He uses his whistle to call the children, explaining it would take too long to use their names – but they march down as if in procession. Maria's hat falling off breaks some of the tension as she meets (in descending order of age) Rupert, Hedwig, Werner, Johanna, Martina and Agathe (who had promised each other not to laugh in front of the new governess). She is then taken to meet young Maria who had scarlet fever two years earlier – and isn't as ill as she makes out. Fräulein Maria, as she becomes known, sees a picture of the Baron's wife and her kind words make young Maria react. However, the Baron isn't impressed by Maria's joking about punctuality.

As the children agree to work together to get Maria out, Maria comes down to dinner and meets Baroness Matilda; Maria isn't happy that young Maria isn't joining them (she's fed in her room) and goes to get her. The girl drops her food, but as Maria talks to her, the furious Baroness walks in . . .

Episode 4: 'The 26th Governess'
Matilda and Fräulein Maria have a set-to over young Maria, and Maria makes it clear that everyone's opinions matter. Matilda sends the governess to her room as she tries to find out from the young girl what happened. The children leave the dinner table, and Hedwig hears Matilda's interrogation of her sister. Meanwhile, Mimi, one of the maids, who was present at the argument, thinks things will be getting interesting.

Hedwig tells young Maria she should have said that the governess dropped the food but Maria knows that's wrong. The others come up, but, hearing someone approaching, Maria hides in the wardrobe. In fact, it's Fräulein Maria who tells them that she's not cross with their sister; she comes out, but as the Baroness comes upstairs, the other children race

to their rooms. Neither Maria hides, and the governess tries
to understand why the girl doesn't want to eat. She says she
wants to stay small forever, and she retreats to her bed, asking
Maria to stay till she drops off. Maria does so, tying a ribbon
gently on the girl's arm.

Matilda tells the Baron that they should get rid of Maria,
but he isn't so sure. Matilda asks about his engagement to
Yvonne, and he says she hasn't responded. He's been a widower for two years, Matilda points out, and she wants to go
back to Vienna: the children need a mother, not a governess.

Rosy, the cook, can't stand Matilda and brings Maria some
food, telling her she knows that young Maria throws her food
away. Maria wonders if the Baron has noticed. Next day she
meets Franz the gardener who encourages her to help and
explains that Maria slept with her mother who died of scarlet
fever. Next morning, Fräulein Maria promises she'll do what
is required, and the Baron says he wants her to stay. Not all
the children are pleased by this . . .

Episode 5: 'Maria is the Cause of Drama'

Hedwig says that her father and Maria are being selfish deciding that Maria will be her sister's governess for the next nine
months without consulting her. However, Georg has to leave
for Linz and Maria realizes that perhaps Hedwig is jealous.
Outside, Hedwig can't stand the thought of nine months of
Maria. Matilda is taking her breakfast in bed, also annoyed
at the prospect, and decides Maria will need to learn how to
behave. Maria goes looking for her young charge, and finds
her in the girls' room making bows for them in the same way
Maria did for her the night before. She tells the girl she'll be
staying, but then the other maid Clarine comes in and sees
that young Maria has been keeping sewing ribbons in a box.
She says Matilda will be cross, but the girl says it was her
mother's box, not Matilda's. Clarine and the girl fight for it,
and Maria falls; Clarine blames Fräulein Maria for the commotion, and she determines to get the box back.

Matilda says it's not appropriate for young Maria to play with it, and points out that Maria won't be there that long. Encouraged by Clarine, Matilda tries to read Maria's fortune in the cards – and becomes confused when there are two birth places. Maria explains she was born on a train, delivered by a guard who had nine children of his own, and she was left with a cousin after her mother's death. Her father returned to look after her, but one day didn't wake up.

Young Maria has sneaked into the room and also hears the tale – and gives Maria the ribbon from her arm as she is also an orphan. Maria makes it clear she will be staying, even though Matilda's cards show 'chaos'. The two Marias talk outside but are summoned in by Matilda: it's far too risky for eight-year-old Maria to be out there . . .

Episode 6: 'The Missing Children and the Hunger Rebellion'

Little Maria tells Matilda she asked Maria to go into the garden; Matilda tells Fräulein Maria that her responsibilities are purely to teach Maria: everything else goes through her. Maria is not to do anything other than acknowledge the other children.

Werner and Johanna are heading back from school but the girl is tired; Werner says he'll run home to get Franz to pick her up. While she waits, a shepherd goes past with his flock but one small lamb is left behind.

The two Marias are ready for lunch as they missed breakfast; Werner gets back and goes in for lunch. The two youngest are brought in by a bickering Clarine and Mimi. When Werner says that Johanna was too tired to walk home, Maria questions him but is told it is not her business. Franz gets back: Johanna wasn't at the crossroads. Matilda tears into Werner and sends him to his room for leaving Johanna. Although Matilda maintains it's not her concern, Maria says she'll help look.

Franz, Werner and Maria go to look but can't find Johanna,

so Franz heads to the school to check if she's returned there. Maria spots fresh sheep droppings and follows the trail, leaving Werner at the crossroads. Faint from hunger, she falls off her bike and meets the shepherd who hasn't seen Johanna but is looking for his lost sheep. When she gets back to the crossroads, Werner has gone. Franz and Hedwig arrive from school, and the girl is furious at Maria. However, Maria hears a dog barking, and finds the shepherd, his dog, the lost sheep – and Johanna, who gives Maria a kiss. Going back to the others, Maria suggests Johanna should go back and Hedwig starts to bluster – as Werner returns after eating too many blueberries.

The Baron has come back early and Matilda needs to talk to him. Little Maria gets a sandwich for Maria, much to Hedwig's annoyance. As Maria waits in her room, the children talk to their father: Hedwig wants Maria out, but the others point out how different she is from the other governesses. Rupert is sent to fetch her . . .

Episode 7: 'I Can Not Trust Adults'

Maria is surprised when Baron Georg asks her to look after Johanna as well as Maria. Hedwig objects – Johanna isn't ill – but the walk has clearly been too much for her. Hedwig bundles Johanna out of the room, insisting they can sort themselves out; Rupert goes to try to calm things down. Maria and the Baron are left alone: Maria knows Hedwig is at a difficult age. They are about to discuss the problem about previous governesses when Georg receives an urgent phone call.

The children are arguing: Werner is pleased he can come home on his own from school; only Hedwig doesn't like the new arrangement. She's convinced Maria will show her true colours sooner rather than later. Maria comes in determined to talk to them all but Hedwig and Rupert start fighting. Hedwig turns on Maria – she won't have an adult she can't trust in the house. She pulls Maria's sleeve off and the ruckus disturbs Matilda. Hedwig knows she's gone too far, but Maria says it can be repaired.

Clarine tells Matilda a garbled version of what's happening as Georg reveals that the bank has cut off financing. Matilda bursts in and says she should have been consulted about Maria's extra responsibilities but Georg hasn't got time to listen.

Rosy and Mimi explain to Maria that the various governesses argued to show who was best, but Hans enters and tells them off for gossiping. Maria understands why Hedwig can't trust adults; she remembers the cruelty she suffered as a child. The other children tell Hedwig that they like Maria, but she goes to her room and lies on her bed looking at a photo of their mother. Maria comes in and explains that the previous governesses were immature. The children were used to nice people like their parents so the nastiness of these others was a shock. Maria says she's an ordinary girl who was orphaned, then brought up by an old lady, and trained as a teacher.

As the Baron leaves, Maria promises him she'll be there till June – and even Hedwig begins to realize that Maria is different . . .

Episode 8: 'Courtesy is Important?!'
(NB the double punctuation is in the Japanese original)

It's the first Sunday since Maria arrived at the von Trapps, and, along with the children and Matilda, she has gone to church. The children show Maria around the garden, but explain they aren't allowed to play in the woods or climb trees – the garden is 'for the purpose of walking quietly'. Maria raises this with Matilda but is told, once more, to confine herself to Maria and Johanna's teaching. Clarine bustles Maria out of the room when she asks if Matilda agrees with the Baron's diktats on their upbringing. Hans calls Matilda to the phone to talk to Earl Belvedere; she is told that Belvedere's daughter, Lady Yvonne, will arrive the next day – the Earl has run out of patience and wants Yvonne to meet the children so the marriage can take place.

In the nursery, Maria discovers that the children don't know the folk songs she sang with the schoolchildren (in episode 2). They do know 'Wild Rose', and she starts to teach them harmony, with even Hedwig joining in. Meanwhile, Matilda and Clarine prepare for Yvonne's arrival – and they storm into the nursery. Why are the children on the floor? They're not like the neighbourhood children, Matilda maintains; Maria argues the opposite. She's told her room has to be vacated for the important guest (although Matilda won't tell the children who it is).

Hedwig is surprised her father hasn't said where he was going, and quizzes Hans. Georg gets back to face an inquisition from Hedwig, but he's more concerned over Yvonne's impending arrival. Hedwig overhears Matilda telling Georg that if he marries Yvonne, his money worries will be over; Georg doesn't want to marry for that. Hedwig bursts in at the thought of the remarriage and runs to her room in tears. Georg calls the children together but Hedwig refuses to come and instead goes and hides.

Matilda tells Fräulein Maria that Yvonne will be the children's new mother – which Hedwig hears and races downstairs to say that the children won't accept any mother in the house other than their own.

Episode 9: 'Baron von Trapp's Fiancée?'

Yvonne is on the way, but young Maria has taken to her bed. Maria understands that the girl doesn't want a replacement mother, and to her and Matilda's surprise, Georg agrees. Maria tries to get her namesake to understand why her father is doing this, meanwhile Yvonne's car passes the three eldest on their way back from school. The boys race ahead, as the staff greet Yvonne, an attractive young blonde, but she doesn't want to meet the children just yet. Hedwig watches as Georg shows Yvonne to her room.

After her many cases are brought up, Yvonne tells Matilda it must be boring living out there in the country, and wonders which restaurant they will go to that evening. Matilda, who's been overseeing a special dinner in the kitchen, is surprised by that, and by Yvonne's clear unwillingness to see the children. Georg summons them (after Hedwig has briefed them all to be cold to Yvonne) and Hedwig brings the picture of their mother down with her, which Matilda then keeps trying to hide. Yvonne doesn't make a good impression on the children. She looks Maria up and down and doesn't see a rival. When Hedwig once again tries to show Yvonne the photo of her mother, Maria defuses the approaching argument by suggesting a trip into Salzburg – something which Matilda grudgingly respects.

They visit Mozart's birth house (their mother loved Mozart, Hedwig points out) and other sights, but as Georg and Yvonne walk off together, Hedwig shouts after them that Father has forgotten about their mother. As Georg goes to talk to her, Yvonne asks Maria why she put Hedwig up to saying that. Alone again with Georg, Yvonne says she came to see him, not play house; she wants a quiet romantic dinner, just the two of them. She drops her handkerchief in front of Georg, but he hesitates to pick it up – so Maria does. When they get back to the villa, Yvonne packs up and leaves – much to the children's delight.

Episode 10: 'Sewing Machine and Violin'
Maria is shocked at how much she's paid: it's far too much. Georg wonders why she hasn't returned to the guest room, but as far as she's concerned, if she's being paid, she's not a guest.

In a storeroom, Mimi shows Maria an old sewing machine, but warns her not to use it without permission. Maria finds an old violin that's not been played for a long time. Matilda gives her permission to teach young Maria the violin, and grudgingly lets her take the two girls shopping. Neither of them knows who the violin belongs to, but in an instrument repair shop, the shopkeeper notices the name 'Agathe' (the girls' mother) on it, and tells young Maria the violin needs playing. (Maria uses her own money for some cloth and the violin repair; the rest she sends to the abbey.)

When Georg gets home, young Maria asks him if the violin was her mother's. The Baron is angry and takes the violin from her, then tells Fräulein Maria that taking things without asking causes trouble. Maria takes offence.

In the study, Georg explains that his wife used to try to encourage the children to play, and seeing it brings back too many memories. Georg thinks young Maria should be trying to forget. Neither Maria is happy with the outcome. After tea, Georg comes up to the nursery and sees Fräulein Maria sewing. He accuses her of dragging up all the memories of his wife – first the violin, now the sewing machine. Maria says she had permission and asks Georg if the person who died might prefer to be remembered rather than forgotten?

Later on, Georg sits in the study looking at the violin and the picture of Agathe. Little Maria comes in and says she wants to learn to play. And a few minutes later, the whole house is amazed to hear expert violin playing coming from the study. Georg also was a violinist, and he gives little Maria permission to learn.

Episode 11: 'Playing in the Mud is Supreme!'

On a lovely day, Maria asks the Baron if he'll buy the children some play clothes. He heads off to work before answering. Maria learns her scales on the violin as Johanna draws. Little Maria is upset that the others aren't allowed to play outside because she's too weak. Her violin practice is upsetting Matilda, who would rather it was in the afternoon. Later on, Georg agrees that the boys should play outside, but he's concerned about little Maria overdoing herself; the others get playtime at school.

Little Maria comes up with an idea – an athletics meeting on the meadow. She can't run so she's come up with the contests.

Later, in Vienna, Georg looks at football kit in a shop window and that night he comes back with a set of boots for everyone, including both Marias, after ringing the clinic and learning that little Maria does need to exercise a bit.

On Sunday, the games begin with the children snuffling for chocolates, and a relay involving everyone, with Maria teaming up with Matilda against Georg and little Maria (whom he carries). Even Martina's teddy wins a medal. After tea, the children go off to play in the meadow, while the Marias go for a walk. Franz tells the Baron it's a long time since they all laughed together.

When Matilda comes to find the children, Werner hides because he has sat in a cowpat – Matilda sees it, chases after him, and then slips in one herself. After a moment, she starts to laugh as hard as everyone else . . .

Episode 12: 'Chocolate Cake: Maria Style'

The Baron is away on business when a telegram arrives for Matilda: her sister Agnes is ill. Hans says that he and Maria can cope till the Baron returns. Matilda refuses to leave the children with Maria. However, after a phone call she decides to go – but leaves Clarine there 'in her place'. Once Matilda has gone, Clarine becomes too high and mighty to help and starts reorganizing everything. The staff complain to Hans who dresses them all down.

Hans asks Maria to look after the house while he visits a lady friend. Mimi overhears, and she and Rosy decide they'll take the day off too. Maria therefore takes the children outside for a picnic, as it's nice and quiet. Then she makes them work for their food in the kitchen, preparing Nonnberg Abbey Chocolate Cake. Werner is playing with the cake and it breaks into pieces when it drops on the floor. The children are down-hearted to begin with, but cheer up as Maria reworks it into 'Maria Cake' – and they invite Clarine and Franz to join them to eat. When Matilda rings for an update, Clarine says all is going well, to everyone's relief.

Episode 13: 'Don Quixote's First Love'
Autumn has arrived, and Georg is giving Rupert a fencing lesson outside to prepare for a forthcoming schools' match. Werner looks forward to having coaching too.

Hedwig's friend Nastassja is sad because her family are moving away to Russia. Hedwig asks her father if Nastassja can come to stay for the weekend. Rupert is delighted at the idea, as he has a crush on her. Nastassja is a little envious of the close relationship between Rupert and Hedwig.

Rupert isn't the only one who has a crush on Nastassja: her friend Anton does, and Hedwig invites him to join the farewell party for her. After Hedwig asks Maria for her advice on the party, the children greet Nastassja with a song and a flower each – all bar Rupert who's not home from school yet. He has other problems: he has to fence against Anton, the school champion, in a practice match.

When he gets home, he looks through the window and sees Anton giving Nastassja a music box as a farewell present; he himself has carved a knight for her, but when he sees Anton's fancy gift, he goes off, dejected, to hide in the shed.

Franz fetches Maria to talk to Rupert. He explains that the knight is meant to be Don Quixote – and that's how Rupert feels going up against Anton in the fencing match. Maria makes Rupert understand that Nastassja's situation is much worse than his, and he needs to get over his self-pity. He doesn't hear Nastassja telling Anton that she doesn't like boys who give love letters – which upsets Anton as he's put such a letter in the music box.

Rupert comes back to the villa but the others are all outside. He picks up the music box, but the arm has broken off – as the others come in through the French windows and find him there looking guilty . . .

Episode 14: 'The Music Box's Secret'
Rupert denies he broke the music box. Maria believes him, remembering that the French windows were locked earlier

when she tried them. Nastassja says she also believes him, which annoys Anton. He taunts Rupert about the fencing match, and says he's glad Nastassja will be gone before he beats Rupert to a pulp. Maria separates the two boys with Anton goading Rupert that he always needs the governess to stand up for him. Rupert challenges him to a duel.

Maria acts as referee, Nastassja stands as witness – as does Georg, who has come home early and stands with Franz, watching his son fight. Anton is wiping the floor with him, but Rupert remembers his father's advice and makes sure he gets at least one point. The weather turns bad as they continue; the others take shelter but Maria and Nastassja stay watching as the boys fight. Rupert falls but won't let Maria help him. Anton wins – but it's Rupert that Nastassja goes to. Anton claims he wasn't fighting properly, which was how Rupert got a point. Nastassja calls him a coward and slaps his face. He runs off.

That night Georg toasts Rupert's first trial in life as the family sit in front of the fire. Nastassja has had to leave early. Werner reveals that he realized earlier that Anton was responsible for the music box being broken. At home, Anton remembers breaking it when he tried to retrieve the letter he hid in the music box, and feels miserable.

The next day, the older children and Maria reach the station just before Nastassja's train pulls out. Anton also arrives and admits what he's done. Rupert and Nastassja both forgive him. The children sing her a farewell song, then Rupert runs down the platform after the train and manages to give her his knight figure.

Episode 15: 'Martina and the Bear, Nikola'

Maria is teaching Johanna and little Maria when they hear a terrible scream: Clarine was going to take Martina's bear Nikola to wash it after she spilled cocoa on it, and Martina bit her. Little Maria persuades Martina to show the bear to Maria, and the governess realizes that Martina was simply trying to give her bear a drink. To persuade her to allow Nikola to be washed,

Maria says mice will go for it (leading to a surrealist mice chasing teddy bear sequence!). They decide to bath the bear but Martina has a cold so she can't get in the bath with her toy.

The children have been asked by their father to come up with a present for Matilda's birthday and they decide to do something that will make her laugh again, as she did at the sports festival. They all go out into the woods near the river to practise a new song, but when Martina spots a rodent, she runs off. The others don't notice. Martina is worried the rodent will eat Nikola, so goes to a bridge and leans over to wash her. But the bear is pulled away by the current – and Martina falls in too. When Maria realizes she's gone, she rushes to find her, but the little girl has been in the water for a long time . . .

Matilda enjoys telling Maria off – she shouldn't have had all the children with her – and sends the children away before making it clear that Maria is not to have anything to do with anyone but little Maria and Johanna, and she shouldn't try to be friends with the others. Mimi comes in to say that Martina has a fever; Maria is banished to her room while Matilda and Mimi care for the girl. The children come in to say they should explain why they went to the river but Maria points out that she is responsible for Martina's accident.

The doctor diagnoses pneumonia, and Georg says he obviously trusted Maria too much. Martina is calling for Nikola in her fever, and Maria goes out to find the now-clean bear, which she dries and repairs. When she takes it up to Martina's room, Georg is there, as he's been all night, and he says the fever is abating. Maria sheds tears of relief – and starts to tell the Baron something. At breakfast, he breaks the news to the children that Maria has gone and little Maria runs up to her governess's now-empty room . . .

Episode 16: 'The House without Fräulein Maria'
Georg tells the children that he thinks Maria has lost a little of her spirit, and she has returned home, to the abbey, to rest.

Little Maria and Johanna miss Maria and ask Matilda when she's returning, but she tells them to forget about Maria; she won't be coming back. Little Maria asks her father if she can call Maria but he explains she can't, but tells her he thinks Maria will be back soon: Maria had told him she wasn't quite ready for what happened with Martina.

Little Maria and Johanna devise a plan to get Maria back. Martina wants to go with them, but they say it's too far and Fräulein Maria would worry. She sends Nikola the bear with them instead. The girls sneak off and catch the bus into Salzburg.

Later, Georg comes out of a bakery with a cake and is about to head home when he sees the bus depositing his two daughters (and a bear). After asking for directions to the abbey, they run up the stairs to the abbey, but are daunted by the (not particularly long) tunnel just before the entrance. When they run through, Maria drops Nikola and bravely goes back for her. They enter the abbey, and are greeted by a nun who fetches the Mistress of Novices; no, they can't see Maria, she tells them, but she'll pass a message. 'Please come home,' is all they can say. They leave Nikola with the Mistress – and walk out to find their father standing there. He takes them home.

Maria is back in her postulant's robes praying for strength – and, as if it's a sign, she is given Nikola. Matilda is given her birthday cake, and the children explain they were going to sing a song for her, and that's why they were by the stream. As they sing, Maria arrives back – and Matilda is convinced she came home because Nikola came to get her! Addressing the Baron as Captain, she says she's reporting for duty, and he welcomes her home.

Episode 17: 'The Wounded Fawn'
Werner and Rupert are climbing trees when they're caught by a teacher, and Werner rips his shorts. When he gets home, he explains that he was investigating a woodpecker's nest; Matilda says he can't have lunch, but his father countermands

that. Matilda says that Georg doesn't know how the discipline of a real baron's household works since he was given his knighthood for his war service; it's her job to ensure things are done properly and aristocratically. She's already been lecturing him about the slipping standards at the villa.

Georg is torn: he left Vienna's high society because of the stifling rules, and he can see that Werner's suffering. Werner is getting it in the neck from his siblings too who think that he's allowed Matilda to humiliate their father. Annoyed, he runs off. In the woods, he finds a fawn that's been injured and Maria spots him later going off with a medicine kit. She follows him to the barn and helps him treat the bite wound, then explains that as a child she often helped small animals and fed the birds. She also recalls constructing a bird food box full of worms that her 'uncle' hated. They make a straw bed for the fawn, and Maria agrees not to say anything to the Baron.

Dinner is roast venison, but Werner claims he has stomach ache. He's sent off for an early night, but Maria makes the connection between the venison and his pet deer. Next morning she finds him in the barn with the fawn and sends him off to school. She then leaves Johanna and Maria to get some straw and water for the fawn – but Clarine has followed them and goes to get Matilda. Maria tries to cover for Werner, but she can't lie effectively, particularly after Matilda shakes her.

At lunchtime, Werner heads home, delighted with life . . .

Episode 18: 'All God's Creatures, Great and Small'

Matilda is furious at Maria and Werner, but Georg thinks that all the children should see wild animals. When Werner reaches the barn, the younger ones and Maria are there and he's furious – Maria promised it would be their secret. He throws straw at them to get them out, and one lot hits Matilda who has come out to say it's lunchtime. She blames Maria for Werner now being rebellious.

Werner locks himself in the barn; Matilda tells the other children to go back to the house and Maria takes them, leaving

Matilda waiting for Werner. She tells the boy he isn't coming out till he apologizes. He realizes that the fawn's family might be looking for it, but when he sneaks out to get some water, Matilda enters the barn. When he returns, they argue and he runs off but Maria hides him from the pursuing Matilda.

Georg has been on a trip to the mountains with Franz, but comes back early; unfortunately they hit a deer and killed it. Georg digs a grave and they bury it. Werner's deer should go back to the mountains, but Werner doesn't want to let it go. His father clips his ear and tells him to think carefully.

The next day Werner isn't smartly dressed for church. He runs off when he's scolded, and Georg asks Maria to look after the children while he goes to look for his son. Werner is with his deer when his father finds him, by the grave. Georg admits he doesn't like the aristocracy either, so Werner shouldn't worry about fitting in. He also says he knows Werner thinks the deer Georg hit is his deer's mother, but he only thinks that because of what's happened to him.

Later Georg, Maria and the children take the fawn up to the mountain, where it joins a herd.

Episode 19: 'Lady Yvonne's Gifts'

The girls and Maria are playing outside when a telegram arrives from Earl Belvedere. He is coming over to celebrate his daughter's impending engagement and is going to talk with Georg about it. Matilda tells Maria there can be no repetition of the bad behaviour of Yvonne's previous visit. Maria asks why the Earl is so keen on the marriage, which would be to someone lower in rank; Matilda explains that it's because Georg doesn't seem to be after the family money. The children aren't happy, and Maria tries to explain that their father has many things to consider; however, the children don't really understand.

Lady Yvonne arrives, together with her own cook – but without her father, who's ill. She says she and Georg will need to go back to Vienna for the engagement party. The Earl has sent presents for the children – a large bear, a train set, a moving toy dog, a doll, a dollhouse, even a fake-silk outfit for Hedwig. Hedwig tries it on, but it makes her miss her mother more. Little Maria doesn't want to go to Vienna if Maria isn't going, but the governess isn't invited. Maria decides she is going to ask Yvonne to explain to the children why she wants to marry their father.

On the landing, Maria asks to talk to Yvonne but the woman brushes her off. Yvonne trips and nearly falls down the stairs, but Maria saves her from a tumble, and asks her to talk to the children, or they'll never accept her. Yvonne tries to push past her, but trips, and the pair fall to the bottom of the stairs . . .

Episode 20: 'Each Person's Life'
Yvonne has hurt her ankle, but Maria bore the brunt of the fall and possibly has concussion. Maria's taken into the drawing room with everyone fussing around her; Yvonne is left alone but for Matilda at the foot of the stairs. Yvonne is taken to the car for transport to the hospital and looks daggers at Maria who's being taken for a check-up. Hedwig invites herself along, leaving the children with Matilda who is furious that Maria has spoiled another engagement party.

Hedwig is honest with her father: even though people have been injured, she's happy because the engagement party won't be happening. When they get home, Hedwig tells the others Maria is staying in hospital and they have a competition to come up with the best thing to take to cheer her up.

Georg worries whether what he's doing is best for the children; Matilda is clear: it's the only solution. They all go off to the hospital, but the children are only interested in seeing Maria. Only when they're threatened that if they don't see Yvonne, they won't be allowed to see Maria, do they go. Yvonne is making the best of what she sees as a terrible situation, and has ordered hordes of flowers to fill the room, but realizes the children want to see Maria and tells them to go.

As she leaves, Hedwig tells Yvonne she's still opposed to the marriage – and Yvonne notes that they're honest.

The children visit Maria and they've all brought the same thing for her, something their mother made for them – a toy which sends things flying out when opened. Matilda ruefully watches them with Maria.

Yvonne tells Georg that she can't be a second mother to his children; she just wants to marry Georg and they can leave the children to Maria. Georg says he won't be ready to remarry for at least a couple of years.

Once the children have gone, Matilda tells Maria she knows she's trying to get the children not to get attached to Yvonne, and she wants Maria to keep her distance with the youngsters. Yvonne goes to see Maria in the hospital and tells her she doesn't want to get hurt by the children, but they can't find a meeting of minds with Yvonne admitting she thinks Maria's overly positive outlook is wearying.

Matilda is plotting with the Earl on the phone – there's only one thing left to try . . .

Episode 21: 'Baron von Trapp's Decision'
At the hospital, Maria and Yvonne are worried about the situation, and Maria suggests Yvonne is more open with the children. Back home, they are practising a song, which Matilda first suggests then demands they are singing for Yvonne. However, they are silent in front of Yvonne when she enters through the front door; they sing for Maria who comes in via the servants' entrance. Matilda is horrified when she comes down, and, remembering her instructions, Maria returns the gifts to the children, and goes to her room.

The children are concerned they've done something wrong; little Maria leaves tea without permission, and Yvonne offers to go and get her. Maria tells little Maria that she's tired and wants to be left alone. Yvonne comes up and sees the girl crying, and goes into Maria's room, telling her that acting coldly towards the children isn't what she wanted. She doesn't need Maria's poorly acted theatrics to get her to spend time with them – but then goes to her room to lie down. The children are delighted that their Maria is back.

A telegram comes which delights Matilda. Yvonne is trying her hardest with Hedwig, but the teenager rebuffs any approach. When the other children and Maria come in, Yvonne admits that she didn't see much of their mother because she had qualities that Yvonne knew she didn't – like kindness and honesty. She wants to marry Georg, not become their mother, and she says they think they own him. Everyone has a right to their own life.

Yvonne tells Georg she realizes she can't do anything too drastic with the children, nor can she force Georg to come to Vienna. She also doesn't want Georg to forget Agathe; Yvonne knows Agathe wouldn't have chosen a bad man.

After Yvonne leaves, Georg tells the children change is afoot: Matilda has been offered a job in Vienna, but won't be leaving till Maria goes back to the abbey in the summer. Oh, and he's getting engaged. Little Maria faints.

Episode 22: 'Can You Live Alone?'

As he leaves for the station, Georg is told by Maria she's changed her nightly prayer: now she prays that the children will get close to Yvonne. However, Hedwig is on the phone trying to get hold of her maternal grandparents: as far as she's concerned her father is going to swap his children for 'Grandma' Yvonne. Little Maria prays for her father to break his engagement, and if he does, she'll enter Nonnberg; when she hears this, Fräulein Maria tells her she needs to experience life, even if she doesn't like the idea.

Next morning Matilda is woken by Clarine: Hedwig has run off and isn't coming home while Georg remains engaged. At the station, Hedwig hasn't got enough money for a first-class ticket, but is told she has enough for third class, travelling with people desperate to find work. A thief steals her bag with all her money but she refuses to go home, despite snow starting. She has a run-in with a beggar and knocks over a milk churn; the young boy carting the milk is Maria's former pupil Thomas. He takes pity on her and takes her to his home.

Believing Hedwig has headed for her grandparents, Matilda wants to wait till they've confirmed she's there before telling Georg; Maria wants to check at the station but Matilda is more worried about the scandal. Against Matilda's direct orders, Maria heads off.

Thomas takes Hedwig to the hut where he lives, and feeds her, but needs her to be out of the way when his grandfather gets back. Hedwig hides when the old man arrives but then comes out, complaining of a stomach ache. Thomas has explained he was at Nonnberg school, and Hedwig asks him to fetch Fräulein Maria.

At the station, Maria learns that Hedwig didn't buy the ticket. Coming out, she sees Raphaela with Thomas and they take Maria to the hut. Hedwig is concerned about her stomach ache, but Maria explains her pains are because she's an adult (i.e. her periods have started). Hedwig doesn't want to go home but Maria reminds her there are people there who love and look after her, and they return, arms around each other.

Episode 23: 'Letters to the Angel'

It's the start of Advent, and the von Trapp children are making a traditional Advent crown, and will light one candle per week. It should go in a room where everyone is, but Georg says it can't go in the living room – and Hedwig says without a family a living room is a façade. Since everyone comes to where Maria is, that's where it's put. Maria goes to talk to Hedwig, trying to explain that her father isn't trying to cast her aside. After Georg hangs the crown, Maria explains that on Sundays, they'll listen to the Gospel and light a candle. The children then sit down to write letters to Christ.

That evening they sing 'Angels from the Realms of Glory' and are about to carry on when Matilda says it's time for bed.

Georg hasn't taken his eyes off Maria the whole time they were singing, and after the children go to put their letters out on their window ledges (Hedwig's is a prayer that her father doesn't stay engaged), he tells her he's looking forward to more songs. He says he's glad God sent her, and there's a moment of silence between them. Maria's a little disturbed by the feelings she's getting but tells herself it's down to Christmas.

Next morning the letters are gone, and Hans is made up as St Nicholas. He arrives with Franz dressed as the Krampus, a creature from Alpine myths who punishes those who have been naughty. Werner has skipped class (Georg secretly approves; Matilda is furious), and Rupert has smoked a cigarette. Martina tells 'St Nicholas' her secret wish is she doesn't need Yvonne because Maria is there, at which Matilda tells them all to go to their rooms. She tells Georg that Maria should be sent back to the abbey, but he points out she's done nothing wrong: the house is brighter with her. That's the problem, Matilda returns, and when Georg doesn't budge, Matilda decides she'll have to make Maria resign. However, when she talks to the governess, Maria doesn't believe that the Baron wouldn't tell her himself if he wanted her to leave. Matilda says she's a hindrance to the Baron's engagement but Maria doesn't understand.

Matilda tells the children Maria will be leaving; little Maria goes to ask her why and Matilda stops her. Martina stamps her foot in anger – and all the children start banging the table. Alerted by the noise, Georg comes up; Matilda's angry they're rebellious, Georg is pleased they have their own opinions. He tells them Maria won't be leaving.

Next day, Matilda watches as the Baron gets in a snowball fight with the children; the phone rings – it's Yvonne . . .

Episode 24: 'Christmas Carol'
The younger children finish making a snowman as Georg receives an invitation to go deer hunting at Earl Belvedere's holiday villa in Hungary. The children don't want him to go

since he'll miss lighting the next candle; Georg asks Maria's opinion. She says that next year there'll be someone new in the family, so this will be the last year for the children with their father. Georg decides not to go. Matilda isn't happy that the children have played outside in the snow.

The children are making presents for their grandparents, when Matilda comes in and bars Maria from seeing any of the children except her two charges, and prevents the children from going into each other's rooms. That's the way it should be in the household of an aristocrat. And if they don't do what she says, Maria will be sent away. Once Matilda has gone, the children complain they won't be able to practise singing, but Maria has a plan.

Georg doesn't think Maria has anything to do with the gap between him and Yvonne and he wants the children to have a happy Christmas, which they will if Maria is there.

Maria puts the music for the carols under the other children's doors and Johanna and the two Marias sing on the landing while the others join in from their rooms. When Clarine is around they hide, but when she's gone they come out – and the practice means the song under the crown that Sunday is excellent. After the children have gone to bed, Maria asks the Baron a favour. They chop down a tree, and put it in one of the rooms, which is deemed off limits to the children.

As they decorate the tree, Georg and Maria talk about their past: he used to decorate the tree with Agathe; Maria reveals how she was abused as a child, but then is embarrassed by what she's said.

On Christmas Eve they all sing 'Silent Night' together before Maria goes back to the abbey. As she prays, her thoughts go to the children and to Georg – but mostly to the children.

Episode 25: 'In the Snow of the Alps'
As the bells ring in the new year, Yvonne calls Georg from the party she's at, inviting them all to go to Kitzbühel for

a ski party. Little Maria will go if Maria's invited, and, to Matilda's annoyance, Georg says she is, at Yvonne's request. They sing a yodelling song as they go by train and car to the resort. Before Yvonne arrives, they start skiing, and Georg takes Werner and Hedwig up on the ski lift while Maria waits with the others. Rupert is distracted about something that he wanted to talk to his father about earlier, but hasn't had the chance.

Georg, Werner and Hedwig enjoy their ski while Rupert asks to speak to Maria, who says he needs to talk to his father rather than her when she learns what it is about. The others see Werner coming down on the injured sled – he jumped and fell in a hole because he was being reckless, and sprained his ankle. That evening, Rupert goes out and mends Werner's broken ski. Maria follows, then tells Georg he needs to talk to Rupert.

Rupert doesn't know what to do for the next year at school, and Georg asks if he's asked Maria's advice. He says he has because his father was too busy. Rupert doesn't think he's cut out for the military, and Georg says he wants both his sons to do something that's useful to others – but otherwise they should choose for themselves.

After the children have gone to bed, Georg tells Maria Yvonne has fallen ill on the journey so isn't coming, and they chat about Rupert: he's very good with his hands, Maria says. Georg agrees and they sit quietly by the fire together.

Episode 26: 'Oranges and Flower Seedlings'
The von Trapps return home early; intriguingly, Matilda had heard a different story about Yvonne's illness.

Maria, Johanna and little Maria plant some seedlings Maria was given. The children want to go mountain climbing, but little Maria thinks she won't be allowed; Maria promises she will. Georg asks Maria which of the children he should take with him to visit Yvonne, but Hedwig says none of them should go, because that means they're agreeing to the marriage. Matilda says it's too late for that; Georg explains the engagement is the time for everyone to get used to the idea. Rupert says they should give their father a break; the others say Yvonne clearly said she didn't want to be their mother. Georg reminds them that Yvonne's mother was widowed and remarried, so she doesn't want to force them into anything. Maria says she doesn't think Yvonne would lie, which upsets little Maria who thinks Maria must be taking Yvonne's side because she wants to go back to the abbey.

Georg leaves alone, although Maria gives him an alpine rose seedling from the children to take. He arrives at Grindelwald Castle and meets Yvonne's aunt, who embarrasses him with a reminder of his heroism during the war. Yvonne doesn't believe Georg's claim that the plant is from the children; she knows it's from Maria herself. Later that night, she tells Georg that she hopes when they're married it will just be the two of them, with the children away at boarding school in Vienna. Georg makes it clear he won't be sending the children away. There's a silence between them before she offers him some fruit, and they sit there eating an orange each.

Maria sings a lullaby to little Maria and tells the girl that she's found the nicer side to Yvonne; so might Maria in time.

Georg leaves the castle and Yvonne's aunt asks what's up between them. Yvonne explains the problem, and it's on Georg's mind as he drives, nearly having an accident. He arrives back and throws each of them an orange he has brought back.

Episode 27: 'Yesterday, Today and Tomorrow'
It's the start of Lent, and Maria asks if she can just be given soup to eat. She is working on a tapestry to be sent back to be sold for the abbey, and they all think of what they can do for Lent. Hedwig suggests that Matilda should give up chocolate, which doesn't go down well.

Maria and her charges go for walks in the fresh air; Hedwig starts doing a tapestry; Rupert decides he will study medicine.

The next evening, when Maria and the children are chatting, Maria recalls running away from home, aged fourteen. Her friend Annie followed, and Maria explained that her uncle was cross because she'd passed the entrance exam to teacher training college. Annie suggested going to work at the resort at Semmelink. Maria took her suitcase, took some money from her uncle's room for the fare, and her aunt wished her luck. She also took her uncle's whip and threw it out of the train.

After Georg comes in with the two little ones, Maria continues her tale. She had problems getting a job initially but after leaving her address at one hotel she was called back when they needed a tennis coach. She learned what to do but was shocked when her uncle showed up – but all he wanted to do was check she was okay. She later learned he had a neurosis and was hospitalized.

Georg says he'll give up smoking for Lent and give the money to Nonnberg. His eye slips from little Agathe who picks up the scissors and starts to cut up Maria's tapestry, nearly dropping the scissors on her foot. Maria doesn't mind restarting from scratch.

Episode 28: 'Naughty Agathe'

Everyone hears Matilda spanking Agathe for wetting the bed five nights in a row. Mimi says it's not the child's fault, but Matilda says her new mother won't love her if she's like this. Maria and Johanna know their sister is only doing it because she's constantly nagged.

Yvonne arrives unannounced, coming in through the servants' entrance. She arrives as Maria is telling Georg she thinks Agathe is being scolded too much, and Georg agrees. Matilda says she hasn't got time for Agathe to learn – it needs to be done before Yvonne becomes his wife. Yvonne makes her presence known, saying she wanted to see Georg in everyday clothes; like Matilda, she can't see why Maria is interfering in something to do with Agathe, who isn't her concern.

Agathe is being naughty again, walking off in Yvonne's shoes which the young woman took off so she could climb the stairs quietly to surprise Georg. She goes outside and uses Yvonne's shoes to pile mud on the front of her car. When she goes to wash one of them in the fountain outside, she nearly falls in – and would have, if Maria didn't catch her. She promises Maria she won't walk on the stone surround of the fountain again. When Georg comes to reinforce that, Agathe hides in Maria's clothes. Johanna fishes the shoe out of the water – and a watching Yvonne is not impressed.

Later on, Maria is singing with the younger children as Georg and Yvonne sit on the balcony; she notices he's tapping his fingers to the music. She tells him she is prepared to compromise and be their mother. At tea, she asks Maria's advice, and then says she'll hire a nanny or a tutor so she only has to do the nice things. Maria points out that she wants to be able to cheer the children up after she's scolded them. Georg agrees – they will raise them together, without outside help. Agathe is nearly four, although she may not make five if she carries on as she is behaving: they realize she has stood on directories to get scissors out of a drawer while the others were talking.

Maria finds her after she's already cut up the tablecloth and is starting on the curtains. She's about to grab the little girl when Johanna appears at the door, and Agathe jumps off a chair, nearly impaling herself on the scissors. They try to get them off her and she runs into the hall, trips, the scissors go flying, and Maria saves her from them. After making sure she's okay, Maria then gives her a severe dressing down. Agathe demands the scissors, and Maria gives her one wallop and tells her to say sorry. She refuses and runs to Yvonne, who takes her away. Maria asks Yvonne not to interfere; Yvonne says it's not her responsibility, and Maria says she'd be irresponsible if she doesn't make sure Agathe realizes the danger. Georg says that Maria does interfere, but she's right in this case.

Agathe becomes Yvonne's best friend and tries to feed her at the dining table, getting gravy on her dress. Yvonne exits without a word.

Episode 29: 'A Wife, A Mother'
Agathe bursts into tears at the look of disgust on Yvonne's face (the scene is expanded from the end of the previous episode). Georg goes after Yvonne while Agathe gets gravy on Matilda's dress too. As Matilda takes Agathe through the hall, Yvonne looks at her silently – then runs outside, telling her chauffeur to drive off quickly. She locks the door against Georg and the car leaves, passing the three eldest at the gate. The younger ones fill them in on what's happened, to Hedwig's delight. Johanna says what they're all thinking – they've got Maria, why do they need a new mother? She says she has to (and they chorus in unison with her) 'go back to Nonnberg Abbey'. Johanna wishes the abbey were gone.

Yvonne is at a hotel in Salzburg, wondering why she acted as she did. Maria is thinking about what the children said, and tells Matilda she's realized that her staying is causing problems for the children in accepting Yvonne. Matilda is delighted.

Georg and Yvonne go out walking; Georg explains that Agathe wasn't trying to be naughty. Yvonne asks if he really wants to get married. Of course, that's why they're engaged, Georg replies; but she thinks he's looking for a mother for the children, not a wife for him. He can't separate the two. They go over to where a couple are coming out from church after their wedding. Yvonne goes to catch the bouquet but misses; Maria picks it up – she'll be the next bride. Matilda has brought Maria so that she can tell them her news – she is going to return to the abbey a month early. Yvonne is delighted, but Georg is furious: how can Maria be so selfish to do this to the children? Yvonne loses it at this point, and drags him away.

She asks him pointedly if he likes Maria – it doesn't matter if she's a nun or someone else's wife; does he like Maria? He says she's twenty years younger and he's marrying Yvonne. She points out he's kidding himself. She tells him to admit it ... and after a long pause, he does. She collapses for a moment, then walks proudly away.

Maria is waiting at her hotel; when Maria tells Yvonne she thinks of the children above anything else, Yvonne can't help laughing. She thinks children are as dishonest as adults, and she's determined to prove the von Trapps are like all other children.

Johanna and little Maria are talking about dreams they had about Maria – fun ones – and one little Maria had about Yvonne, who was insisting on talking an odd language with their father. They don't realize Yvonne and Maria are standing behind them, and on hearing what the children say, Yvonne leaves. Maria races to the car, and Yvonne says she's heading home. Maria is the right person to be their mother, she says, and drives off, leaving Maria dumbfounded.

Episode 30: 'Would You Marry Me?'

Matilda is reading a newspaper report of Yvonne with her new fiancé, an English noble, coming out from the opera at Vienna. It's two weeks since she cancelled her engagement to Georg. Maria comes to get her up, but Matilda would rather stay in bed than go to church. (Maria's planned return to the abbey hasn't happened.)

Werner is tossing a coin and Johanna is determined to do so too but swallows her coin. Maria comes out of church to find her, and although Johanna seems fine, they call Dr Voltman who confirms she was lucky it landed in her mouth vertically. Maria says she could have killed herself; Georg agrees, and Maria tells her to promise her father she won't do it again. Dr Voltman has told Georg the treatment, but he says a maid should do it. Maria insists it's her job.

The children are singing outside when Johanna feels ill. She has to use a chamber pot and isn't too happy. While she does so, Maria reminisces about her arrival at the von Trapp house and about Yvonne's last words. The coin doesn't appear this time. The other children don't continue singing; it's not fun without Maria, and they hate that she's only there for ten more days . . . but Hedwig has a plan.

Maria asks the Captain if she can borrow a ladder to clean the house before she leaves; he says he'll help her. The children come to help but Johanna has to go to the toilet again. While Maria is sorting through the chamber pot's contents to look for the coin, the children talk to their father. They all want him to marry Maria. He admits he likes Maria but he doesn't know whether the feeling is reciprocated. The children go to ask Maria if she likes them, but Georg doesn't feel he can ask such a question. The children each ask Maria if she likes them (she does), and if she likes their father (she says she does) – and off they run to tell him. He goes to talk to Maria, and Hedwig stops the others from following. Georg asks Maria if she'll marry him, and she's shocked; he thought that's what the children had asked her. She says she hasn't thought about it before . . .

Episode 31: 'God's Decree'
Maria says she came to Salzburg to be a nun; Georg points out that in ten days she'll never see him or the children again. Before Maria can reply, the children run in: Hedwig and little Maria are fighting with Matilda over whether Georg can marry Maria. As far as Matilda is concerned, the Baron was only engaged three weeks previously, Maria is twenty years younger and not of noble blood. Hedwig points out that Yvonne is now engaged; Georg says that if being a noble means you have to marry someone you don't like, he'll stop being a noble. He wants to marry Maria because she's important to him and the children. Matilda shakes Maria to get her to say no; Georg says Matilda is the one being stubborn. Maria has never been happier but she's going back to Nonnberg to talk to the Abbess. With a smile, she leaves.

But she's conflicted. Raphaela is delighted to see her back

at the abbey, and now she's back, it feels like home. She tells the Abbess she should become a sister, but that's not what the Abbess asked – she wants to know what Maria *wants*. Maria can't explain how she feels, so they kneel in front of the crucifix. Maria admits she's afraid and the Abbess tells her to pray till she gets an answer.

As all the children pray for her return (Johanna so the coin can come out of her stomach), Georg is loitering in the hall and gets a chair to wait more comfortably on – to Matilda's incredulity. Maria prays in the abbey church, asking out loud if God doesn't need her anymore; Sister Dolores, never Maria's best friend, is the one who points out that God is near her always. The eight people need her and God meant her to be with them – and off Maria trots, down through Salzburg, arriving back at the villa at sunrise. The back door hasn't been unlocked so she comes through the front – to see Georg there. He asks if it's good news, and Maria, crying, says yes – and as the children come down, she says she's home.

Episode 32: 'A Bride in July'

The Abbess may have given her blessing, but Matilda won't have it. She says there's gossip about Georg and Maria already. Georg realizes he has to go away until the wedding; he has to go to Vienna to see Agathe's parents. Matilda agrees to stay, but she thinks Agathe's parents will dissuade Georg from the marriage. Johanna and Maria have been eavesdropping and decide to send their grandparents a letter.

Georg leaves with a tender farewell to Maria (to Matilda's disgust), and Maria starts to learn about running a household from books in the library. A few days later Maria takes Rupert to the train station for his entrance exam in Innsbruck and when she gets back there's a letter from Georg: even the salutation makes her blush. He's been gone a week, and tells her his in-laws agree with the marriage. To keep gossip at bay, he is going cruising for a month, and he hopes that Matilda will wait till he's back.

Maria shows Matilda the letter, and the older woman admits that she lied about the job at a prestigious school; it was the only way to force the marriage between Georg and Yvonne. Her concern about Georg and Maria's marriage is that it'll prevent the children from marrying into a noble family. Maria tells Matilda that Yvonne told her to be their mother. Matilda says it's getting late so Maria leaves her, and Matilda gets out her cards to do a reading. She sees the marriage will face difficulties but they'll be fruitful and happy.

Agathe's parents send a gorgeous wedding dress for Maria; Matilda feels faint when she sees it. Georg returns, tanned and bearded. It's Maria's turn to go – she returns to Nonnberg to meditate for ten days. The night before the wedding, Matilda puts the children to bed, and Georg thanks her for all she's done; however, she won't come to the ceremony.

Georg and Maria exchange vows at the abbey church with the children and the nuns all sitting watching. When they come out, Matilda and Clarine are waiting; Matilda has a word of advice about each child, and gives Maria her watch, as it's been very useful to her. Maria sheds a few tears as she goes – and so does Matilda.

Episode 33: 'A True Family'

The children come on the honeymoon trip, as Maria and Georg get used to not calling each other 'Fräulein Maria' and 'Captain von Trapp'. The children decide to call her 'Mother Maria'. When they get back, there's a letter for Rupert – he's passed the entrance exam to medical school. And there's a phone call for Georg: the Ranmel Bank has gone bankrupt. He explains to Maria that Austria was already pressurizing Germany and so he helped the Ranmel Bank by transferring money from England – but now it's all gone. Maria may be right that he's done nothing wrong, but it doesn't alter the fact that they're bankrupt. Maria says he'll have to work rather than live off the interest of his stocks and shares. They still have the house but will have to cut back the staff.

She's so excited Georg feels like he's not gained a life mate, but another child!

Maria says she'll go out first thing to find some work, and she runs back from the abbey a bit later. Georg has gone out too, and Franz asks her if they can talk. The children have picked up on something being wrong. None of Georg's friends will lend him money – to Maria's delight – but Franz gives them a sheaf of money he's saved. She's also been told the Catholic university is looking for a boarding house for professors and students, as is the Benedictine church – they can all run it as a family. Rupert offers not to go to medical school but Maria says he can work to put himself through school.

The family move to the third floor, as the guests will use the first two, and Georg and Maria realize how much this is bonding them all. Rupert goes to work in a bookstore while at Innsbruck, and a chapel is approved by a priest at the villa ready for the students – their first boarder will be the priest in charge of it.

Episode 34: 'The Trapp Family Singers'

Maria overhears an argument between Mimi and her fiancé Karl about whether she should stay working for the von Trapps. In the chapel the children are singing 'New Every Morning is the Love' for morning Mass. Father Wasner, the priest, gives the children singing lessons, and then they go to clean the third floor – but Mimi has already done it. The children therefore decide to clean the second floor, where the students are studying, but they don't do it properly and object when Mimi shows them how.

Mimi, Rosy and Hans sit down with the von Trapps. There isn't work out there, but they don't want to be a drain on the family, and Georg wouldn't want them to stay out of sympathy. Maria wants the children to learn to be self-sufficient like Mimi (who later starts to think the children have grown up and don't need her).

Opera star Lotte Lehman comes to stay on the recommendation of the archbishop for the duration of the Salzburg Festival, and hears the children singing. She wants them to enter a contest; Georg isn't happy about the idea but she thinks they should share their gift. They may not be professional but they sound like they're singing as one, maybe because they're a family. Father Wasner thinks they'll have fun, and be a contrast to church choirs. Georg thinks it'll be too hard, but everyone – including Nikola the bear – wants to try. Rupert comes back and is dragged into joining in.

Mimi decides she'll like being a goatherd in the Tyrol valley. She and Karl decide to go together.

The children practise, although Georg is clearly still unhappy, and at the music festival (at the Rehearsal Halls in Salzburg) they are discouraged by what they hear. They come out and Martina waves Nikola's arm at Father Wasner in the audience; Johanna then bows as Georg shakes his head before they start. They receive rapturous applause. Mimi and Karl come to say goodbye after the performance.

Episode 35: 'Singing In The Wind'
On a windy, rainy day, Salzburg Radio Station calls Maria asking them to come in on Saturday for a broadcast, and they'll be paid. Georg is really unhappy about this.

A parcel comes from Matilda that the children want to open; she's also written to say their grandmother is ill. They can't afford to go to Vienna, but Maria thinks she could hear the children sing on the radio. Georg is still against it, but since it's for the children and their grandmother, he agrees.

At the radio station they perform with Father Wasner conducting: Matilda and Clarine listen in, as do Rupert and his classmates – and the Austrian Chancellor (called 'President' in the subtitles) Kurt von Schuschnigg, who calls, asking them to sing for him. They think it must be a joke, but a week later an official invite arrives, along with rail tickets, which will allow them to see their grandmother as well.

Matilda – now very happy – and Clarine meet them at Vienna station and take them to the official event. The Chancellor wants Georg to sing as well, and the little ones take him up to the stage where they all sing 'The Linden Tree'. The manager of the Vienna concert hall asks them to perform there, but Georg doesn't want them performing for money. The Chancellor points out that the Third Reich is causing Austrians economic problems because tourists have stopped coming and he wants the singers to help cheer the people up. Georg says yes, as long as it's not for profit.

After that, they visit the children's grandmother who is pleased to see all of them, especially Maria.

Episode 36: 'The Nazi Invasion'

It's winter and Father Wasner is practising the songs for the concert with the whole family. Rosy has prepared food for the journey, and Maria hopes they can earn enough money for a turkey for Christmas. Rosy and Hans are left behind; Hans doesn't think their singing will help Austria's present position.

When the family reach the concert hall, American star Marian Anderson is singing so there's a huge interest. The children lose their confidence when they know a great singer is in the same building, but Father Wasner and Maria remind them they sing joyfully, so they go out, in front of the Austrian flag, to perform. Johanna misses her solo because a mosquito flew into her throat, which Maria explains, to the audience's amusement. She realizes that they have made a connection.

After the concert they are congratulated by the Chancellor's aide, and Mr Wagner, a pushy American agent, says they must come and tour. Neither Georg nor Maria like the idea; they're not making their living from singing, and the children have school. However, they keep his card and put it in their scrapbook, which they go back and look at as midnight approaches for the new year of 1938 (the first time the year is specifically given). Rupert has to go back to Innsbruck the next morning.

March 11 1938: on the radio, the family hear the Chancellor surrendering to Germany (although it's early evening as the children are still up). The German army has invaded, and Georg sends a telegram to the Chancellor wishing him safety. Hans wonders if it will be sent: there is no Austria, nor a Chancellor of Austria any more. They go outside to hear the bells pealing – on Gestapo orders, Franz tells them, to 'welcome' the army into Salzburg.

Arrive it does in force: swastikas are soon everywhere. The family and the staff go to pray in the chapel; all except Georg – who looks up at his Austrian flag and says Austria will never die, it's just sleeping – and Hans, who listens to the news with glee, a swastika badge on his shirt . . .

Episode 37: 'The New Salute'

Hans suggests that the Austrian flag should be moved somewhere less conspicuous. Georg's refusal and the ensuing argument can be heard by everyone. Hans' Nazi sympathies are becoming clearer and he warns Georg that if he speaks out, not only he, but the family, will suffer. Hedwig tries to explain what's happening to the younger ones, and they don't dare say anything negative even in front of their friends. There's a huge swastika over the school entrance, they have new teachers and are taught the new 'Heil Hitler' salute. Johanna doesn't join in when they're being taught but under peer pressure gives in.

When the children come home and say what they've been taught, Georg becomes increasingly angry and says he'd rather drink wine with crushed glass in it than do the salute. The others say they cheated, and Johanna feels guilty that she gave in. Maria tries to cheer them up by singing, but neither Johanna nor Georg are mollified.

Next morning, Johanna's teacher greets the class with a salute, but Johanna refuses, saying her father doesn't like it. The teacher says her parents are old-fashioned; what the children are learning is the new, the right way. The school summons Maria who leaves Georg to look after Agathe and Martina. Maria is delighted when one person she passes exchanges a Good Afternoon rather than a Heil. The principal tells Maria to watch what the children say. Maria says she prays at home, which brings the teacher's wrath: faith is no part of life any more, only strength matters. He warns her that people with suitable views are rewarded.

That night Maria advises Georg to keep his opinions away from the children because it will be hard for them to keep it secret at school. Johanna is seriously upset by what has happened, and comes to their bed in floods of tears. The next morning the other children tell her how to cheat – they say 'Tail Hitler' not 'Heil'.

Georg hopes that the Nazi problem will be over soon, but it's just starting – a Gestapo officer arrives at the door . . .

Episode 38: 'Hans' Secret'

Maria and Georg see the Nazi car as Hans tells Georg he has a guest. The SS officer says that they should have a Nazi flag; Georg says he hasn't got any money to buy one – so they give him a flag. Hans accepts it on their behalf. Georg explains that they have their own flag, but when he takes the SS officer to show him the Austrian banner, it's gone. The Nazi advises not holding on to the old flag but putting up the new; Georg says he'll never do so. Meanwhile Agathe is trying to get the Nazi driver to play with her; he ignores her, and Maria grabs her. The SS officer warns Maria that resisting is futile and she collapses by the door. Franz tries to contact Dr Vortman, but he's a Jew and has been taken away by the Nazis.

Georg and Maria take a train to Munich; Georg has kept Vortman's fate hidden from Maria and just said they're seeing an old friend instead. The doctor says Maria has been working too hard: her kidneys are weak and she's pregnant. They're delighted, but the doctor warns that she may not carry to term and suggests aborting. Maria flatly refuses. Before they catch the train, they visit an art museum and find Nazis heiling in front of a bad painting of Hitler as a Wagnerian hero. They go for a meal, and find themselves in the same restaurant as Hitler himself. They leave, feigning illness, as Hitler behaves like a lunatic and then has everyone chanting 'Sieg Heil'.

They get home to find that the huge Nazi flag is draped outside. Georg pulls it in as Hans explains he promised the Gestapo he'd put it up in return for them not reporting the Captain for non-cooperation. Hans admits he's a Nazi party member and has been for two years; Maria faints but tries to rally as the children see her.

Episode 39: 'Pride and Belief'

Maria takes the children away, leaving Georg, Franz and Hans. Georg dismisses Hans but the servant warns that he's the only thing keeping them all safe. Georg cuts the Nazi flag in two over Hans's protestations, but doesn't fire him.

Although the children are nervous now because they can't trust Hans, they are delighted when Maria tells them she has good news, and Hedwig deduces she's pregnant. Rosy is worried that Georg will speak openly and get himself in trouble; the Nazis don't like them renting rooms to priests. Maria starts to dig out the baby clothing and bedding (which Hans notices).

Salzburg is changing; they can only walk a certain way up streets, and there's a near-confrontation with Nazi soldiers. It's not the only change: Georg receives a letter from the German navy appointing him captain of a new submarine, but when Agathe and Matilda inadvertently find the old Austrian flag, Georg realizes he can't take the appointment. They decide to name the baby after the guardian angel of the Austrian navy, St Barbara.

A few days later, on Hans's day off to go to a Nazi meeting, Rupert comes home; the Nazis have taken over Innsbruck. The Gestapo officer arrives, again noting the lack of a flag, and presenting an invitation for the von Trapps to sing at the Führer's birthday. A family council follows; this will be their third refusal and Georg tells them they will have to leave.

To allay suspicion, Rupert returns to Innsbruck, and Maria asks the Abbess to ask the archbishop for permission for Father Wasner to come with them or he'll be in danger. They know they need to move quickly.

Episode 40: 'Farewell to My Country'

Georg is explaining the plan to Franz: they'll meet Rupert on the train, then go to the village where Mimi lives in the Tyrol, and from there go over the Alps into Italy. Franz offers to come with them to help, but Georg tells him he needs to remain behind or Hans will know they've escaped. If it looks as if the family is just going hiking, they may get away with it.

Maria and Father Wasner act out a charade for Hans's benefit: the priest is 'going to a monastery' for an overnight stay while the family go hiking. Franz goes to Innsbruck and briefs Rupert to catch the Oetztal train the next morning. That night they're all packing as Hans asks for a day off since everyone is going to be away.

In the morning, Rosy brings some food for them to take on their hike; for her own protection she doesn't know what's happening, but the children can't leave without saying goodbye, and Hedwig gives her a brooch. She silently asks Maria if they're going, and she nods.

Hans is waiting at the bus stop, and notices little Maria has her violin in her knapsack. Franz arrives saying he has relatives arriving, and Hans says he's off to see his mother. Franz salutes as they get on the bus and tells them everything is ready; Georg throws him his pipe. The bus takes them to Salzburg station where they depart successfully.

However, Rupert has problems: an accident prevents his bus from reaching Innsbruck station in time. Maria leaves with the children on the train while Georg waits for Rupert. The children, Father Wasner and Maria arrive at Mimi's home, and her husband Karl says they can't stay at the local inn; it'll be too dangerous.

On the train, Georg and Rupert hear that the border

is about to be closed, and back at the villa, Hans sees the Austrian flag is gone, and puts two and two together. Georg and Rupert make it to Mimi's village where they are met by Karl. They need to go now so Karl finds a car – or rather a hearse. Karl drives, with Georg and little Maria in the front. They are stopped by a Nazi patrol and explain they are taking a dead man back to his birthplace in Italy. It has to be done overnight as the body's decaying.

When the Nazi opens the back of the hearse, Father Wasner is praying over the coffin, with Maria, Rupert, and Werner. The other girls are hidden inside. Father Wasner asks if the guard is going to disrespect the dead, and he backs off. They reach Italy, and get a train to Switzerland. They have tickets from Mr Wagner, the American agent, to get to America by boat. As they stand on the boat deck and think of the people they've left behind – Franz and Rosy; Mimi and Karl; Matilda and Clarine – they sing a song of farewell.

And we leave them as they enter New York Harbour, amazed at the Statue of Liberty, ready to start a new adventure.

In some ways, *Trapp Ikka Monogatari* stands as the most faithful of the adaptations of Maria von Trapp's memoirs, but it does play with the narrative as much as the others. We realize late on in the proceedings that the early episodes are set between September 1936 and June 1937 rather than a decade earlier; the events of the years between the von Trapps' marriage and the Anschluss are compressed into less than six months – which means that Rosemarie and Eleonore disappear from the picture completely; the sequence leading up to the decision to leave follows Maria's original version even though it can't possibly work out chronologically. The children's names and ages are changed around – Agathe goes from being the oldest to the youngest – and the characters of Franz and Hans are based on just one person. A couple of incidents drawn from later in the von Trapps' tour of America (the mosquito in Johanna's throat – although it was Maria herself in reality who nearly choked – and the hearse as an unconventional means of transport) slot in neatly to the story.

Where *Trapp Ikka Monogatari* scores is in its characterization of Maria: more than in any other version, you see the tomboy who becomes a nun who becomes a mother. The dramatization of her early life is drawn from the 1972 autobiography – the German movies and the musical's 'Maria Rainer' come from happy backgrounds, which simply wasn't the case – and while Maria doesn't go into details regarding her differences with Baroness Matilda (and it's Agathe's book that tells us how much they were at odds), what's here is a good extrapolation, even if the real Matilda did leave the villa much earlier than suggested here. Yes, some incidents in this are magnified from the reality, or manufactured completely, but at the end of over eight hundred minutes you get more of a feel of what the tale was really like than from any other production.

PART FIVE: THE TRAPP FAMILY SINGERS LIVE AGAIN!

19
TWENTIETH-CENTURY REVIVALS

It's perhaps a little disingenuous to suggest that at any stage *The Sound of Music* has needed a revival. It is one of the most popular pieces in the Rodgers and Hammerstein canon, and licences for performances are regularly granted by the Rodgers and Hammerstein Organization. A new Polish production *Dźwięki Muzyki* opened in Gliwice in March 2014, while in June 2014, as this book was completed, there were thirteen separate amateur English-language versions being staged around the world, from Patcham High School near Brighton, England, to the Act 1 Theatre Company in Great Falls, Montana. Full orchestral arrangements, or a simpler version for two pianos, can be hired, along with banners, headers, posters, and specific imagery for use on Facebook and elsewhere online. A quick look at the Cast Album database reveals that there have been at least 116 different cast albums released around the world, commemorating everything from the original releases (which intriguingly included a German edition of the movie soundtrack – given the film's negative reception, one has to wonder how many copies of this RCA sold!) to the 2009 Icelandic *Söngvaseiður* and the 2011 Russian production of *Зуки Музыки*. The original cast album has never gone out of print and a copy of it was among those records approved to be played to the British public in the event of a nuclear strike to maintain some semblance of normality!

However, while *The Sound of Music* has never really gone away, it has certainly had peaks and troughs of popularity. The original British stage production continued running after the movie was released in 1965, eventually closing in 1967. The movie received a re-release around the world in 1973, and the screen siblings were asked to help promote it in February and March, travelling around North America – their European tutor, Jean Seaman, accompanied Debbie Turner and her mother (although the publicists managed to misspell her surname!).

The ABC network in America was the first to broadcast the movie, airing it on 29 February 1976 to record ratings: 'a total-household rating of 33.6 and a 49 share' in broadcast-speak, which means that, at any point during the broadcast, over a third of houses with televisions (which formed part of the media agency's sample) were watching the film, and just under half of all the TV sets in America (that they monitored) were on during the film.

The rights then went to NBC, who premiered it on 11 February 1979, reaching 30 per cent of the audience watching TV at the time (and that was against the highly publicized sequel to the slavery drama *Roots* running on ABC). The film's home was on NBC for the next two decades, although after 1987, it was frequently heavily edited to bring it down to a three-hour running time including commercials, rather than four hours. Portions of the nuns' initial Alleluia, 'I Have Confidence', and 'So Long, Farewell' were lost, as well as various dramatic scenes, some of which – such as the Captain explaining at dinner that he is going to Vienna the next day – must have made the film difficult for new audiences to follow. That version was ditched in 1995, when Julie Andrews introduced a nearly full-length broadcast (the intermission was deleted), although NBC decided not to renew its contract a few years later after ratings continued to slip.

The Fox network broadcast *The Sound of Music* once in 2001, in truncated form (their editor apparently decided that the wedding scene could be dispensed with to fit the film to the slot) before the film returned to its original home at ABC. A full-length broadcast is now scheduled on the main network annually, and on the sister network, ABC Family, periodically across the year; since 2008, these have been in high definition. The 2012 broadcast achieved considerably higher ratings than previous years, averaging 5.2 million viewers in the key 18–49 demographic (against 3.7 million in 2011), and 2013 went even better, some of which was attributed to a knock-on effect from the NBC live version of the stage show (discussed in the next chapter).

The film was released to the home entertainment market in each new successive format – from a two-tape VHS version in 1986, to laserdisc two years later, then DVD in 2000 (to mark the thirty-fifth anniversary), and most recently Blu-ray in 2010, which was the most detailed transfer of the negative yet. It's also available for download.

There were plenty of touring productions of the stage show around the United States and United Kingdom during the 1960s and 1970s, with Barbara Cook, Barbara Eden, Florence Henderson, Shirley Jones, Maureen McGovern, Marie Osmond, Roberta Peters and Constance Towers amongst those who picked up their guitar and played Maria. However, *The Sound of Music* hadn't been heard on Broadway or in London's West End for fourteen years when the next big production opened on 17 August 1981.

British singing star Petula Clark headlined the cast at the

Apollo Victoria Theatre, with Michael Jayston as Captain von Trapp, and *The Avengers'* Honor Blackman as the Baroness. Even without its incredible success, the staging would have been notable as it was the first time that an actor had transitioned from playing Maria to the Mother Abbess in professional productions. June Bronhill, the original Australian Maria, had trained in London and regularly appeared on the West End stage; she was delighted to switch sides, although the tinnitus from which she suffered in later life would affect her performance.

Clark was in her late forties, and despite Mary Martin making a success of the role at a similar age, she took some convincing to take the part. She made it her own – and even received high praise from Maria von Trapp herself, who said that Ross Taylor's production was the best she had ever seen. It made musical history, playing to 101 per cent capacity every week for over a year, and over the half-term holiday week at the end of October 1981 it had the highest attendance record for a single week up to that point.

The musical, which closed on 18 September 1982, was an interesting hybrid of the stage and film versions. It started with the 'Preludium' and then 'The Sound of Music' preceded 'Maria', per the stage libretto, but then rather than having the Abbess and Maria singing 'My Favourite Things', director John Fearnley and musical director Cyril Ornadel opted to give them 'A Bell is No Bell' as a duet. This is the lead-in to the reprise of 'Sixteen Going on Seventeen', whose lyrics were originally intended for use in 'Climb Ev'ry Mountain'. The four lines are sung alternately, and then as a duet with a small snippet of dialogue between the verses. This then led into the movie song, 'I Have Confidence'. 'Do Re Mi' was used to introduce Maria to the children, but 'My Favourite Things' also assumed its movie position during the thunderstorm. In the second half, Clark and Jayston sang about 'Something Good' rather than 'Ordinary People'. (The cast album CD is a little misleading: it has two extra songs on it:

Clark's rendition of 'Edelweiss', and an extra song 'Darkness', a sub-James Bond theme tune number that is spectacularly out of place!)

A very different production was put on by the Snow Troupe, one of the five groups that form the Takarazuka Revue in Japan, in 1988 at the Bow Hall. The Revue is an all-female musical theatre troupe, based at Takarazuka in Hyōgo Prefecture, and founded in 1913. Competition for places in the five troupes that make up the Revue is very keen, with only forty to fifty students a year being accepted from the thousands who apply to the Takarazuka Music School. This leads to a very high standard for their productions, which are drawn from Japanese stories, as well as Western plays, films and musicals – *An Officer and A Gentleman*, *Casablanca* and *Gone with the Wind* have all been adapted. It's possible that the success of this production led to the green light being given to the anime version of the story, which premiered three years later (see chapter 18).

The 1990 stage production by New York City Opera at the Lincoln Center's New York State Theatre was most notable for its director: Oscar Hammerstein II's son James. Described by the *Christian Science Monitor* as a 'handsome, admirably performed revival' of the musical, it featured Christian music star Debby Boone as Maria with Laurence Guittard as Captain von Trapp. Gone were the references to the film: this was Lindsay and Crouse/Rodgers and Hammerstein, pure and simple. There were plans for this production to extend into the summer of 1990 beyond its run over Easter, but they didn't materialize – it would be another eight years before *The Sound of Music* made a proper return to the Great White Way.

Susan H. Schulman's 1998 production was heralded as the triumphant return of the musical nearly forty years after it premiered. Rebecca Luker was cast as Maria, with Michael Siberry initially playing Captain von Trapp (Dennis Parlato and *The Thorn Birds*' Richard Chamberlain took over the role through the run). The show also amalgamated material from

both film and stage, with 'I Have Confidence' and 'Something
Good' appearing, but both of Elsa and Max's songs, 'How
Can Love Survive?' and 'No Way to Stop It', also featured.
Their cynicism was something star Luker welcomed: 'I think
it's a needed ingredient in the show that the movie doesn't
have,' she told the press at the time. (As a result of the success
of this production, Schulman was asked by Andrew Lloyd
Webber to prepare an American run of his musical of *Sunset
Boulevard* featuring another former Maria, Petula Clark.)

The production was opened in style. Four of the surviving
von Trapp children – Johannes, Maria, Agathe and Rosmarie
– went to the premiere on 12 March 1998, and then in
December, a grand reunion was arranged. The four children,
and their two siblings Werner and Eleonore, returned to New
York where they were joined by the seven actors who had
appeared as the von Trapp children in the 1965 film. The (real)
von Trapps were given the Golden Decoration of Honour by
Dr Arno Gasteiger, the governor of the state of Salzburg,
to mark the work that the Trapp Family Relief Effort had
carried out in the period after the war. The family then surprised the guests at the ceremony by singing 'Silent Night' in
German, followed by a rendition of 'Edelweiss'. Then all thirteen 'von Trapps' – real and fictional – went to see the show.
At the curtain call, three 'generations' of von Trapps lined up:
the originals, the movie siblings, and their 1998 counterparts.
(The movie brothers and sisters were once again cooperat-
ing with publicity for the film; when they met up in London,
shortly after the twenty-fifth anniversary, they decided they
should be paid for their efforts, and after some friction, this
was agreed.)

Over fifty years had passed since the end of the Second
World War, which meant that the Broadway production
could be more open about the Nazi menace than its prede-
cessors had been. The idea of a swastika forming part of the
background set is in Lindsay and Crouse's original notes for
the show, but had not featured in an American production

previously – although the British version directed by Wendy Toye for Sadler's Wells, with Christopher Cazenove and Liz Robertson in the leads, had done so (part of the changes from the 'cardboard inadequacies' of the previous production noted by the *Spectator*'s critic, Sheridan Morley). After it had run in New York for fifteen months, during which time it was nominated for a Tony award, the production was transported across to Australia, where it played in Sydney for three months before going on tour.

However, as the twentieth century drew to its close, the most unusual version of *The Sound of Music* was gaining momentum . . .

20

THE STORY THAT NEVER DIES

Dubbed 'The Rocky Horror Show on Prozac' by Variety, there's one version of The Sound of Music that allows everyone to join in – from a small boy dressed as Scooby Doo (his logic for the choice was that the cartoon Great Dane was one of his favourite things) to a group of people singing as if they're in a communal shower. It's the madcap Sing-A-Long-A Sound of Music, which takes audience participation to a whole new level.

First seen at the London Gay and Lesbian Film Festival in London in 1999, prompted by one of the organizers noticing that the residents of an old people's home had been singing along to a broadcast of Seven Brides for Seven Brothers, the Sing-A-Long-A has been a feature at the Prince Charles cinema in Leicester Square, London, ever since. Ben Freedman, director of Singalong Productions Ltd, the company behind the show, explained in an interview for this book that 'it very quickly captured everybody's imagination. It's still showing at the Prince Charles one Friday a month. We booked it into some live theatres around the UK at the beginning of 2000, then we opened in America later on in 2000, and in Canada and Australia beginning of 2001. It's been going and going ever since – to New Zealand, Sweden, Holland, Switzerland, Austria, Asia and Malaysia.'

One of the few places it didn't work well was Miami, after the producers learned that the original film had not been distributed in Cuba so the émigrés who had crossed to the United States were not aware of it. The producers even tried taking it to Salzburg, but it wasn't that successful there either. 'We found that people come to Salzburg on day trips; they don't tend to stay over. So we weren't able to generate as good an audience in Salzburg as we'd hoped; that was a bit disappointing but you have to accept it.

'The key thing about our shows is that the auditorium has to be full,' Freedman continues. 'Unless we start to advertise a show at least three months in advance, it doesn't tend to sell out or sell well. In somewhere like Salzburg where you get people coming in twos or threes, they don't organize ahead of time.

'The core audience is groups of women – six, eight, ten women who come from work or for a hen party, birthday party, some sort of celebration. Somebody sees it and then speaks to their friends to organize it. The hard-core audience for this film is women. Within probably two to three shows, the audience shifted to what it has consistently been everywhere in the world, which is ninety per cent women between the ages of thirty and sixty/sixty-five.'

In America, the *Sing-A-Long-A* debut was timed to coincide with the launch of the thirty-fifth anniversary DVD of the movie, showing the strong relationship right from the start between the *Sing-A-Long-A* team and those who control *The Sound of Music*: 20th Century Fox and the Rodgers and Hammerstein Organization. 'Rodgers and Hammerstein have been fantastic,' Freedman notes. 'Bert Fink, their head of marketing, heard about it on the internet, and to his great credit in our eyes, understood that it was a good thing for the title. As a result he came to London from New York with Ted Chapin, the chief executive and [Richard Rodgers' daughter] Mary to see the show. They gave us their blessing and have been very supportive over the past fifteen years.

'20th Century Fox basically allowed us to get on with it. I think they had got to a point with the title where it was sitting within their library but not a huge amount was happening with it. There is a *Sing-A-Long-A* special feature on the DVD, which I've been told is the most successful of the DVD versions. They've understood that it is a tremendous marketing benefit.'

Although the movie's stars Charmian Carr, Daniel Truhitte and Kym Karath attended that first performance, and have from time to time acted as hosts, Freedman is clear about one aspect of the show that sets it apart. 'We've always said that the host is not the star; the audience is the star. Therefore we need to have hosts who recognize that – they are there as enablers rather than getting people to look at them. If Charmian said she wanted to do it, that would be fantastic, but generally we just have somebody local who is used to doing a bit of improv and work with what the audience gives them.'

The *Sing-A-Long-A* is included in the fortieth and forty-fifth anniversary editions of the movie, and the general air of abandon – what Freedman calls 'giving the audience permission to behave in a way they're not used to behaving and enabling them to feel comfortable about that' – shows how much people enjoy the chance to be part of their favourite movie. 'It's not going to go away,' Freedman concludes. 'It's a universal story, lovely music and there's a constant regeneration of the audience.

A few months before the 2005 Hollywood Bowl performance of *Sing-A-Long-A Sound of Music* shown on the DVD, (at which not only the cast of the film but also a younger generation of von Trapp singers appeared), the musical broke through one of its biggest obstacles and started playing to a German-speaking audience. There had always been resistance to both the film and the stage incarnation in Austria and Germany, in part because there were already two good German films about the von Trapp family, and this was seen as a needless Americanization (or worse, Disney-fication) of the story, but also because there was a certain amount of resentment still at the family for getting out soon after the Anschluss while others had to stay behind. (The good that the Trapp Family Relief Fund achieved wasn't necessarily taken into account.) There was also a feeling in Austria that *The Sound of Music* perhaps talked too much about the way in which the Austrians had welcomed the Nazis, rather than being their first victims, as was often claimed. A small production in Innsbruck and a satirical version in Vienna in 1993 were about the only times Rodgers and Hammerstein's show had been seen or heard in the countries in which it was set.

The production at the Volksoper, which began in February 2005, put the Nazi element front and centre, with a huge swastika over the stage during the festival rendition of 'Edelweiss'. The new German-language translation (*'Die Dinge, die ich gerne mag'* is the new title for 'My Favourite Things', while *'Du bist sechzehn. Beinah schon siebzehn'* is 'Sixteen Going on Seventeen') didn't shy away from Lindsay and Crouse's charting of the rise of Nazism within Austria prior to the Anschluss – although it did correct Richard Rodgers' combination of Schnitzel and noodles (which you will not find anywhere in Austria) to the more gustatorily accurate *Gulasch mit Nockerln*.

The translations of the songs weren't the same as those used for the movie in its short-lived appearance in German cinemas: in that, 'The Sound of Music' had been *'Die Täler entlang'* (now it begins 'The most beautiful music is the song of the mountain'), and 'My Favourite Things' was translated as *'Finde ich schön'*. Ute Horstmann and Eberhard Storch were responsible for the new translations, bar 'Edelweiss', whose translator is unknown, and 'Something Good,' which was translated by Peter Pikl and Christoph Wagner-Trenkwitz as '*Gut gemacht*'. 'Do-Re-Mi' underwent a drastic change, becoming 'C, D, E'.

The French-Canadian duo of director Renaud Doucet and set and costume designer André Barbe prepared their production with the leitmotiv that 'freedom is something we have to fight for every day,' according to the comments on their website. 'We felt it was crucial to look at the piece with open-mindedness and a lack of irony to more honestly address the political and social choices that were made in Austria during the war.'

However well-intentioned, the show was greeted in the same rather haughty way by critics as many previous productions – *Die Presse* called it a 'boring two and a half hours' while another magazine, *Kurier*, moaned that 'Edelweiss' was 'an insult to Austrian musical creation' – but it was a popular success, adding extra performances to the initial twenty-two, and eventually becoming part of the Volksoper's regular repertoire. English surtitles are provided for the many tourists who now go to see *The Sound of Music* close to the real locations.

The Volksoper production paved the way for a second stage incarnation, even closer to the home of the story: after eighteen months' preparation, the Salzburg Landestheater began their own production on 23 October 2011, which is now in its fourth year. One of its attractions for locals is the number of their own children who audition for parts as the von Trapp siblings.

It's not the only way you can see *The Sound of Music* live in Salzburg. Those who don't want to watch it sung in German, or would rather not sit in their hotel rooms and choose it from the entertainment selection, can pop down to the Salzburg Marionette Theatre by the River Salzach. The adaptation by Richard Hamburger is performed in English and is an abridged and occasionally altered version of the stage show – with some surprises, such as a rather outsized marionette of the Mother Abbess or a version of 'Do-Re-Mi' where the puppets quite literally swing from one side of the villa's hall to the other – which has also toured successfully around the United States. Running at only 105 minutes, it's another very different kind of show. (Highlights can be seen on their website.)

Andrew Lloyd Webber had wanted to bring *The Sound of Music* back to the West End of London for a long time before he finally achieved his dream in November 2006. His production would be spectacular, justifying its home at the London Palladium, where director Jeremy Sams had worked on the stage version of Ian Fleming's *Chitty Chitty Bang Bang*. He would headline an American actress who would be guaranteed to bring fans flocking to the box office. However, Scarlet Johansson – who went on to gain cult fame later as the Black Widow in Marvel's *Avengers* films – couldn't commit to the nine-month run that would be required, nor could Lloyd Webber and her management come to mutually agreeable terms.

Rather than go through the normal audition process, Lloyd Webber and his team at the Really Useful Group came up with a new twist – the auditions for the critical role of Maria would be televized. In fact, not only would they be televized, but they would be the focal point of a new Saturday evening entertainment programme.

The eight-part BBC One series, *How Do You Solve A Problem Like Maria?*, was the first time such an idea had been tried out (the format has since been replicated for productions of *Oliver!*, *The Wizard of Oz* and *Jesus Christ Superstar*, amongst others). The panel consisted of Lloyd Webber, musical performer John Barrowman, producer David Ian, and voice coach Zoe Tyler. The ten finalists who appeared on television were whittled down from two hundred chosen at open auditions to fifty, who attended 'Maria school' (and a few extras who got passes for various reasons). From that fifty, twenty were chosen to sing in front of an audience of entertainment professionals; half of them were eliminated. The series began on 29 July 2006, and ended on 16 September, when a public vote chose call-centre worker Connie Fisher as the new Maria.

Although the initial plan was for Fisher only to sing at six performances a week, she eventually ended up singing at all eight until advised to cut back on medical grounds. The £4 million production took £10 million in advance sales and opened on 15 November 2006; Fisher remained with the production until February 2008, when Summer Strallen took over. This followed another unusual TV tie-in: her character on soap opera *Hollyoaks* had approached Lloyd Webber (playing himself on the programme) asking for a chance to sing and he cast her in the Palladium show. Simon Shepherd originally was cast as Captain von Trapp but was replaced by Alexander Hanson after previews; Simon Burke and Simon MacCorkindale also took the role. Opera singer Lesley Garrett was the original Mother Abbess, replaced by Margaret Preece.

The London show closed on 21 February 2009 but the production opened on a UK-wide tour five months later, starting at the Millennium Centre in Cardiff. Connie Fisher played Maria until February 2011 when Verity Rushworth took over; Kirsty Malpass had covered when Fisher was getting married. *Robin of Sherwood* star Michael Praed played Captain von Trapp, with Jason Donovan taking over in January 2011 and continuing until the final performance on 22 October 2011.

The production followed the now familiar pattern, adding 'I Have Confidence' and 'Somewhere Good' from the movie soundtrack, but also retaining 'How Can Love Survive' and 'No Way to Stop It' from the original show. 'Do-Re-Mi' turned up to accompany Maria's introduction to the children, but the thunderstorm had 'My Favourite Things' rather than 'The Lonely Goatherd', which made an appearance later in the first act.

Lloyd Webber repeated the televized audition process in 2008 in preparation for the Canadian production of the show, which ran for sixty-nine weeks in Toronto from 3 October 2008 to 10 January 2010 (a further week's run was added by public demand, for which tickets were sold at a reduced rate). Lessons were learned from the British run: both the winner of the TV series (also entitled *How Do You Solve A Problem Like Maria?*) Elicia MacKenzie and the runner-up Janna Polzin were cast as Maria, with the former doing the bulk of the performances.

The production also travelled to South Africa in the first part of 2014, with shows at the Artscape in Cape Town and the Teatro at Montecasino, Johannesburg.

2013 saw two high-profile stagings of the original musical, one on either side of the Atlantic. Regent's Park Open Air Theatre put on their version directed by Rachel Kavanaugh from 25 July to 14 September, with Charlotte Wakefield credited as Maria Rainer and Michael Xavier as Captain von Trapp. Although the show included the film songs, Wakefield felt that it had a fresh approach, partly caused by her own age (twenty-two at the time): she told *What's On Stage* that they had stripped it back. 'Instead of it being a fluffy musical it's more like a play with very prestigious music, so the dialogue is just as important as the songs, which is great.' This was recognized by the *Guardian*'s Michael Billington, who commented that it 'respects the story's integrity'.

The American production had considerably more money thrown at it. NBC decided that they were going to broadcast a live version of the stage musical, with country singer Carrie Underwood as Maria. Announcing the project in June 2012, producer Craig Zadan explained that 'It isn't our intention to produce a remake of the movie version of *The Sound of Music* – that would be artistic blasphemy. What we want to do, instead, is to give audiences a completely fresh experience of this great Tony Award-winning stage musical in the form of a classic television event, combined with the spontaneity of a live performance. And all of the actors will be singing live; there will be no lip-synching to pre-recordings.'

With a $9 million budget, the live *Sound of Music* was broadcast from a specially built soundstage at Grumman Studios in Bethpage, New York, on 5 December 2013, with a repeat nine days later. Underwood was joined by *True Blood* star Stephen Moyer as Captain von Trapp, with three Broadway and Tony Award winners to back them up: Audra McDonald, Laura Benanti and Christian Borle. The stage show placements of the songs were retained, although 'Something Good' did replace 'An Ordinary Couple'.

The broadcast was deemed a success: it was the most watched programme of the night (although in the key 18–49 demographic, it was beaten by geek comedy *The Big Bang Theory*), and although it didn't receive critical acclaim (like virtually every other production of *The Sound of Music* over the preceding forty-eight years), Carrie Underwood's singing was singled out for note. It won the Emmy Award for Outstanding Technical Direction, Camerawork, Video Control for a Miniseries, Movie or a Special, and was also nominated for Outstanding Music Direction, Outstanding Directing for a Variety Special and Outstanding Special Class Programme. A live broadcast of *Peter Pan* followed in December 2014.

Craig Zadan may not have wanted to produce a remake of the movie of *The Sound of Music*, but there are very few stage or stage-based productions which don't make reference to the visual iconography of the 1965 film. Julie Andrews gave her seal of approval to Underwood's performance (although some of her colleagues in the original cast were less generous) and she continues to cast a shadow over everyone else who plays Maria. And perhaps in this fiftieth anniversary year, that is how it should be.

AFTERWORD

Everyone involved with the story of *The Sound of Music* on stage or screen seems to get asked the same question at some point – what is it about this story that keeps it bringing in new audiences? After spending some time reading Maria von Trapp's accounts in her own words (even counterpointing those with the reminiscences of her stepchildren), and watching the many different versions of the tale, one answer springs to mind: it's the character of Maria herself.

Whether it's the real Maria Augusta Kutschera refusing to be browbeaten by her 'uncle' into not following her dreams of being a teacher, the stage musical's Maria Rainer who acts impetuously in joining a convent, the film's Fräulein Maria who shows steel when faced with Nazis preventing her and her new family from leaving the country, or the anime Maria who is determined to get through to the family's eldest daughter Hedwig, she is a strong woman who will not be pushed around by anyone. She's someone who would rather save the day than have her day saved for her by others.

Those who have told her tale have recognized that. She's the one constant throughout all the different variants; the children may be called by different names; twelve years' events might be compressed into one; the Captain with whom she eventually falls in love may be a doting father or a military martinet; but at the heart of the tale is a tomboy who sees the best in people and situations, and is adamant that God will lead her on the right path. As Ernest Lehman and Robert Wise recognized when they made the choice not to shy away from the inherent religious content of the tale, Maria may have only been at the convent for a few months, but it was a critical time that formed her. Watch the footage of her chatting with Julie Andrews in 1973 (the programme is on the anniversary DVDs) and you get a sense of the strength of the woman.

And she has been served well by those who have relayed her story: the creators of the 1950s German movies recognized that they didn't need to embellish it. Howard Lindsay and Russel Crouse wove a tale around the central pillars of the truth, which Richard Rodgers and Oscar Hammerstein II added to immeasurably with some of their finest music. Lehman and Wise opened that story out, and the writers of the Japanese anime extrapolated incidents which might not have happened to Maria, but feel as if they should. With Hollywood's current penchant for remaking everything, chances are that there'll be a new Maria at some point soon with yet another version of her tale – but at its heart it will still be that tomboy who turned up at Nonnberg Abbey, ice pick in hand and rope over her shoulder, wanting to serve her God.

Long may that story be told.

APPENDIX

The names of the von Trapps and their friends and families change considerably between versions of the story: overleaf is a quick guide to the main characters and their equivalents.

Name	Real life	Die Trapp-Familie	The Sound of Music	Trapp Ikka Monogatari
Maria	Maria Kutschera	Maria Kutschera	Maria Rainer	Maria
Georg	Georg Johannes, Ritter von Trapp	Baron Georg von Trapp	Baron Georg von Trapp	Baron Georg von Trapp
Rupert	Rupert	Agathe	Liesl	Rupert
Agathe	Agathe	Rupert	Friedrich	Hedwig
Maria	Maria	Werner	Louisa	Werner
Werner	Werner	Hedwig	Kurt	Maria
Hedwig	Hedwig	Maria	Brigitta	Johanna
Johanna	Johanna	Rosemarie	Marta	Martina
Martina	Martina	Martina	Gretl	Agathe
Rosmarie	Rosmarie	Johannes	n/a	Barbara
Eleonore	Eleonore	n/a	n/a	n/a
Johannes	Johannes	n/a	n/a	n/a
Yvonne	Princess Yvonne	Yvonne	Baroness Elsa Schraeder	Lady Yvonne
Baroness	Baroness Matilda	Baroness Matilda	Frau Schmidt	Baroness Matilda
Hans	Hans	Franz	Franz	Hans & Franz
Mr Wagner	Charlie Wagner	Mr Samish	n/a	Mr Wagner
Father Wasner	Father Wasner	Dr Wasner	Max Detweiler	Father Wasner

ACKNOWLEDGEMENTS

After a quartet of books which have seen me return to the worlds of science fiction and fantasy, it has been a refreshing change to work on something very different for my last couple of projects, and my thanks, as ever, to Duncan Proudfoot and Clive Hebard at Constable & Robinson (now Little, Brown) for asking me to delve into the very varied history of the von Trapp family.

My thanks also to:

Scott Harrison and Brian J. Robb for their usual excellent job reading through the draft of this manuscript, and my copy-editor Gabriella Nemeth, for ensuring that I didn't put whiskers on roses, or dewdrops on kittens (as Margo Leadbetter famously did in *The Good Life*), or kill off a studio doctor accidentally!

Brian Sibley for generously sharing his interviews with both Robert Wise and Julie Andrews – when I spoke with Mr Wise in 2001, we concentrated on his SF credentials, and I regret now not taking the chance to talk about his work on the classic musicals.

Jonathan Clements, for the insight into the creation of the

Japanese anime of the von Trapp story and how it fits into the history of the form there.

Ben Freedman of Singalong Productions Ltd. for his time discussing the history of that variant of the show.

The extremely helpful people who created the subtitles for the version of *Die Trapp-Familie* uploaded to YouTube; and those who carried out the translation and subtitling of *Trapp Ikka Monogatari* without whom the detailed synopses simply wouldn't have been possible.

Brett Harriman for his excellent book *Salzburg, Lake District & The Sound of Music*, which was an invaluable guide during our time following in the footsteps of the production team in Salzburg and environs (and for permission to adapt one of the gags).

Louise Donaldson, Sam Dorset, Adina Mihaela Roman, Kayla-Mae Alexandria, Patricia Hyde, Sophie Parsons, Monica Derwent and Jessica Bridges for their assistance.

Lee Harris, David Moore, Nicola Budd, Tracy Stanley and Erik Gilg for helping to keep the wheels of finance turning.

Fellow writers Karen Lord and Robert Shearman who separately, within the space of three hours partway through the writing of this book, provided me with some interesting insights into Maria von Trapp.

The members of ASCAT church choir and All the Right Notes singers for providing further musical outlets, and for expressing the joy in their singing which the von Trapps clearly felt in theirs.

The staff at the Hassocks branch of the West Sussex public library who are getting very good at guessing what my next project is from the books that regularly appear on the reserved shelf. More than on most volumes, this Brief Guide has referenced books published in the 1950s–1970s, which are out of print and as yet unavailable digitally, and without the library's central stock it would have been much poorer. Your local library needs every single person who reads this book to support it, no matter where you live in the world.

Last but definitely not least, my partner Barbara and my daughter Sophie, who give me the time and space to work on these books; I couldn't do it without your love and support. And of course, our faithful terriers Rani and Rodo, who would have thoroughly enjoyed visiting Salzburg with us, but had their own holiday instead.

BIBLIOGRAPHY

AboutGerman.net. The Sound of Music German Lyrics Trivia http://www.aboutgerman.net/AGNlessons/sound-of-music-trivia.htm

Baer, William. *Classic American Films: Conversations with the Screenwriters*. Praeger, 2008.

Barbedoucet.com. The Sound of Music. http://www.barbedoucet.com/en/productions-the-sound-of-music.php.

BBC News, 19 March 2005. 'Austria discovers The Sound Of Music'.

Behind the Arras. 'How did they solve a problem like Maria?' http://www.behindthearras.com/Reviewspr/Features%20pro/BaylessH06-10.html

Bronson, Fred. *The Sound of Music Family Scrapbook*. Carlton, 2011.

Carr, Charmian with Jean A.S. Strauss. *Forever Liesl: My Sound of Music Story*. Sidgwick & Jackson, 2000.

Christian Science Monitor, 19 March 1990. '"Sound of Music" Wins New Fans'.

Daily Express, 15 March 2014. 'Whatever happened to . . . Rolfe from The Sound Of Music' http://www.express.co.uk/life-style/life/464618/What-happened-to-Liesl-Von-Trapp-boyfriend-Rolfe-Gruber.

Deadline, 23 December 2013. ' "The Sound Of Music" Continues To Echo Across The Ratings Landscape'.

Denkert, Darcie. *Hollywood & Broadway: A Fine Romance*. Watson-Guptill, 2005.

Entertainment Weekly, 4 December 2013. ' "The Sound of Music": We rank every song'.

Financial Times, 3 March 2005. 'The Sound of Music, Vienna Volksoper'.

Gehring, Wes D. *Robert Wise: Shadowlands*. Indiana Historical Society Press, 2012.

Gray, Edwyn. *The Devil's Device: Robert Whitehead and the History of the Torpedo* (Naval Institute Press edition, 1991 – originally published as *The Devil's Device: The story of the invention of the torpedo* in 1975).

Haaretz, 25 May 2006. 'To Sing Through the Night'.

Harriman, Brett. *Salzburg, Lake District & The Sound of Music* Harriman Travel Books, 2014.

Herman, Jan. *A Talent for Trouble*. Da Capo Press, 1997.

Leonard, Hal. *The Sound of Music: Vocal Selections* (uncredited biography and introduction). Williamson Music, 2004.

Martin, Mary. *My Heart Belongs*. William Morrow & Company, 1976.

Maslon, Laurence. *The Sound of Music Companion*. Pavilion, 2006.

Mordden, Ethan. *Rodgers & Hammerstein*. Harry N. Abrams, 1992.

The New York Times, 17 November 1959. 'Theatre: The Sound of Music'.

The New York Times, 24 March 2005. 'In Austria, "The Sound of Music" is a curiosity'.

The New York Times, 24 December 2008. 'Von Trapps Reunited, Without the Singing'.

Nolan, Frederick. *The Sound of their Music*. J.M. Dent & Sons, 1978.

Plummer, Christopher. *In Spite of Myself*. JR Books, 2010.

Robert Whitehead. A Brief History (at http://www.hansonclan.co.uk/Royal%20Navy/rw.htm).

Rodgers, Richard and Oscar Hammerstein II. *The Sound of Music Libretto*. Williamson, 1960.

Sibley, Brian. *Century of Cinema*. BBC Radio 2, 1999.

Sibley, Brian. *Simply Julie*. BBC Radio 2, 1998.

Stirling, Richard. *Julie Andrews: An Intimate Biography*. Portrait, 2007.

The Sound of Music: 45th Anniversary Edition Blu-ray. Robert Wise, Julie Andrews, Christopher Plummer commentary tracks.

The Spectator, 4 July 1992. 'What Larks'.

Time magazine, 19 December 1938. 'Music: Family Choir'.

Time magazine, 30 November 1959. 'The Theater: New Musical on Broadway, Nov. 30, 1959'.

Time magazine, 12 March 1979. 'Chaos in Television'.

Time magazine, 5 November 1990. 'Mary Martin, 76, First Lady of Musicals, Dies'.

Variety, 2 July 2001. 'Review: "Sound of Music" '.

Von Trapp, Agathe. *Memories Before and After* The Sound of Music. HarperCollins, 2010; self-published 2004.

Von Trapp, Georg, translated by Elizabeth M. Campbell. *To the Last Salute*. Bison Books, 2007.

Von Trapp, Maria. *The Story of the Trapp Family Singers*. J. B. Lippincott, 1949.

Von Trapp, Maria. *Maria: My Own Story*. Creation House, 1972.

Von Trapp, Maria with Ruth Murdoch. *The Trapp Family on Wheels*, 1959.

Wall Street Journal Marketwatch, 24 December 2012, 'ABC's "Sound of Music" ratings up 22% over 2011'.

Author's interview with Ben Freedman, 2 June 2014.